ADAM SMITH AND THE PHILOSOPHY OF LAW AND ECONOMICS

Law and Philosophy Library

VOLUME 20

The titles published in this series are listed at the end of this volume.

ADAM SMITH AND THE PHILOSOPHY OF LAW AND ECONOMICS

Edited by

ROBIN PAUL MALLOY

College of Law, Syracuse University, New York, U.S.A.

and

JERRY EVENSKY

Department of Economics, Syracuse Univeristy, New York, U.S.A.

KLUWER ACADEMIC PUBLISHERS

DORDRECHT / BOSTON / LONDON

A C.I.P. Catalogue record for this book is available from the Library of Congress.

ISBN 0-7923-2796-9

Published by Kluwer Academic Publishers,
P.O. Box 17, 3300 AA Dordrecht, The Netherlands.

Kluwer Academic Publishers incorporates
the publishing programmes of
D. Reidel, Martinus Nijhoff, Dr W. Junk and MTP Press.

Sold and distributed in the U.S.A. and Canada
by Kluwer Academic Publishers,
101 Philip Drive, Norwell, MA 02061, U.S.A.

In all other countries, sold and distributed
by Kluwer Academic Publishers Group,
P.O. Box 322, 3300 AH Dordrecht, The Netherlands.

Printed on acid-free paper

Printed in the Netherlands

To Margaret and Gina for their support and understanding.
RPM

To my parents, Herbert and Sylvia Evensky, with appreciation and love.
JME

TABLE OF CONTENTS

PREFACE

More than two hundred years after the publication of the first edition of *The Wealth of Nations*, Adam Smith continues to be a central figure in discussions concerning the philosophy of law and economics. It is the purpose of this book to explore some of the contemporary issues and controversies surrounding these discussions. We have not attempted to produce a definitive work on Adam Smith's entire philosophy of law and economics. Instead we have pursued a series of important issues that we believe are central to understanding the relevance of Smith to contemporary discourse.

In preparing this book we made a conscious effort to obtain contributions from scholars that represented different disciplines and academically different approaches to Adam Smith's work. This is reflected in the styles of each individual contributor. We also set out to present the material in a somewhat unique manner. We wanted to capture both the academic analysis of Smith's work and also show Smith as a 'living' participant in the ongoing public policy debates of law and economics. This objective lead to the division of the book into two parts. The first part of the book presents some important new essays on Adam Smith's work. The second part of the book centers on a debate between two leading advocates of law and economics. In this second part of the book Smith is brought to life by his contextual presence in opposing positions by each of the debate participants. On the surface the debate is directed at contemporary disputes over the direction of law and economics, however, it becomes clear that a major separation between the views of the two antagonists relates to their distinct interpretations of Adam Smith's work. With this debate as the backdrop, further analysis is presented which both critiques the debate and connects the themes of part two with those of part one of the book.

As editors of this volume we have also taken the liberty of being major contributors. In addition to our own contributions we are delighted to be able to include insightful essays by Dr. John W. Cairns of the University of Edinburgh (Scotland), Dr. J. Ralph Lindgren of Lehigh University (U.S.A.), Professor Kenneth A.B. Mackinnon of the University of Waikato

(New Zealand), and the Honorable Richard A. Posner of the United States 7th Circuit Court of Appeals.

In making this project a reality we have many people to thank. Most importantly, we thank Margaret A.P. Malloy for contributing her computer expertise in preparing the final edit and formatting of the book. Thanks also go to Mary Ann McClanahan, Lynn Oatman and Cathie Soccocio for initial word processing assistance and to Dave Longeretta and Anthony Calabrese for aid in proof reading and cite check work. In addition, we thank the people at Kluwer Academic Publishers, in particular Peter de Liefde, Nicola Berridge, and Isabella C. Key for their support and patience in guiding us through the publication process. Finally, we thank the *Valparaiso University Law Review* for releasing their interest in the reprinted debate included in this volume. The debate was originally reported in Vol. 24 Number 2 of their *Law Review* in the winter edition, 1990.

Robin Paul Malloy, & Jerry Evensky
Syracuse University
Syracuse, New York U.S.A.

ROBIN PAUL MALLOY

INTRODUCTION TO THE VOLUME

Discussions on the philosophy of law have seldom included one of the most important figures of the modern age. A figure made ever more relevant by recent work in critical legal theory and in law and economics. Both critical theorists and legal economists have linked economics, in one way or another, to law, legal institutions, and dominant legal theory. Casting an imposing shadow over all such debates, although seldom adequately addressed, is the work of Adam Smith. Smith was among the grand philosophers of his time and yet today he is seldom studied outside of circles composed of those interested in the history of economic thought. Modern textbooks on economics give short mention to Smith other than to note his place in the developmental history of that science. Philosophers have done little better in the attention they have given to Smith's work. Likewise, lawyers, even those interested in legal theory, spend little time reading or thinking about Smith's contributions to the philosophy of law. All of this lack of attention, however, has never seemed to stop countless such people from cavalierly citing Smith as their patron Saint. There is no shortage of opinion regarding the pros and cons of Smith's legacy as it is embodied in the ideology of western capitalist economies. It seems therefore that while many are willing to speak directly or indirectly regarding Smith on any matter at hand, or to claim or disown his intellectual inheritance depending on the particular situation, it is seldom a scholarly as opposed to popular inquiry that ensues.

The contributors to this book uniformly believe that Smith's work is invaluable if one is seeking to gain a better understanding of the nexus between philosophy, economics and the law. As legal economists and critical theorists expound on the relationship between economic and legal ideology, it becomes ever more important to explore the legal philosophy of the acknowledged leading figure in the development of our economic tradition. Smith's work is more than foundational, however, for it continues to play a role in current debate on legal theory. Smith's work finds its place amidst the intellectual clashes over natural rights, the role of values and morals in law, and the tension between individualist, communitarian, and altruistic frameworks in shaping social organization.

This book addresses Adam Smith's philosophy of law and economics

R.P. Malloy and J. Evensky: Adam Smith and the Philosophy of Law and Economics, 1–5.

and seeks to shed important new light on the complexity and relevance of Smith's work. Brought together for this project are scholars on Adam Smith including Jerry Evensky, and J. Ralph Lindgren, from the United States; John W. Cairns from Scotland; and Kenneth A. B. Mackinnon from New Zealand. This volume also includes works from two major contributors to the discourse in law and economics, Robin Paul Malloy and Richard A. Posner. The contributors to this volume represent a variety of disciplines including law, legal history, economics, and philosophy. All of the contributors do cross-disciplinary work and bring fresh intellectual vigor to their topics. We believe that this represents the first attempt to bring such a diverse set of scholars together for the purpose of exploring Adam Smith's contribution to the philosophy of law and economics.

Since the genesis of this project the goal has remained constant and clear. We wanted to explore Adam Smith's contributions to the philosophy of law and economics by looking at three distinct but related subject matters. First, we wanted the book to address Smith's views of law and of the legal system. Second, we wanted to further investigate Adam Smith the philosopher as his philosophy related to both legal and economic considerations. Third, and finally, we wanted to explore Smith's evolving role in the development of a new and specialized subdiscipline referred to as law and economics. While this one book cannot cover all issues related to these three distinct areas of inquiry we have nonetheless raised points which we believe are of central significance for present and future debates.

In Part One of the book we present a series of essays on specific elements of Adam Smith's work. In 'Setting the Scene: Adam Smith's Moral Philosophy', Jerry Evensky presents a framework for understanding the relationship between Smith's views on the functioning of the economy, the role of law, and moral philosophy. Evensky demonstrates the evolutionary nature of Smith's ideas on ethics, economics, and jurisprudence. He shows how Smith's moral philosophy was central to his vision on each of the relationships evident in law and economics. With important historical references he thereby sets the stage for the materials that follow.

John W. Cairns pursues Smith's conception of the proper role and function of the judiciary in his chapter titled 'Adam Smith and the Role of the Courts in Securing Justice and Liberty.' Cairns uses a general discussion of Smith's thought on the relationship between wealth, commerce, and liberty to launch into a new and detailed analysis of Smith's writing on the relationship between the legislative and judicial branches of government. He provides valuable insight into the historical distinction between the incorporation of Roman Civil Law into most of Europe and the development of the Common Law in England. Smith's work is explored for commentary on the importance of this distinction as well as for the influence of his moral philosophy in shaping his understanding of the consequences of each tradition.

In 'Adam Smith's Treatment of Criminal Law,' J. Ralph Lindgren explores Smith's views on a theory of criminal law and punishment. He uses this chapter to go beyond the work of Knud Haakonssen and to argue for a different conclusion regarding Smith's approach. Lindgren is interested in Smith's detailed treatment of criminal laws and examines them from the perspective of resentment theory and utility theory. He uncovers a complexity to Smith's work in this area that had not been explored and by so doing presents a more complete picture of Smith's jurisprudence. He discusses crimes against both person and property as well as crimes of intent and anticipation. Lindgren concludes that Smith's arguments relied more on considerations of utility than retribution.

Kenneth A.B. Mackinnon contributes 'Adam Smith on Delictual Liability' which is a subject matter known more familiarly to Common Law lawyers as torts. The law of delict is the Roman Civil Law approach to the subject matter of private causes of action for injuries resulting from acts of commission or omission. Mackinnon provides historical information on the relationship between the Common Law and Civil Law traditions in this area and explains how Smith was in contact with both systems as a result of the differences between the Scottish (Civil Law) and English (Common Law) approach. He uses the opportunity presented by Smith's work to explore the standard of the impartial spectator as a legal standard and to illustrate the connection between Smith's moral, economic, and legal theories.

In the concluding essay to Part One Robin Paul Malloy discusses the relevance of Smith's work in the growing discourse of Law and Economics. In his chapter 'Adam Smith and the Modern Discourse of Law and Economics,' Malloy provides a detailed discussion of important moral and economic themes from Smith's work as they have a bearing on the law. He discusses the importance of Smith's rejection of social contract theory and of his views on natural liberty, self interest, and social evolution through individual and collective experience. This discussion is then put into context by exploring the way in which particular modern day legal theorists invoke Adam Smith's memory in their own discourses about the relationship between law and economics.

Part Two of the book presents another aspect of Adam Smith's legacy. In the second part of the book we look at how Adam Smith's work is imported into the actual discourse of contemporary legal, economic, and philosophical dispute. Disagreements involving interpretations of Smith's work turn out to be at the root of many current controversies. Such controversies go beyond issues of natural rights, morality and ethics, and explore the more concrete problems of family, housing, medical care, affirmative action, and surrogate motherhood. These issues and more are explained in Part Two of the book which begins with a brief introduction by Malloy.

The Malloy/Posner debate which follows the introduction to Part Two, forms an important part of the book because it illustrates the continuing relevance of Adam Smith's work to core understandings regarding law and economics. In Malloy's opening statement and in his response to Posner, the argument is made that Smith's work on law and economics must be understood by way of, and in connection with, Smith's work on moral philosophy. Malloy argues that Smith's dynamic system of evolutionary development would lead to a value based and humanistic conception of law and economics. And, that a market economy, in the Smithian sense, requires a firm grounding in moral discourse and normative consensus building. Richard A. Posner answers Malloy by presenting a different view of Smith in both his opening statement and his reply essay. Posner finds no need to link an understanding of Smith's economics, as expressed in *The Wealth of Nations*, to his earlier work in *The Theory of Moral Sentiments*. Furthermore, Posner states clearly and expressly, for the first time in print, that he does not find appeals to moral argumentation to be useful. Posner thereby rejects Malloy's call for moral discourse and separates Adam Smith's contributions to economic science from Smith's other interesting, but 'less fruitful,' philosophical endeavors.

Underlying both positions in this debate are differences between the participants concerning their philosophy of law and their understanding of Smith's original ideas. In this light, Jerry Evensky's 'Comments on the Debate' helps to highlight the various express and implicit allusions to Smith's work made by both Malloy and Posner. Evensky points out the way in which he believes Smith's work is both used and misused by each participant. Finally, in an effort to advance the debate beyond the confines pursued by Malloy and Posner, Evensky offers his own thoughts on Smith's possible role and importance in understanding current controversies in law and economics.

In the final essay of Part Two, Jerry Evensky brings a sense of closure to the subject matter discussed throughout the entire book. He revisits the essays from Part One and ties them together with the themes of Part Two.

While each contributor to this volume brings a different perspective to his work all share a common recognition of the importance of Smith's views on the philosophy of law and economics. This book does not represent the definitive word or conclusion on this subject but rather a beginning of a new discourse. It is the hope of the editors that this effort will inspire further inquiry and debate.

Syracuse University, College of Law

JERRY EVENSKY

SETTING THE SCENE: ADAM SMITH'S MORAL PHILOSOPHY

1. INTRODUCTION

The subject of our book is Adam Smith and the Philosophy of Law and Economics. As the title of this chapter suggests, its purpose is to set the scene for what is to follow.

Smith's views on the functioning of an economy and the role of law are subsets of his moral philosophical vision. In order to set that topic into its proper context, it is important that we first review Smith's views on philosophy in general and on moral philosophy in particular. Sections two and three of this chapter address each of these topics in turn. In Sections four, five, and six I focus in more detail on the dimensions of Smith's moral philosophical vision: ethics, economics, and jurisprudence. In Section seven I show how Smith's moral philosophy evolved over time, and I conclude in Section eight with thoughts on the importance of filling in gaps in our understanding about Smith's views on jurisprudence.

2. ADAM SMITH ON PHILOSOPHY

Philosophy is the science of the connecting principles of nature. (Smith, 1980, p.45)

Adam Smith's conception of philosophy is framed by his conception of the origin of the universe. He is a believer in the view that the universe is the product of the hand of a designer who arranged the mechanism and set the system in motion. The classic statement of this 'design argument'[1] position is that made by the character Cleanthes in David Hume's *Dialogues Concerning Natural Religion*:

Look round the world: contemplate the whole and every part of it: you will find it to be nothing but one great machine, subdivided into an infinite number of lesser machines, which admit of subdivisions, to a degree beyond what senses and faculties can trace and explain. All of these various machines, and even their most minute parts, are adjusted to each other with an accuracy which ravishes into admiration all men, who have ever contemplated them. The curious adapting of means to ends, throughout all nature, resembles exactly, though it much exceeds, the productions of human contrivance; of human design thought, wisdom, and intelligence.

R.P. Malloy and J. Evensky: Adam Smith and the Philosophy of Law and Economics, 7–29.

Since therefore the effects resemble each other, we are led to infer, by all rules of analogy, that the causes also resemble; and that the Author of Nature is somewhat similar to the mind of men; though possessed of much larger faculties; proportioned to the grandeur of the work, which has been executed. By this argument *a posteriori*, and by this argument alone, do we prove at once the existence of a Deity, and his similarity to human mind and intelligence. (Hume, 143)

This argument *from design* (or, one based on the notion that it took a Deity *to design* certain purposefulness into what exists (e.g., the ability of the eye to see)), provided a proof according to Cleanthes, and many including Sir Isaac Newton, that there was a Deity.

Hume goes on in the *Dialogues* to destroy the logic that underlies this "proof" and Smith is well aware of Hume's argument.[2] But this has no bearing on Smith's conception of the Deity's role in the design, for Smith did not conceptualize the Deity or the design in terms of proof or capital-T, Truth.

Smith's belief in the Deity derives from the same source as that represented by Demea in Hume's *Dialogues*: faith. Smith's rejection of the notion that the design argument provides proof of the Truth of the existence of the Deity is consistent with his view of the role of Truth in philosophy in general. There is no proof of Truth, either of the Deity or of the shape and structure of the design of the Deity.

All that we know, according to Smith, is effects of the design. The actual pins and wheels of the mechanism that the Deity designed lay out of sight. The machine that moves nature lays behind the face of nature, just as the pins and wheels that move the hands of a watch lie behind the face of the watch. In both cases, the elegance of the design that provides the dependability and elegance of what we actually observe is ascribed to the designer.

The wheels of a watch are all admirably adjusted to the end for which it was made, the pointing of the hour. All their various motions conspire in the nicest manner to produce the effect. ... Yet we never ascribe any such desire or intention to them, but to the watch-maker .... (Smith, 1976B, 87)

And in both cases, the watch and the universe, the internal structure and thus the design are invisible to one who can only see the face of it.

The difference lies in the fact that in the case of the watch we can open it up and analyze its internal structure. We can observe its design and the connecting principles that give rise to the motion we observe on its face. So too, to use another example from Smith, the wonder we feel at the illusion created by the facade of an opera set vanishes when we are allowed to see the mechanisms that create that illusion:

Upon the clear discovery of a connecting chain of intermediate events, it [(our wonder)] vanishes altogether. Who wonders at the machinery of the opera-house who has once been admitted behind the scenes?

But, Smith continues, it is not so with nature:

In the Wonders of nature, however, it rarely happens that we can discover so clearly this connecting chain. With regard to a few even of them, indeed, we seem to have been really admitted behind the scenes. (Smith, 1980, 42-3)

For Smith, nature's Truth lies in the machinery, the connecting principles, that lie behind the scenes, and the subject of philosophy is those connecting principles of nature.

Individuals are drawn to the study naturally, for it is our nature, according to Smith, to look upon nature with wonder when we see 'extraordinary and uncommon objects, at all the rarer phaenomena of nature, at meteors, comets, eclipses, at singular plants and animals, and at every thing, in short, with which we have before been little or not at all acquainted ....' (Smith, 1980, p.33) The philosopher, having an image of a coherent design in mind, rejects the notion that there are in fact any singularities or leaps in nature. But having no direct access to these connecting principles, the philosopher's work becomes a process of creative imagination.

Philosophy, by representing the invisible chains which bind together all these disjointed objects, endeavours to introduce order into this chaos of jarring and discordant appearances, to allay the tumult of the imagination, and to restore it, when it surveys the great revolutions of the universe, to that tone of tranquility and composure, which is both most agreeable in itself, and most suitable to its nature. Philosophy, therefore, may be regarded as one of those arts which address themselves to the imagination .... (Smith, 1980, p. 45-6)

Philosophy ... *pretends* [emphasis added] to lay open the concealed connections that unite the various appearances of nature." (Smith, 1980, 51)

A great philosopher is one who has the creativity to imagine what the 'concealed connections' might be. And, in Smith's view, the greatest of all philosophers was Sir Isaac Newton.

In his 'History of Astronomy' Smith asserts that Sir Isaac Newton's work 'prevails over all opposition ... with principles [that], it must be acknowledged, have a degree of firmness and solidity that we should look in vain for any other system'.(Smith, 1980, 104-5) Newton's work seems to reflect the Truth about the connecting principles of nature, but lest we be seduced to make that leap from admiration for Newton's imagination to enshrinement of his ideas as Truth, Smith reminds us not to do so:

And even we, while we have been endeavouring to represent all philosophical systems as mere inventions of the imagination ... have insensibly been drawn in, to make use of language expressing the connecting principles of this one, *as if* [emphasis added] they were the real chains which Nature makes use of to bind together her several operations. (Smith, 1980, 105)

Newton's work is so powerful that it is easy to use the language of Truth when one describes it, but even his philosophical triumph is simply a work of a creative imagination. Its power comes from its ability to sooth our imagination and to give us the feeling that it reflects the connecting principles we cannot actually observe.

Smith's objective is to do for moral philosophy what Newton had done for natural philosophy. He has a vision of the invisible chains that form the connecting principles of the human order. He wants to tell his story with the same persuasive power.

3. ADAM SMITH'S MORAL PHILOSOPHY: BACKGROUND

Triangulating from his three key frames of reference, Deism, Classical Liberalism, and evolutionary thought, allows us to locate Adam Smith's moral philosophy.

As noted above, Smith believes in the existence of a Deity and that the universe is the product of that Deity's design. The domain of Natural Philosophy covers all of that universe which surrounds the human condition. Newton provided us with a powerful story describing what he imagined the connecting principles of that domain are. Moral philosophy is the study of the connecting principles that underlie the structure and evolution of the human order. Much of Smith's career is devoted to the work of moral philosophy: representing the connecting principles of that human order.

Smith's belief in the Deity has significant implications for his conception of those connecting principles. Not only does that belief anchor his position that there is an order, it justifies Smith's faith in the notion that the order was inherently good: That the order, when functioning in harmony with the Deity's design, is one in which individual humans would find much for which to give thanks. This is so because Smith's Deity is a benevolent Deity:

> The happiness of mankind, as well as of all other rational creatures, seems to have been the original purpose intended by the Author of nature, when he brought them into existence. No other end seems worthy of that supreme wisdom and divine benignity which we necessarily ascribe to him .... (Smith, 1976B, 166)

This 'mankind' of which Smith speaks is made up of 'rational creatures' who exist as autonomous Beings and interact with one another within the context of a political state. In the ideal, design case, the political state created by these Beings exists for the sole purpose of insuring that the requisite definitions necessary for commercial intercourse, and the institutions necessary to resolve issues of definition, are in place. Smith's ideal state is a classical liberal state in which individuals interact within the context of a nonintrusive, instrumental political structure.

But this is not where the human condition begins. This is an ideal, a limit, that human society evolves toward through the course of human history. No state actually reaches the limit, and no one state follows an unbroken path toward the limit. Any given state may move forward and then stagnate (e.g., China, according to Smith (Smith, 1976A, 89)) or even regress (e.g., Bengal, according to Smith (Smith 1976A, 91)). But through the course of time, the overall path of human history brings the maturing of the human condition from the rude state of hunting and gathering, through the successively more advanced states of pasturage and agriculture, to the most advanced state: commercial society. It is in that last stage that the classical liberal political structure must emerge, for an effective commercial society depends on the presence of such a structure.

Smith presents his moral philosophy, his ideal classical liberal vision and the forces that propel the evolving human condition, in his two great works: *The Theory of Moral Sentiments* (hereafter *TMS*) and *The Wealth of Nations* (hereafter *WN*). He had in mind a third work on 'the general principles of law and government, and of the different revolutions which they had undergone in the different ages and periods of society' (Smith, 1976B, 342), but as of 1790 he writes that 'the theory of jurisprudence, which I have long projected, I have hitherto been hindered from executing'. (Smith, 1976B, 3) Unfortunately, he dies in 1790 never having completed the task. In the next two sections (IV. 'Ethics' and V. 'Economics') we will examine the elements Smith does present, his social and economic analysis, in more detail. In section VI., 'Jurisprudence' we will review Smith's general views on the nature of law. In last section VII., 'The Evolution of Smith's Moral Philosophy', we will describe the evolution of Smith's views on these dimensions of his moral philosophy. All this will set the scene for the remainder of the book which is dedicated to filling in the unfinished pages of Smith's story: The place of jurisprudence in his moral philosophy.

4. ADAM SMITH'S MORAL PHILOSOPHY: ETHICS

Adam Smith began his published work on moral philosophy with *The Theory of Moral Sentiments*, because ethics is the foundation of his moral philosophical vision of a constructive classical liberal society. As described above, that vision is a product of Smith's mind's eye, his imagination. What he imagines is the connecting principles that are assembled by a benevolent Deity make up the immense machine of the universe. In his moral philosophy he represents his image of that machine as it functions to define the human condition. For the wheels of human society to turn easily, for that machine to run smoothly, there must be virtue. Human virtue, ethics, is the *sine qua non* of the Smith's constructive classical liberal society. The source of the divergence between the real and the ideal is very simple: humans are subject to human frailty.

> Human society, when we contemplate it in a certain abstract and philosophical light, appears like a great, an immense machine, whose regular and harmonious movements produce a thousand agreeable effects. As in any other beautiful and noble machine that was the production of human art, whatever tended to render its movements more smooth and easy, would derive a beauty from this effect, and, on the contrary, whatever tended to obstruct them would displease upon that account: so virtue, which is, as it were, the fine polish to the wheels of society, necessarily pleases; while vice, like the vile rust, which makes them jar and grate upon one another, in as necessarily offensive. (Smith, 1976B, 316)

The 'abstract and philosophical light' is the light of the moral philosopher describing his mind's eye view of the ideal. The 'noble machine that was the production of human art' is the case of the real. For a moral philosopher such as Smith to present a full and coherent vision of the human condition, he must represent the ideal and the source of the distortion that deflects the real from the ideal. And if that moral philosopher has a sanguine view of the ultimate state of the human condition, as Smith does given his faith in a benevolent Deity, he must explain how it is that the real state of society approaches the limit of the ideal over time. This is what Smith does in the *Theory of Moral Sentiments*.

Smith's ideal of human moral behavior is based on several concepts that he weaves together. First there are sentiments. Foremost among the sentiments are self-love, justice, and benevolence. Each of these sentiments serves a crucial function in the formation of human action. Self-love is the motive force for individual betterment, and as such it is the motive force behind all the activity that gives rise to the creativity and productivity of a commercial society. The classic line from Smith in the *Wealth of Nations* tells us that:

> It is not from the benevolence of the butcher, the brewer, or the baker, that we expect our dinner, but from their regard to their own interest. We address ourselves, not to their humanity but to their self-love, and never talk to them of our own necessities but of their advantages. (Smith, 1976A, 26-7)

But while self-love is necessary for the existence of a constructive commercial society, it is not sufficient. Indeed, if allowed to run unbridled, it can become the source of destructive behavior that is inimical to the kind of constructive competition through which the ideal classical state enriches itself and all who participate in it. As Smith writes:

> In the race for wealth, and honours, and preferments, he may run as hard as he can, and strain every muscle, in order to outstrip all his competitors. But if he should justle, or throw down

any of them, the indulgence of the spectators is entirely at an end. It is a violation of fair play, which they cannot admit of. (Smith, 1976B, 83)

Society sees such behavior as reprehensible because it is destructive. 'In the race for wealth, and honours, and preferments' the more any individual exerts herself to get ahead by doing her best, the greater the social product at the end of the day. When any individual deflects energy to justling or throwing down and opponent, she not only reduces her own productivity, she reduces the productivity of her opponent as well. In a footrace, this simply means that the relative positions at the finish line will be different and the times will be less impressive. But in the 'race for wealth, and honours, and preferments' it means there will be less social product.[3]

The justice of an individual is an important balance to one's sentiment of self-love. If the balance between these two is appropriate, the motive forces generated by self-love will be channeled into constructive pursuits that will contribute to the well being of the individual and of society. If all individuals have that proper balance, then society can achieve much of its potential.

Society ... cannot subsist among those who are at all times ready to hurt and injure one another. The moment that injury begins, the moment that mutual resentment and animosity take place, all the bands of it are broke asunder, and the different members of which it consisted are, as it were, dissipated and scattered abroad by the violence and opposition of their discordant affections. If there is any society among robbers and murders, they must at least, according to the trite observation, abstain from robbing and murdering one another. ... Society may subsist, though not in the most comfortable state, without beneficence; but the prevalence of injustice must utterly destroy it. Justice ... is the main pillar that upholds the whole edifice [of society]. ... [S]ociety cannot subsist unless the laws of justice are tolerably observed .... (Smith, 1976B, 86, 87)

But while justice is necessary for the cool efficiency of a classical liberal society, '[m]ere justice is, upon most occasions, but a negative virtue.' (Smith, 1976B, 82) It is not sufficient for the warmth of human caring that is the foundation of personal attachment and in turn the primary source of social bonds and individual happiness.

It is thus that man, who can subsist only in society, was fitted by nature to that situation for which he was made. All members of human society stand in need of each others assistance, and are likewise exposed to mutual injuries. Where the necessary assistance is reciprocally afforded from love, from gratitude, from friendship, and esteem, the society flourishes and is happy. All the different members are bound together by the agreeable bands of love and affection, and are, as it were, drawn to one common centre of mutual good offices. (Smith, 1976B, 85)

Thus, the ideal classical liberal society is one in which each individual embodies each of these sentiments in proper balance - one to the others. Moral sentiments, as in the title *The Theory of Moral Sentiments*, are just that: sentiments properly balanced.

> Concern for our own happiness recommends to us the virtue of prudence: concern for that of other people, the virtues of justice and beneficence; of which the one restrains us from hurting, the other prompts us to promote that happiness. (Smith, 1976B, 262)

> The man who acts according to the rules of perfect prudence, of strict justice, and of proper benevolence, may be said to be perfectly virtuous. (Smith, 1976B, 237)

But how is an individual to know what balance of sentiment is proper and therefore moral? What is the standard? What is the measure? The standard is consistency with the Deity's design. The measure is the sympathy of an imagined impartial spectator, 'the well informed spectator ... the man within the breast, the great judge and arbiter of their [individuals'] conduct.' (Smith, 1976B, 130)

The impartial spectator stands in a unique position: able to see what balance of sentiments would be in harmony with the Deity's intention and able to see into the Being of an individual to discern what actual balance of sentiments motivates individual action. To the degree that these two scales show the same balance, the impartial spectator is in sympathy with the intentions and action of the individual. And to the degree that the individual enjoys that sympathy, she is acting morally. Thus, for an individual to act ethically, ideally she must have the ability to step outside herself and take that position as the impartial spectator. This is necessary, but not sufficient for ethical behavior, for

> the most perfect knowledge of those rules will not alone enable him to act in this manner: his own passions are very apt to mislead him; sometimes to seduce him to violate all the rules which he himself, in all his sober and cool hours approves of. The most perfect knowledge, if not supported by the most perfect self-command, will not always enable him to do his duty. (Smith, 1976B, 237)

These then are the prerequisites for a perfectly ethical individual: the ability to determine the proper balance of sentiments by taking the position of an impartial spectator and the self-command to impose those moral sentiments on herself. Such individuals are the stuff of a constructive classical liberal society. But as Smith recognized all too well, no such individuals exist. The closest he had seen was David Hume. In a letter William Strahan (Kirkaldy, Fifeshire, 9 Nov. 1776) offering 'some account of the behavior of our late excellent friend, Mr. [David] Hume, during his last illness ....' Smith concludes: 'Upon the whole, I have always considered him, both in his lifetime and since his death, as approaching as nearly to the idea of a perfectly wise and virtuous man, as perhaps the nature of human frailty will permit.' (Smith, 1977, pps. 217, 221)

Virtue, that proper balance of sentiments described above, is a limit.

Due to human frailty it is a point beyond reach, a point that few (a la Hume) even approach. But approaching that limit on a broad scale is precisely what is necessary if a society is to approach the limit represented by the ideal constructive classical liberal society. So, from whence Smith's sanguine view? How is it that society could eventually come to be populated by a multitude of David Humes?

Smith's answer lies in what he sees as the dynamic of social evolution. While no one can ever actually take the position of an impartial spectator, over time there evolves in society a proxy for the dictates of that impartial spectator. Smith calls it duty:

> [G]eneral rules ... universally acknowledged and established by the concurring sentiments of mankind. ... Those general rules of conduct, when they have been fixed in our mind by habitual reflections, are of great use in correcting the misrepresentations of self-love concerning what is fit and proper to be done in our particular situation.
>
> ...
>
> The regard to those general rules of conduct, is what is properly called a sense of duty, ... the only principle by which the bulk of mankind are capable of directing their actions. (Smith, 1976B; 160, 162)

But as with the impartial spectator, so too duty is not sufficient to insure ethical behavior by an individual. It is not enough to know what should be done, one must have the wherewithal to do it. Given human frailty, we cannot rely on self-command:

> There are situations which bear so hard upon human nature, that the greatest degree of self-government, which can belong to so imperfect a creature as man, is not able to stifle, altogether, the voice of human weakness, or reduce the violence of the passions to that pitch of moderation, in which the impartial spectator can entirely enter into them. (Smith, 1976B, 26)

To fill this gap, Smith turns to the power of social approbation and socialization. The insatiable need of individuals for the former can be exploited by society to effect the latter. To the degree that socialization inculcates a definition of duty that is consistent with the balance of self-love, benevolence, and justice necessary for a constructive classical liberal society, the society will enjoy that fruitful condition.

Much of Smith's work focuses on the power, methods, and consequences of socialization; and the role of socialization in the scheme of the Deity's design. Socialization is nature's (the Deity's - since the Deity is the designer) way of accommodating for human frailty:

> Nature, however, has not left this weakness, which is of so much importance, altogether without remedy; nor has she abandoned us entirely to the delusions of self-love. Our continual observations upon the conduct of others, insensibly leads us to form in ourselves certain general rules concerning what is fit and proper either to be done or to be avoided.
>
> ...

The regard to those general rules of conduct, is what is properly called a sense of duty, a principle of the greatest consequence in human life, and the only principle by which the bulk of mankind are capable of directing their actions.

...

The coarse clay of which the bulk of mankind are formed, cannot be wrought up to such perfection [as Hume]. There is scarce any man, however, who by discipline, education, and example, may not be so impressed with a regard to general rules, as to act upon almost every occasion with tolerable decency, and through the whole of his life to avoid any considerable degree of blame. (Smith, 1976B; 159, 161-2, 162-3)

'The coarse clay of which the bulk of mankind are formed' does not change with time. The essence of Being, the array of sentiments embodied in us, the capacity for self-command and self-delusion, the desire for approbation are common to all Beings. Indeed, it is our nurturing and not our nature that accounts for most of the variation that emerges as we grow into adulthood:

The difference of natural talents in different men is, in reality, much less than we are aware of; and the very different genius which appears to distinguish men of different professions, when grown up to maturity, is not upon many occasions so much the cause, as the effect of the division of labour. The difference between the most dissimilar characters, between a philosopher and a common street porter, for example, seems to arise not so much from nature, as from habit, custom, and education. (*WN*, 28-29)[4]

What matters is the way in which individuals are molded. Society provides the mirror in which we see ourselves:

Were it possible that a human creature could grow up to manhood in some solitary place, without any communication with his own species, he could no more think of his own character, or the propriety or demerit of his own sentiments and conduct, of the beauty or deformity of his own mind, than of the beauty or deformity of his own face. All these are objects which he cannot easily see, which naturally he does not look at, and with regard to which he is provided with no mirror which can present them to his view. Bring him into society, and he is immediately provided with the mirror which he wanted before. (*TMS*, 110)

Society has the power to shape us because we are social by nature, and because we desire to be accepted and admired by those we accept and admire:

Nature, when she formed man for society, endowed him with an original desire to please, and an original aversion to offend his brethren. ... She rendered their approbation most flattering and most agreeable to him for its own sake; and their disapprobation most mortifying and most offensive. (Smith, 1976B, 116)[5]

...

This natural disposition to accommodate and to assimilate, as much as we can our own sentiments, principles, an feelings, to those which we see fixed and rooted in the persons whom we are obliged to live and converse a great deal with, is the cause of the contagious effects of both good and bad company. (Smith, 1976B, 224)

As the individual is shaped by society, so too the society is shaped by the individuals who make it up. Smith did not see the motive force for evolution as an either/or proposition: it is not driven either by entirely autonomous individuals or by all powerful social forces. His vision is more complex. He sees a coevolution of individual and society. The socialization of society does shape the clay of the individual, but the individual is shaped by more than society. Her personal experience will include interactions with other societies or with natural phenomena that impact on and shape her Being. The individual is thus shaped by society and, in turn, as she grows she becomes a source of change within society. The degree to which individuals are shaped by forces that are exogenous to their primary social environment determines the degree to which the society is subject to change from such forces. Smith's model must be so, for both the individual and society must evolve if individuals and societies are to pass through the stages he envisioned toward the desired limit he envisioned, the Deity's design.

At each stage in this coevolution the character of Being that is held in esteem will be different. The nature of the virtues held in high regard will be directly related to the material conditions of the society:

> Every age and country look upon that degree of each quality, which is commonly to be met with in those who are esteemed among themselves, as the golden mean of that particular talent or virtue. And as this varies, according as their different circumstances render different qualities more of less habitual to them, their sentiments concerning the exact propriety of character and behavior vary accordingly.
>
> ...
>
> In general, the style of manners which takes place in any nation, may commonly upon the whole be said to be that which is most suitable to its situation. (Smith, 1976B; 204, 209)

As the shape of Being begins to approximate the model, the perfectly ethical Being, simultaneously the society is approaching that ideal limit, the constructive classical liberal society.

Smith's sanguine view of society derives from his faith in the invisible hand. That image, the invisible hand, is generally associated with Smith's economics, and the elegant and efficient functioning of a market system that he described so powerfully in *The Wealth of Nations*. But Smith's invisible hand lies behind the face of all we observe, including the evolution of society. Recall, the invisible hand is that of the benevolent Deity as designer. If indeed the Deity is benevolent, then the Deity must have provided a mechanism for society to move from its rude state through the stages Smith envisions toward that ideal limit: the constructive commercial society. Smith's evolution analysis is his representation of the machine the Deity designed to carry human society through those stages.

As we have seen, the *sine qua non* of this evolutionary process is the development of progressively more refined ethics: An appropriate ethical system is the necessary and sufficient condition for the existence of the Deity's ideal case: human happiness and the greatest possible wealth for the nation.

How does the economy produce such wealth without anyone in charge? The Deity has arranged the mechanism. All we need do is insure that it is well polished with human virtue. In that case the economy moves with the smoothness and steadiness of the hands of a watch; guided, like those hands by an invisible hand. Smith, the moral philosopher, describes this part of the machine of the universe in his *Wealth of Nations*. In the next section we turn to Smith's economics.

5. ADAM SMITH'S MORAL PHILOSOPHY: ECONOMICS

Smith's moral philosophical vision is, in the language of modern discourse, a general equilibrium system. Indeed, it is much more *general* than what is today referred to in modern neoclassical economics as general equilibrium analysis. This is so because the scope of Smith's systematic simultaneous analysis encompasses the social, political, and economic dimensions of the human condition.

As in any general equilibrium framework, partial analysis is a ceteris paribus analysis. Those forces that emanate from the other dimensions, are to be taken as given. If one wants to generalize what is initially a partial analysis, one relaxes the givens and explores the implication of these 'exogenous' changes. In reality, however, nothing that is exogenous for all dimensions of the system are simultaneously determined.

Smith understood this very well. When he turns to his analysis of the economy, he treats it at two levels.

His ideal representation of the economy assumes that the political and social dimensions are perfectly aligned with the Deity's design. In this case perfectly ethical beings pursue their own self-interest within the context of natural jurisprudence. Natural jurisprudence provides the instrumentation for a classical liberal society: the definitions necessary for individuals to act and interact with perfect liberty, and the arbiters necessary to interpret those definitions when an honest dispute arises.

Given this assumption the general condition of the economy is determined. Each participant will use the resources at her disposal to her greatest advantage. In doing so the micro system will be most efficient and the aggregate effect of this micro efficiency will be the greatest possible wealth for the nation. Smith writes:

The whole of the advantages and disadvantages of the different employments of labour and stock must, in the same neighborhood, be either perfectly equal or continually tending to equality. If in the same neighborhood, there was any employment evidently either more or less advantageous than the rest, so many people would crowd into it in the one case, and so many would desert it in the other, that its advantages would soon return to the level of other employments. This at least would be the case in a society where things were left to follow their natural course, where there was perfect liberty, and where every man was perfectly free to chuse what occupation he thought proper, and to change it as often as he thought proper. Every man's interest would prompt him to seek the advantageous, and to shun the disadvantageous employment. (Smith, 1976A, 116)

And in the course of doing so:

As every individual, therefore, endeavours ... to employ his capital ... he intends only his own gain, and he is in this, as in many other cases, led by an invisible hand to promote an end which was no part of his intention. ... By pursuing his own interest he frequently promotes that of the society more effectually than when he really intends to promote it. (Smith, 1976A, 456)

The invisible hand is that of the designer, the benevolent Deity who created the mechanism and the connecting principles for the purpose of providing humankind this wonderful opportunity. To the degree that virtue provides the fine polish that keeps the mechanism running smoothly humankind will enjoy this gift. To the degree that vice creates that vile rust which causes the gears of the machine to grate and jar on one another, humankind misses that opportunity. The sanguine, evolutionary Smith saw society as moving from the former toward the latter case. Much of *The Wealth of Nations* is dedicated to describing what Smith imagines as the mechanism and the connecting principles of that ideal design case.

He begins with the ultimate source of human productivity: the division of labor. Chapter I, 'Of the Division of Labour' opens:

The greatest improvement in the productive powers of labour, and the greater part of the skill, dexterity, and judgement with which it is any where directed, or applied, seem to have been the effects of the division of labour. (Smith, 1976A, 13)

This division of labor is necessary for the enhancement of society's productive capacity, but it is not sufficient for society to enjoy the fruits of that increased productivity. At the end of a production process that embodies the division of labor, each individual is overabundently supplied with a product the production of which is her specialty; but she has nothing of the other products that are necessary for subsistence or the enhancement of life. Smith understood that for individuals to enjoy the benefits of the division of labor, Beings must be inclined to exchange and there must be a mechanism which coordinates the exchange of surpluses in a coherent way. He took the inclination to exchange as a given, part of the Deity's design:

The division of labour, from which so many advantages are derived is not originally the effect of any human wisdom, which foresees and intends that general opulence to which it gives occasion. It is the necessary, thought very slow and gradual consequence of a certain propensity in human nature, which has in view no such extensive utility; the propensity to truck, barter, and exchange one thing for another. (Smith, 1976A, 25)

The mechanism that provides the medium for this coordination of exchange of surpluses is the market. Each individual comes to the market with her surplus for exchange. The test of whether her time and resources have been well spent is the markets response to her product: a response that is determined not by the benevolence but by the self-interest of those with whom she seeks to exchange.

[M]an has almost constant occasion for the help of his brethren, and it is vain for him to expect it from their benevolence only. He will be more likely to prevail if he can interest their self-love in his favour, and shew them that it is for their own advantage to do for him what he requires of them. Whoever offers to another a bargain of any kind, proposes to do this. Give me that which I want, and you shall have this which you want, is the meaning of every such offer; and it is in this manner that we obtain from one another the far greater part of those good offices which we stand in need of. It is not from the benevolence of the butcher, the brewer, or the baker, that we expect our dinner, but from their regard to their own interest. We address ourselves, not to their humanity but to their self-love, and never talk to them of our own necessities but of their advantages. (Smith, 1976A, 26-7)

Thus in pursuit of our own advantage, we serve the needs of others. This then is the magic of a market system in the design case:

It is the great multiplication of the productions of all the different arts in consequence of the division of labour, which occasions, in a well-governed society, that universal opulence which extends itself to the lowest ranks of the people. Every workman has a great quantity of his own work to dispose of beyond what he himself has occasion for; and every other workman being exactly in the same situation, he is enabled to exchange a great quantity of his own goods for a great quantity, or, what comes to the same thing, for the price of a great quantity of theirs. He supplies them abundantly with what they have occasion for, and they accommodate him as amply with what he has occasion for, and a general plenty diffuses itself through all the different ranks of society. (Smith, 1976A, 22)

The only limit on this being the extent of the market, for

[w]hen the market is very small, no person can have any encouragement to dedicate himself entirely to one employment, for want of the power to exchange all that surplus part of his produce of his own labour, which is over and above his own consumption, for such parts of the produce of other men's labour as he has occasion for. (Smith, 1976A, 31)

But this constraint becomes less and less onerous and the division of labor becomes more and more fine as the size of the market grows. And in Smith's design case, the market will grow progressively larger, thanks to the accumulation that created by the parsimony of the populace.

Parsimony, is part of that 'balance' that makes for moral Beings. It implies intertemporal balance in the expression of self-love. Resisting prodigality, the properly parsimonious individual will not consume all the stock that is generated by the gains from trade. She will consume some and accumulate the rest. This accumulation will in turn provide the capital that makes possible the expansion of the market and the progressively finer division of labor:

Capitals are increased by parsimony, and diminished by prodigality and misconduct.

...

Parsimony, by increasing the fund which is destined for the maintenance of productive hands, tends to increase the number of those hands whose labour adds to the value of the subject upon which it is bestowed. It tends therefore to increase the exchangeable value of the annual produce of the land and labour of the country. It puts into motion an additional quantity of industry, which gives an additional value to the annual produce.[6] (Smith, 1976A, 337)

Here again we see the nexus between Smith's economics and his ethics that underlies the whole of his moral philosophy. Even self-love, in and of itself, must be properly balanced intertemporally if prodigality is to give way to the prudence (parsimony) that is a necessary condition for the ideal classical liberal society.

And we also see here the nexus between Smith's economics, and his social and political analysis. In the design case, the benefit of the gains from the trade is the increased opulence that all participants enjoy. But it comes with a potential cost:

The man whose whole life is spent in performing a few simple operations, of which the effects too are, perhaps, always the same, or very nearly the same, has no occasion to exert his understanding, or to exercise his invention in finding out expedients for removing difficulties which never occur. He naturally loses, therefore, the habit of such exertion, and generally becomes as stupid and ignorant as it is possible for a human creature to become. The torpor of his mind renders him, not only incapable of relishing or bearing a part in any rational conversation, but of conceiving any generous, noble, or tender sentiment, and consequently of forming any just judgement concerning many even of the *ordinary duties of private life*. [emphasis added] ... His dexterity at his own particular trade seems, in this manner, to be acquired at the expence of his intellectual, social, and martial virtues. But in every improved and civilized society this the state into which the labouring poor, that is the great body of the people, must necessarily fall, unless government takes some pains to prevent it. (Smith, 1976A, 782)

The problem created by the economic dynamic is an erosion of virtue (that fine polish) at the most basic level: duty. Smith's solution is public education and participation in a militia. (Smith, 1976A, pps 784-8) Through these two contexts the government can empower the 'common people' to think in ways that are requisite for the inculcation of duty. This in turn makes it possible to socialize the common people with that sense of duty which is requisite for the smooth functioning of a classical liberal society.

A properly socialized populace will follow the dictates of duty, and duty is a proxy for the dictates of an impartial spectator. Thus a properly socialized populace will, to the degree the proxy approximates the ideal, embody the ethics that are necessary for the realization of the ideal state, the Deity's design.

But ethics, while necessary, is not sufficient. A constructive classical liberal society must also have in place a system of instrumentation that facilitates exchange among individuals: the definitions necessary for individuals to act and interact with perfect liberty, and the arbiters necessary to interpret those definitions when an honest dispute arises. 'It is the end of jurisprudence to prescribe rules for the decisions of judges and arbiters.' (Smith, 1976B, 330) Smith refers to the ideal version of this system of instrumentation as 'natural jurisprudence.'

6. ADAM SMITH'S MORAL PHILOSOPHY: NATURAL JURISPRUDENCE

'The two useful parts of moral philosophy ... are Ethics and Jurisprudence.' (Smith, 1976B, 340) Smith's first book, *The Theory of Moral Sentiments*, is on ethics. As noted above, he closes that book with a promise to return to the discussion of jurisprudence that he begins in the last chapter. But he never does so. Thus, what we know of Smith's views on jurisprudence must be culled from the lecture notes of his students, the *Lectures on Jurisprudence*; and from what he writes on jurisprudence in the *Theory of Moral Sentiments* and the *Wealth of Nations*.

Smith begins his 1766 lectures on Jurisprudence: 'Jurisprudence is that science which inquires into the general principles which ought to be the foundation of the laws of all nations.' (Smith, 1978, 397) Note the words: 'general principles which ought'.[7] Smith's conception of jurisprudence is embedded in his lager moral philosophy which envisions a design case applicable to all humankind. Thus the rules of jurisprudence are 'general', because they are universal; and they 'ought' to be followed, because they reflect the intentions of the Deity. When the actual rules are consistent with the Deity's design case, they are in harmony with nature. Smith refers to this ideal of jurisprudence as natural jurisprudence. Given human frailty, humankind can only approximate the ideal of natural jurisprudence:

> Every system of positive law may be regarded as a more or less imperfect attempt towards a system of natural jurisprudence, or towards an enumeration of the particular rules of justice. As the violation of justice is what men will never submit to from one another, the public magistrate is under the necessity of employing the power of the commonwealth to enforce the

practice of this virtue. Without this precaution, civil society would become a scene of bloodshed and disorder, every man revenging himself at his own hand whenever he fancied he was injured. To prevent the confusion which would attend upon every man's doing justice to himself, the magistrate, in all governments that have acquired any considerable authority, undertakes to do justice to all, and promises to hear and to redress every complaint of injury. In all well-governed states too, not only judges are appointed for determining the controversies of individuals, but rules are prescribed for regulating the decisions of those judges; and these rules are, in general, intended to coincide with those of natural justice. ... In no country do the decisions of positive law coincide exactly, in every case, with the rules which the natural sense of justice would dictate. Systems of positive law, therefore, though they deserve the greatest authority, as the records of the sentiments of mankind in different ages and nations, yet can never be regarded as accurate systems of the rules of natural justice. (Smith, 1976B, 340)

In keeping with his sanguine, evolutionary view of the human condition, at least until the 1770s Smith believed that the development of positive law had been a progressive process and that over time it would come to approximate the requirements of natural jurisprudence.

But, while justice 'is the foundation of civil government' it is not the only purpose of law. 'The four great objects of law are Justice, Police, Revenue, and Arms.' (Smith, 1978, 398) Given ethical Beings and natural jurisprudence, the activity of government in the exercise of police, revenue, and arms would be proper, for it would be carried out in a personal and institutional context that assured it would be so. To the degree that the ethics of individuals are not perfect and the jurisprudence of the society is not natural, the effects might be reflected in arbitrary or capricious exercise of the government's function in the areas of police, revenue, and arms.

Smith recognized that the personal and institutional settings may not be ideal, however, and he highlights examples of distortions that would be the consequence of skewed government policy. Regarding revenue, the government might impose taxes that are distortionary and unjust (Smith, 1976A, 865), accumulate public debt to the detriment of private borrowing (Smith, 1976A, 925), spend out of all proportion to its reasonable requirements (Smith, 1976A, 346), or it might create all three of these distortions.

With regard to police, by which Smith meant regulation, the government might use its power to regulate for the good of particular interests rather than for the general good. Smith identified the array of extant Mercantilist policies as cases of this kind of distortion. (Smith, 1976A, 429)

So we see that for Smith it is with government as it is with individuals: to the degree that government contributes a fine polish to the wheels of society, the society will be productive and good; and to the degree that government is creating a vile rust, the society will be unproductive. The issue for Smith is not whether government serves a purpose, it is what purpose and whose interest will government serve.

As with the rest of his moral philosophy, into his fifties Smith maintains a sanguine view that society is evolving in a progressive way toward the ideal. This sanguine view included the constructive evolution of government, for society could not progress without progressive more constructive government. From his fifties onward, however, Smith seems to become more skeptical.

7. ADAM SMITH'S MORAL PHILOSOPHY: ITS EVOLUTION

In a letter to William Pultney written from his home in Kirkcaldy, Scotland and dated 3 Sept. 1772, Smith writes:

> My book [the *WN*] would have been ready for the Press by the beginning of this winter; but the interruptions occasioned partly by bad health arising from want of amusement and from thinking too much upon one thing; and partly by the avocations above mentioned [(helping friends through difficult times)] will oblige me to retard its publication for a few months longer. (Smith, 1987, 164)

Smith left for London in April 1773 prepared to publish *The Wealth of Nations*. There was a long delay, and it was not published until 9 March 1776. Why the delay when, as reflected in the letter cited above, he felt so close to completion in 1772? I believe that Smith's exposure to the realities of London political intrigue and parliamentary influence caused Smith to rethink his views. 'Interests', especially Mercantile interests, were different in their strength and character than Smith had anticipated. His initial reaction to this was to extend the section of his book related to the mercantile system. The longer term effect was a fundamental shift in thinking about the development of a classical liberal society.

The source of this shift is his emerging concern that the dynamics of society are not inherently constructive. In terms of the imagery presented above, he began to doubt the ability of the invisible hand to carry society through the commercial stage to the ideal society. The concern was motivated by his new view of mercantilism.

Mercantilist obstacles to commerce were a large part of his story from the very beginning. He saw the virtue of a commercial society as being one in which these largely historical artifacts would be eroded away. But therein lay the problem he confronted when he arrived in London in 1773. What he found was not a society that was positioned to slowly crush the old mercantilist obstacles as it moved forward toward the classical liberal ideal of the free flow of all individuals, ideas, resources, and goods. Instead what he discovered was a world in which the mercantile interests were dynamic players and seemed, indeed, to be becoming stronger not weaker over time.

Michael Kammen in *Empire and Interest* refers to 1763-1783 as the 'Age of Interests', a period during which this new kind of interest was gaining influence in Parliament. This new kind of interest was the commercial mercantilist. The emerging ascendancy of this group and its power in parliament is what so disturbs Smith.

This is not to imply that Smith was entirely uninformed about the world of London prior to his arrival. He was simply not prepared for the degree of dynamic mercantilist power he found. In terms familiar to those who observe the political scene in the United States of the 1990s, Smith's experience was analogous to a thoughtful political observer arriving in Washington, DC ('inside the beltway'): By all accounts, it is an eye opening experience, because the nature of that 'inside' world cannot be appreciated until one observes it first hand in action. In effect, Smith arrived 'inside the beltway' and was jarred by the true dynamic nature of the mercantile interests.

When Smith arrives in London the colonial question was heating up. The power of the mercantilists to protect their interests by pressuring parliament to pursue a very expensive war with the colonies clearly distressed Smith greatly.

In his most significant revisions to the *Wealth of Nations*, published in 1784, the largest addition was a new chapter titled 'Conclusion of the Mercantile System'. In these 'Additions and Corrections' he makes to the *Wealth of Nations*, Smith attacks the mercantile system with great venom. In those pages he specifically writes that Parliament has 'wasted' a fortune in pursuit of a colonial policy that benefits only those mercantile interests:

> A great empire has been established for the sole purpose of raising up a nation of customers who should be obliged to buy from the shops of our different producers, all the goods with which these could supply them. For the sake of that little enhancement of price which this monopoly might afford our producers, the home-consumers have been burdened with the whole expence of maintaining and defending that empire. For this purpose, and for this purpose only, in the two last wars, more than two hundred millions have been spent, and a new debt of more than a hundred and seventy millions has been contracted over and above all that had been expended for the same purpose in the former wars. The interest of this debt alone is not only greater than the whole extraordinary profit, which, it ever could be pretended, was made by the monopoly of the colony trade, but than the whole value of that trade or than the whole value of the goods, which at an average have been annually exported to the colonies.
>
> It cannot be very difficult to determine who have been the contrivers of this whole mercantile system: not the consumers, we may believe, whose interest has been entirely neglected; but the producers whose interest has been so carefully attended to; and among this latter class our merchants and manufacturers have been by far the principal architects. (Smith, 1976A, 661)

This change of perspective, his shaken faith in the ability of the invisible hand to guide society toward the ideal, ultimately drives Smith back to the foundation of his argument. Recall that at the heart of his ideal case and of the evolutionay course he envisions is, respectively: a society of perfectly ethical individuals, and an evolution of a socially defined and inculcated sense of duty that will begin to approximate the ideal. His view that the ideal requires a perfectly ethical Beings as a foundation remains unaltered. What is altered is his faith that natural forces within society (the invisible hand) will drive an evolution toward that ideal. The absence of such faith has two effects on Smith. His heart becomes less sanguine, and his mind searches for a solution to his moral philosophical dilemma: the natural, ideal case requires an ethical foundation; but nature has not provided the means of establishing such a foundation.

Smith's recognition of this dilemma and his prescription for dealing with it are embodied in his last work, the revisions he makes in the last year of his life to *The Theory of Moral Sentiments*.

For thirty years Smith had made no significant revisions to the *Theory of Moral Sentiments*. Then, in spite of his advanced years and poor health, he does so. He writes in a letter to Mr. Thomas Cadell, Bookseller, Strand, London, that the cost of this effort has been high: he has given up a more mellow life and his health. In that letter, Smith also hints at the solution he sees to the dilemma his moral philosophy faces. He writes:

Custom-house, Edinburgh, 31 Mar. 1789

Dear Sir,

Ever since I wrote to you last I have been labouring very hard in preparing the proposed new edition of the Theory of Moral Sentiments. I have even hurt my health and have been obliged to return, within these few days, to my usual attendance at the Custom house (from which the indulgence of my colleagues has excused me) I may say principally for the sake of relaxation, and a much easier Business. Besides the Additions and improvements I mentioned to you; I have inserted, immediately after the fifth part, a compleat new sixth part containing a practical system of Morality, under the title of the Character of Virtue. ... After all my labours, however, I am afraid it will be Midsummer before I can get the whole Manuscript in such proper order as to send it to you. I am very much ashamed of this delay, but the subject has grown upon me. I would fain flatter myself that your Profit from the additions will fully compensate the loss you may have suffered by the delay. Let me hear from you as soon as you conveniently can. Remember me to Strahan and Believe me

ever yours

Adam Smith

(Smith, 1977, 319-320)

His hope for a solution to the classical liberal dilemma lies in 'a practical system of Morality, under the title of the Character of Virtue.'

Smith's revisions to the *Theory of Moral Sentiments* represent his appeal to the citizenry to place the interests of society ahead of the interest of any faction to which they might be attached. Beyond that, Smith makes a plea to the future statesmen of the nation to lead by moral example and deed. Having lost faith in the invisible hand's ability to guide society to the ideal, he turns to the visible hand of moral leadership to guide society toward the ideal. As he began, so too he ends his career with his eyes on the central determinate of the well-being of society: the heights of wealth and well-being to which a community may rise is determined by the strength of its ethical foundation[8]. This is the core of Smith's moral philosophical vision.

8. CONCLUSION

At the close of his first edition of *The Theory of Moral Sentiments*, Smith wrote:

> I shall in another discourse endeavour to give an account of the general principles of law and government, and of the different revolutions they have undergone in the different ages and periods of society, not only what concerns justice, but what concerns police, revenue, and arms, and whatever else is the object of law. (Smith, 1976B, 342)

Thirty years later, in his 'Advertisement' to the sixth edition of the *Theory of Moral Sentiments*, he writes:

> In the last paragraph of the first Edition of the present work, I said, that I should in another discourse endeavour to give an account of the general principles of law and government. ... In the *Enquiry concerning the Nature and Causes of the Wealth of Nations*[9], I have partly executed this promise; at least so far as concerns police, revenue, and arms. What remains, the theory of jurisprudence, which I have long projected, I have hitherto been hindered from executing .... Though my very advanced age leaves me, I acknowledge, very little expectation of ever being able to execute this great work to my own satisfaction: yet, as I have not altogether abandoned the design, and as I wish still to continue under the obligation of doing what I can, I have allowed the paragraph to remain as it was published more than thirty years ago, when I entertained no doubt of being able to execute everything which it announced. (Smith, 1976B, 55)

Adam Smith died on 17 May 1790. He was weakened by the efforts that went into revising the *Theory of Moral Sentiments*, and never regained his energy. Thus, we never received the long promised and much hoped for third volume on his theory of jurisprudence. We can, nevertheless, say much about his views on the law based on the sources that influenced him, his published work, and the reports of his lectures. This chapter has set the scene for such speculation by outlining Smith's moral philosophy. In the next four chapters Smith's views on the law are examined in detail. Following this is Part II of this book, where we see the work of Smith used in the discourse of current controversies in law and economics.

NOTES

1. See (Hurlbutt, 1965).
2. Indeed, as he was dying Hume asked Smith to insure the publication of the *Dialogues*. Smith's equivocal reply, based on his concern about the furor Hume's work might generate, motivated Hume to relieve Smith of this burden. Instead, Hume prevailed upon his nephew.

Hume reasoned that his nephew could plead family obligation in the face of any criticism of his facilitating the publication of the piece. See (Smith, 1987, p.205 and 205fn).

3. The rent-seeking literature is a valuable (albeit often distorted) exploration of this issue.

4. David Hume writes in a similar vein: 'When we consider how nearly equal all men are in their bodily force, and even in their mental powers and faculties, till cultivated by education ....' Cited in (Smith, 1976A, 28 fn. 11).

5. Elsewhere Smith writes 'Man naturally desires, not only to be loved, but to be lovely: or to be that thing which is the natural and proper object of love. He naturally dreads not only to be hated, but to be hateful: or to be that thing which is the natural and proper object of hatred.' (Smith, 1976B, 113-114).

6. Anticipating Say's law, Smith argues that this savings does not represent a leakage of demand from the economy: 'What is annually saved is as regularly consumed as what is annually spent, and nearly in the same time too; but it is consumed by a different set of people.' (Smith, 1976A, 337-8).

7. He begins his earlier lecture series (Report of 1762-3) on Friday Decr. 24. 1762 with the statement: 'Jurisprudence is the theory of the rules by which civil governments ought to be directed.' (Smith, 1978, 5) In the *TMS* Smith writes: '[N]atural jurisprudence [is] ... a theory of the general principles which ought to run through and be the foundation of the laws of all nations.' (Smith, 1976B, 341) In both of these cases we see the "general" and 'ought' language.

8. Note: Smith would distinguish between the values that hold within any particular family or group within the community, and those held by the community at large. Family values may vary, this is the beauty of a classical liberal society that is nurtured by the diversity of its members. Those values need only be consistent with (i.e., not undermine) the core values on which the community is constructed. For example, Smith was a proponent of religious diversity, but he would see any religion that honored dishonesty as a problem for the community.

9. A variation on the original title: *An Inquiry into ...*

REFERENCES

Evensky, Jerry. (Forthcoming). 'Adam Smith on the Human Foundation of a Successful Liberal Society.' *History of Political Economy.*

——. (1992A). 'Ethics and the Classical Liberal Tradition in Economics,' *History of Political Economy*, 24(1), 62-77.

——. (1992B). 'The Role of Community Values in Modern Classical Liberal Economic Thought,' *Scottish Journal of Political Economy*, 39(1), 21-38.

——. (1990). *Economic Ideas and Issues: A Systematic Approach to Critical Thinking*, Englewood Cliffs: Prentice-Hall.

——. (1989) 'The Evolution of Adam Smith's Views on Political Economy,' *History of Political Economy*, 21(1), 123-145.

——. (1987). 'The Two Voices of Adam Smith: Moral Philosopher and Social Critic, *History of Political Economy*, 19(3), 447-468.

Hume, David. (1947). *Dialogues Concerning Natural Religion*, Introduction by Norman Kemp Smith. Indianapolis.

Hurlbutt, Robert H., III. (1965). *Hume, Newton, and the Design Argument.* Lincoln.

Kammen, Michael. (1970). *Empire and Interest, the American Colonies and the Politics of Mercantilism.* Philadelphia.

Smith, Adam. (1980). *Essays on Philosophical Subjects*, Edited by W.P.D. Wightman and J.C. Bryce; Vol. 3 of *The Glasgow Edition of the Works and Correspondence of Adam Smith*, General editing by D.D. Raphael and Andrew Skinner, Oxford: Clarendon

Press.
——. (1978). *Lectures on Jurisprudence*, Edited by R.L. Meek, D.D. Raphael, and P.G. Stein; Vol. 5 of *The Glasgow Edition of the Works and Correspondence of Adam Smith*, General editing by D.D. Raphael and Andrew Skinner, Oxford: Clarendon Press.
——. (1977). *The Correspondence of Adam Smith*, Edited by E.C. Mossner and T.S. Ross; Vol. 6 of *The Glasgow Edition of the Works and Correspondence of Adam Smith*, General editing by D.D. Raphael and Andrew Skinner, Oxford: Clarendon Press.
——. (1976). *An Inquiry into the Nature and Causes of the Wealth of Nations*, Edited in two vol.by W.B. Todd; Vol. 2 of *The Glasgow Edition of the Works and Correspondence of Adam Smith*, General editing by D.D. Raphael and Andrew Skinner, Oxford: Clarendon Press.
——. (1976). *The Theory of Moral Sentiments*, Edited by D.D. Raphael and A.L. Macfie; Vol. 1 of *The Glasgow Edition of the Works and Correspondence of Adam Smith*, General editing by D.D. Raphael and Andrew Skinner, Oxford: Clarendon Press.

Syracuse University, Maxwell School, Department of Economics

JOHN W. CAIRNS

ADAM SMITH AND THE ROLE OF THE COURTS IN SECURING JUSTICE AND LIBERTY

1. INTRODUCTION

Adam Smith wrote in the *The Wealth of Nations* that: 'The second duty of the sovereign, [is] that of protecting, as far as possible, every member of the society from the injustice or oppression of every other member of it, or the duty of establishing an exact administration of justice ....'[1] He had made similar remarks to his moral philosophy class in Glasgow in his *Lectures on Jurisprudence*, though there making the maintenance of justice the 'first and chief design of every system of government'.[2] Smith returned to the point in the final chapter of the *Wealth of Nations*, where he commented:

> Commerce and manufactures can seldom flourish long in any state which does not enjoy a regular administration of justice, in which the people do not feel themselves secure in the possession of their property, in which the faith of contracts is not supported by law, and in which the authority of the state is not supposed to be regularly employed in enforcing the payment of debts from all those who are able to pay. Commerce and manufactures, in short, can seldom flourish in any state in which there is not a certain degree of confidence in the justice of government.[3]

Numerous passages allude to this necessity.[4] At first sight, such statements might suggest that Smith considered the administration of justice to be the merely technical matter of facilitating the operation of the market. Knud Haakonssen, however, has rightly stressed that Smith's 'regular administration of justice' was 'a guiding ideal' that could 'lead and direct a political process', commenting that '[t]he system of natural jurisprudence was in itself a *political* challenge'.[5] More was at stake for Smith in the proper administration of justice than simply aiding the market to increase the opulence of individuals and government. It is easy to point to a passage in the *Wealth of Nations* that demonstrates this. Smith discussed the effect of the poor laws in England on the price of wages and the free circulation of labor. As well as noting economic detriments, he commented:

> To remove a man who has committed no misdemeanour from the parish where he chuses to reside, is an evident violation of natural liberty and justice. The common people of England,

R.P. Malloy and J. Evensky: Adam Smith and the Philosophy of Law and Economics, 31–61.

however, so jealous of their liberty, but like the common people of most other countries never rightly understanding wherein it consists, have now for more than a century together suffered themselves to be exposed to this oppression without a remedy. Though men of reflection too have sometimes complained of the law of settlements as a publick grievance; yet it has never been the object of any general public clamour, such as that against general warrants, an abusive practice undoubtedly, but such a one as was not likely to occasion any general oppression. There is scarce a poor man in England of forty years of age, I will venture to say, who has not in some part of his life felt himself most cruelly oppressed by this ill-contrived law of settlements.[6]

The relationship in Smith's thought between wealth, commerce, and liberty has often been discussed, and I do not propose to add to that literature -- though some of what follows will have at least a tangential bearing on it,[7] since Smith believed that 'commerce and manufactures gradually introduced order and good government, and with them, the order and security of individuals'.[8] Instead, this paper is devoted to the narrower theme of the role of courts in securing justice and liberty -- an obvious aspect of the administration of justice. This has been discussed to some extent by, above all, Haakonssen.[9] I hope to provide, however, a development and perhaps reformulation of Haakonssen's remarks, and to build on some comments made by myself in another paper, and thus deepen our understanding of Smith's view of courts.[10]

Smith regarded courts as central to the administration of justice. This, though obvious, is worth stressing. Much recent discussion of Smith's work has located it against the eighteenth-century concern with the science of legislation.[11] This is undoubtedly how Smith himself saw the *Wealth of Nations*,[12] and this aspect of it was readily appreciated by his contemporaries.[13] For Smith, the purpose of natural jurisprudence was to provide 'a theory of the general principles which ought to run through and be the foundation of the laws of all nations.'[14] To the unwary legal historian, this suggests a link with the legislative projects of codification associated with Jeremy Bentham and the Enlightened absolutists of late-eighteenth-century Europe. Indeed, Smith's definition of 'what are properly called laws' as 'those general rules which the sovereign lays down to guide the conduct of his subjects' might seem to prove the connection.[15] Though Smith was sometimes arguing for legislative reform, his legal theory, as Haakonssen has pointed out, led him to favour development through common law.[16] Thus, when Smith wrote that '[i]n other countries the unfortunate constitution of their courts of judicature hinders any regular system of jurisprudence from ever establishing itself among them',[17] he did not simply mean that this thwarted the enforcement of legislation, but rather that the courts themselves could not develop such a system to regulate and bind their own practice. It is as well in this context to recall the additions made to the sixth edition of the *Theory of Moral Sentiments*, published in 1790, in which Smith commented that '[t]he man of system ... is apt to be very wise in his own conceit; and is often so enamoured with the supposed beauty of his own ideal plan of government, that he cannot suffer the smallest deviation from any part of it.' Applying these general remarks he added:

> Some general, and even systematical, idea of the perfection of policy and law, may no doubt be necessary for directing the views of the statesman. But to insist upon establishing, and upon establishing all at once, and in spite of all opposition, every thing which that idea may seem to require, must often be the highest degree of arrogance. It is to erect his own judgment into the supreme standard of right and wrong. It is to fancy himself the only wise and worthy man in the commonwealth, and that his fellow-citizens should accommodate themselves to him and not he to them. It is upon this account, that of all political speculators, sovereign princes are by far the most dangerous.[18]

These remarks serve to remind us that Smith was far from the rationalism or utopianism of a Bentham or a Joseph II. But as Donald Winch has pointed out, Smith was very much in favour of reform: that was a major purpose of the *Wealth of Nations*.[19] Haakonssen likewise has convincingly argued that Smith's natural jurisprudence was a critical jurisprudence.[20] Smith's natural jurisprudence was intended to assist legislators (in a narrow sense); it was also a guide as to how courts should operate.

It is accordingly important to place Smith's views on legislation and courts in the context of Hanoverian Britain. David Lieberman has demonstrated that among Smith's contemporaries there was widespread concern about the confused state of the statute book and the haphazard system of legislation.[21] Legislation was in the hands of politicians and their party interests rather than in those of statesmen or legislators. Furthermore, at the time Smith was active as a scholar, a commercial law was being created for England primarily by Lord Mansfield.[22] One obvious theme of both the *Wealth of Nations* and the *Lectures on Jurisprudence* is the need for a commercial society to have an appropriate commercial law, and such was being created in England in the courts, not the legislature. Smith's connections with the Scottish judiciary, notably with Lord Kames and Lord Hailes,[23] mean that he must have been aware of the significant role of judges in law making. Smith's recognition of this role explains his concern with courts, and should help us understand the remarks he made about the constitution of courts hindering the development of a system of jurisprudence.[24] If courts did more than technical application of existing law to given facts, their structure and proceedings were of vital importance.

Winch has perceptively remarked of the *Wealth of Nations* that '[i]t emerged as a natural by-product of the Glasgow moral philosophy curriculum, a framework which Smith was remarkably content to use for all his writings. Smith never appears in mufti; he is always in full academic dress.'[25] The Scottish academic context is thus important in understanding Smith's thoughts on the operation of the courts. Smith was elected Professor of Logic in Glasgow on 9 January 1751.[26] The Professor of Moral Philosophy, Thomas Craigie, had become ill, however, and had left for Lisbon to recover his health. Smith accordingly agreed to teach natural jurisprudence and politics to Craigie's class when he arrived in Glasgow.[27] Craigie died in Lisbon in late November; Smith was elected to the vacant chair on 22 April 1752 and translated seven days later.[28] He seems to have developed the ideas underlying his general intellectual project during his period as a professor in Glasgow. He had earlier given lectures on rhetoric and belles lettres and on jurisprudence in Edinburgh between 1748 and 1751;[29] these presumably contained matter subsequently followed up in Glasgow, as Smith in fact claimed,[30] though it is unclear exactly which elements of his maturer thought then existed.[31]

At Glasgow, Smith's main duty was to teach the class on moral philosophy. The description of this class by John Millar is familiar:

> His course of lectures ... was divided into four parts. The first contained Natural Theology ... The second comprehended Ethics, strictly so called, and consisted chiefly of the doctrines which he afterwards published in his Theory of Moral Sentiments. In the third part, he treated at more length of that branch of morality which relates to *justice*, and which, being susceptible of precise and accurate rules, is for that reason capable of a full and particular explanation.
>
> Upon this subject he followed the plan that seems to be suggested by Montesquieu; endeavouring to trace the gradual progress of jurisprudence, both public and private, from the rudest to the most refined ages, and to point out the effects of those arts which contribute to subsistence, and to the accumulation of property, in producing correspondent improvements or alterations in law and government ... .
>
> In the last part of his lectures, he examined those political regulations which are founded, not upon the principle of *justice*, but that of expediency ... . What he delivered on these subjects contained the substance of the work he afterwards published under the title of An Inquiry into the Nature and Causes of the Wealth of Nations.[32]

Millar's account is generally accurate, though it may be pointed out that Smith included political regulations founded on justice and those on expediency together in his *Lectures on Jurisprudence*, which he finished with an account of the law of nations.[33] According to Stewart, the balance between the elements of the course altered after the publication of *The Theory of Moral Sentiments* in 1759.[34] Smith's class thus followed and developed on the traditional structure of the moral philosophy curriculum established in Glasgow by Gershom Carmichael.[35] Smith also continued to teach rhetoric and belles lettres in Glasgow, and student notes of these lectures dating from the session of 1762-63 survive.[36] Thus, Smith's views of the role of courts, whether to be found in his published works or in student notes, ultimately stemmed from his classes, especially that in moral philosophy, in Glasgow.

Moral philosophy was a central discipline in the curriculum of the Scottish universities in the eighteenth century. Nicholas Phillipson has suggested that its professors were 'practical moralists who had developed a formidable and complex casuistical armoury to instruct young men of middling rank in their duties as men and as citizens of a modern commercial polity.'[37] Practical moralising as a duty of such a professor has also recently been stressed by Richard Sher.[38] While Paul Wood has rightly argued that 'we must guard against simply focusing on moral didacticism, as if this were the hitherto unrecognised key to the Scottish "school" of philosophy',[39] there can be no doubt that moral philosophy was a practical as well as a theoretical discipline (not that such a distinction would have made sense). In teaching moral philosophy, Smith was engaged not only in metaphysics but also in instructing his class in how to behave and in providing them with a critique of existing ideas and institutions from a philosophical perspective. Moral philosophy in the sense of natural law was regarded as an important adjunct to legal study in Scotland, and had been so regarded since at least the beginning of the century.[40] Smith could have expected some of his students not only to go on to study law but also already to be law students. Thus the future Earl of Buchan attended Smith's class in 1762-63 while simultaneously taking John Millar's class in Civil law: a combination of subjects of which his cousin, John Erskine, Professor of Scots Law in Edinburgh, particularly approved.[41] For one of Smith's reforming frame of mind, such a situation presented an opportunity to influence how future lawyers and statesmen saw their legal system and to suggest remedies for deficiencies in it both at the level of its individual laws and at that of its institutions such as courts. In this paper, I shall suggest that Smith offered his students an (at least) implicit criticism of the main Scottish civil court, the Court of Session.

What follows will mainly draw on the published *Theory of Moral Sentiments* (paying attention to developments through the editions), the *The Wealth of Nations*, the student notes of the *Lectures on Rhetoric and Belles Lettres*, and the two student reports of Smith's *Lectures on Jurisprudence* dating from the sessions of 1762-63 and 1763-64. Comparing these two latter sets of student notes with one another and with Smith's published works tends to support the view that they are a good guide to the content of Smith's classes. There are indeed intriguing differences between them, such as the change in structure between the two sets of lecture notes, but they do not have a particular bearing on the subject of this paper.

The argument will be developed in three stages. First, I shall explain Smith's theory of justice indicating why it tended to lead to a favoring of common law over legislation. Secondly, I shall discuss Smith's views of natural jurisprudence and of the origin and development of courts. In the third stage of the argument, I shall discuss his analysis of the English and Scottish courts and his views on how their structure and proceedings promoted or hindered justice. There will finally be some brief, more general, conclusions.

2. SMITH'S THEORY OF JUSTICE

Towards the very end of *The Theory of Moral Sentiments* Smith wrote that: 'Every system of positive law may be regarded as a more or less imperfect attempt towards a system of natural jurisprudence, or towards an enumeration of the particular rules of justice.'[42] He pointed to various factors that tended to prevent 'the decisions of positive law [from] coincid[ing] exactly, in every case, with the rules which the natural sense of justice would dictate.'[43] He went on to comment that one would have expected 'the reasonings of lawyers, upon the different imperfections and improvements of the laws of different countries' would have led them 'to aim at establishing a system of what might properly be called natural jurisprudence, or a theory of the general principles which ought to run through and be the foundation of the laws of all nations.' He noted that Grotius was the first to attempt this.[44] Smith thus set out the task of natural jurisprudence, and though in *The Theory of Moral Sentiments* he noted that he would deal elsewhere with 'the general principles of law and government',[45] it none the less has to be the starting point for a discussion of Smith's jurisprudence, as the *Lectures* assume a knowledge of what is there stated.

The Theory of Moral Sentiments is largely devoted to answering the question: How is moral judgement possible? As is well known, Smith answered by putting forward his notions of sympathy and the impartial spectator.[46] He argued that as human beings we had the capacity to enter sympathetically into the feelings of others: we could appreciate their pains and their pleasures by an act of imagination, though we experienced their feelings less keenly than they did themselves. Furthermore, we found pleasure in the agreement of our sentiments or feelings with those of others. We also judged the propriety or impropriety of another's sentiments by their correspondence or otherwise with our own. When, however, we felt some passion, we wished spectators to feel the same, but we could only achieve this by reducing our passion to the pitch of that of the spectators.[47]

Smith applied these basic ideas to the forming of moral judgments about the behaviour of others. There were two ways in which we made such judgements: first, we could judge the propriety of others' behaviour; secondly, we could judge its merit or demerit. Our sense of the propriety of behaviour was socially created through the mechanism of mutual sympathy:

> Upon these two different efforts, upon that of the spectator to enter into the sentiments of the person principally concerned and upon that of the person principally concerned, to bring down his emotions to what the spectator can go along with, are founded two different sets of virtues.

The ... amiable virtues, the virtues of candid condescension and indulgent humanity, are founded upon the one: the great, the awful and respectable, the virtues of self-denial, of self-government, of that command of the passions which subjects all the movements of our nature to what our own dignity and honour, and the propriety of our own conduct require, take their origin from the other.[48]

Judgement of merit or demerit, in contrast, arose out of observations of sentiment that gave rise to an action. Approval of that sentiment meant the action was meritorious or deserving reward, disapproval meant it was demeritorious or deserving punishment.[49] Smith explained:

The sentiment which most immediately and directly prompts us to reward, is gratitude; that which most immediately and directly prompts us to punish, is resentment.

To us, therefore, that action must appear to deserve reward, which appears to be the proper and approved object of gratitude; as, on the other hand, that action must appear to deserve punishment, which appears to be the proper and approved object of resentment.[50]

Smith argued that we entered into the feelings of gratitude of a person whom we had seen benefited, and that we also entered into those of resentment against whoever or whatever had wronged him;[51] but we only did this where, in the former case, we approved of the conduct of the person conferring the benefit, and, in the latter case, disapproved of the conduct of the person committing the wrong.[52] Smith stated in his analysis of merit and demerit that 'the sense of merit' was 'a compounded sentiment' made up of two emotions: 'a direct sympathy with the sentiments of the agent, and an indirect sympathy with the gratitude of those who receive the benefit of his actions.'[53] Demerit was also 'a compounded sentiment': 'a direct antipathy to the sentiments of the agent, and an indirect sympathy with the resentment of the sufferer.'[54]

This is where justice entered the argument in *The Theory of Moral Sentiments*. Beneficent actions might deserve reward, but such reward, if not forthcoming, could not be extorted by force. Refusal by a person to reward his or her benefactor might cause disapprobation, and '[t]he heart of every impartial spectator rejects all fellow-feeling with the selfishness of his motives'; such an ungrateful person was not, however, the object of resentment, since 'mere want of beneficence tends to do no real positive evil'.[55] It was otherwise with hurtful actions. Smith had a little earlier commented that: 'The natural gratification of this passion [of resentment] tends, of its own accord, to produce all the political ends of punishment; the correction of the criminal, and the example to the public.'[56] In comparing the virtues of justice and beneficence Smith wrote: 'Resentment seems to have been given us by nature for defence, and for defence only. It is the safeguard of justice and the security of innocence.'[57] He commented that 'the violation of justice is injury: it does real and positive hurt to some particular persons, from motives which are naturally disapproved of. It is, therefore, the proper object of resentment, and of punishment, which is the natural consequence of resentment.'[58] Furthermore, in contrast with other virtues, we felt particularly bound to observe justice, and even the person committing an injustice was sensible of the propriety of the use of force to obstruct him or to punish him. We felt greater sympathy with a person's pain than with a person's joy: it was a stronger, more universal sympathy that we appreciated more keenly.[59] Smith stressed that the foundation of punishment in the sentiments of the person wronged and the sympathetic sentiments of the spectators was 'natural':

> Among equals each individual is naturally, and antecedent to the institution of civil government, regarded as having a right both to defend himself from injuries, and to exact a certain degree of punishment for those which have been done to him. Every generous spectator not only approves of his conduct when he does this, but enters so far into his sentiments as often to be willing to assist him.[60]

Though there was propriety in practising justice, it deserved little gratitude: 'Mere justice is, upon most occasions, but a negative virtue, and only hinders us from hurting our neighbour. The man who barely abstains from violating either the person, or the estate, or the reputation of his neighbours, has surely very little positive merit. ... We may often fulfil all the rules of justice by sitting still and doing nothing.'[61]

Smith's discussion has tended to switch between spectators considered as real individuals acting sympathetically to aid a wronged individual, and impartial spectators, the latter the more abstract concept he was ultimately to conceive of as conscience. He called on the latter concept to explain our sense of justice and remorse and our consciousness of merit. He pointed out that the only proper motive for hurting another individual was 'just indignation for evil which that other has done to us'. Individuals, however, preferred their own happiness to that of others but to injure others to promote our own happiness was 'what no impartial spectator can go along with'. We had to view our actions not in the light in which they appeared to ourselves but in that in which they appeared to others. An individual might naturally prefer himself to all mankind 'yet he dares not look mankind in the face, and avow that he acts according to that principle'. The mutual sympathy mechanism operated:

> If he would act so as that the impartial spectator may enter into the principles of his conduct, which is what of all things he has the greatest desire to do, he must, upon this, as upon all other occasions, humble the arrogance of his self-love, and bring it down to something which other men can go along with.[62]

The spectatorial test provided a measure for just punishment:

The most sacred laws of justice, therefore, those whose violation seems to call loudest for vengeance and punishment, are the laws which guard the life and person of our neighbour; the next are those which guard his property and possessions; and last of all come those which guard what are called his personal rights, or what is due him from the promises of others.[63]

Smith argued that a society could not exist unless the laws of justice were 'tolerably' (an important adverb) observed, as justice supported 'the immense fabric of human society'.[64] Yet despite the evident utility of justice, we upheld it not for this reason, but because of our abhorrence of injustice.[65]

The spectatorial test for justice thus gave rise to rights: initially natural rights to defend oneself against injury and to punish someone who had injured one. It is important to note that Smith argued that these rights arose out of concrete instances and experiences of injuries, which gave rise to the general rules of justice as a virtue. He wrote (talking of rules of morality generally):

They are ultimately founded upon experience of what, in particular instances, our moral faculties, our natural sense of merit and propriety, approve, or disapprove of. We do not originally approve or condemn particular actions; because, upon examination, they appear to be agreeable or inconsistent with a certain general rule. The general rule, on the contrary, is formed, by finding from experience, that all actions of a certain kind, or circumstanced in a certain manner, are approved or disapproved of.

He gave as an instance the man who first saw a murder:

His detestation of this crime, it is evident, would arise instantaneously and antecedent to his having formed to himself any such general rule. The general rule, on the contrary, which he might afterwards form, would be founded upon the detestation which he felt necessarily arise in his own breast, at the thought of this, and every other particular action of the same kind.[66]

Such general rules arising in this fashion would then serve as guides to others for conduct.[67] One special feature of the rules of justice thus developed was that they were very exact: 'The rules of justice are accurate in the highest degree, and admit of no exceptions or modifications, but such as may be ascertained as accurately as the rules themselves, and which generally, indeed, flow from the very same principles with them.' The good man kept precisely to the rules of justice; to indulge in chicanery about them was a first step to other enormities.[68] Smith compared the rules of justice to those of grammar: they were 'precise, accurate, and indispensable'.[69]

The purpose of natural jurisprudence was to elaborate and explain the rules of justice thus arising from the moral sentiments. In doing so it provided, as noted above, 'a theory of the general principles which ought to run through and be the foundation of the laws of all nations.'[70] Natural jurisprudence was in this sense a practical discipline. Smith wrote in the discussion 'Of the Character of Virtue' added in the 1790 edition:

The wisdom of every state or commonwealth endeavours, as well as it can, to employ the force of the society to restrain those who are subject to its authority, from hurting or disturbing the happiness of one another. The rules which it establishes for this purpose, constitute the civil and criminal law of each particular state or country. The principles upon which those rules are, or ought to be founded, are the subject of a particular science ... that of natural jurisprudence ....[71]

The task of natural jurisprudence was thus to explain what the laws ought to be. It is important to bear in mind that for Smith this meant not just aiding legislators, but also judges. Elsewhere in *The Theory of Moral Sentiments* he wrote that '[i]t is the end of jurisprudence to prescribe rules for the decisions of judges and arbiters.'[72] To examine Smith's attempt at natural jurisprudence it is necessary next to turn to the *Lectures*.

3. NATURAL JURISPRUDENCE AND THE ORIGIN OF COURTS

We have seen that in *The Theory of Moral Sentiments* Smith put forward an abstract account of justice based on rights not to be injured. His discussion focussed on the 'natural' right not to be injured in one's person; but he also alluded to rights not to be injured in one's property and possessions, and in one's personal rights. Government had the task in civil society of protecting rights through the enforcement of justice. It was these ideas which Smith elaborated in the *Lectures on Jurisprudence*.

It is not necessary to discuss in detail Smith's analysis of rights; nor do I propose to discuss the connection between justice and police. Smith pointed out that civil government preserved justice by protecting perfect rights: 'Justice is violated whenever one is deprived of what he had a right to and could justly demand from others, or rather, when we do him any injury or hurt without a cause.'[73] A 'man' (as Smith put it) could be injured: first, as a man; secondly, as a member of a family; and thirdly, as a citizen or member of a state.[74] As a man he could be injured in his body, reputation, or estate. Injuries to a man's estate were further subdivided into injuries to real rights and injuries to personal rights. Real rights arose from property, servitudes, pledges, and exclusive privileges. Personal rights arose from contract, quasi-contract, or delinquency. Injury to a man's body or reputation were injuries to natural rights. Injury to a man's estate were injuries to adventitious rights.[75] Some aspects of this analysis may require clarification. First, when Smith talked of 'natural' rights, he did not allude to some supposed state of nature.[76] Such rights were rights which existed in any society, and which would always be recognised by spectators: and indeed we have seen that Smith's discussion of justice in *The Theory of Moral Sentiments* mainly focused on such rights. Since this was the meaning of 'natural' rights, it followed that adventitious rights were dependent on social development: not being 'natural', they would not be universally recognised by spectators. Secondly, he is reported, however, as referring at one point in the earlier set of student notes to property as a 'natural' right: 'The only case where the origin of naturall rights is not altogether plain, is in that of property.'[77] In the second set of notes, Smith quite plainly is reported as considering property an adventitious right.[78] Nothing of great moment follows from this. For Smith the distinction between natural rights and adventitious rights was simply that the latter were dependent on historical development: both were ultimately recognised by spectatorial sympathy. Furthermore, later in the first set of notes, Smith is recorded as describing property as an adventitious right.[79] In any case, property could be viewed as 'natural' in the sense that it was necessary to sustain life: there was always a need for individuals to have rights to clothing, food, and other prerequisites of human existence. If there is an apparent terminological muddle either by Smith or the student it is unimportant. Thirdly, in Smith's extended analysis, the violation of 'natural' rights was treated alongside the violation of 'adventitious' rights, where he discussed rights arising out of delinquency or delict.[80] Given the *schema* into which he fitted his analysis of rights this is correct, though at first sight odd. A fourth and final potential problem is that 'natural' rights were not always enforced or enforceable. I shall return to this below: again it relates to historical development. These apparent problems are not really such.

Smith explained different types of society using the analytic device of four stages. The first was that of hunters and fishers, of which he is reported as stating in one set of notes: 'among hunters there is no regular government; they live according to the laws of nature.'[81] If a population were too large to be sustained by this way of life, it would domesticate animals and be a pastoral society. The domestication of animals required a notion of ownership beyond immediate possession and a more developed form of government. Thus came into existence the more extended adventitious right of property. Should a pastoralist society increase in size so as not to be able to maintain itself in this fashion, it would turn to agriculture. This extended the conception of ownership and created further adventitious rights. As an agricultural society improved its techniques of cultivation, surpluses would be created, leading to trading. This growth of commerce would finally usher in commercial society, further multiplying adventitious rights.[82]

Rights accordingly developed historically, being recognised by the spectatorial test. Thus, in a society of hunters, when property was limited to possession, spectators would protect that possession.[83] But we may note that in the same age, because government was weak, natural rights were not fully enforced. Thus, according to Smith, death was the natural punishment for murder as judged by the spectatorial test. But in the earliest state of society the community could not enforce this, but would impose a compromise to ensure peace.[84] Similarly, in an age of shepherds, propriety would require the recognition of acquisition of property by accession as well as by occupation.[85] Agriculture would multiply the opportunities for acquisition by accession.[86] Eventually, spectators would recognise acquisition of property by prescription and succession.[87] Ultimately the impartial spectator would recognise rights arising out of contracts.[88] What then became crucial was the enforcement of rights, and this was a matter of government and related to social development.

Smith analysed government into three types: monarchical; aristocratic; and democratic. The latter two were republican. The sovereign power of government had three aspects: legislation; judging or establishing judges; and making peace or war.[89] Here I shall trace Smith's views on the development of courts and of legislation. His account of this is found in his discussion of government, and it is neither entirely clear nor easy to disentangle, but the main outlines are discoverable. It is important to stress that Smith did not closely map the development of courts onto his analytic device of the four stages: thus, though in what follows the stages will play some part, they do not in themselves explain the origin and development of courts. Smith had a sophisticated view of history and did not see the four stages as necessarily following on from one another to provide a crudely determinist theory of social change.

Smith argued that in an age of hunters there was very little government, but what there was would be democratic. The judicial power, in so far as it existed, would be exercised by the whole community collectively. Family matters would be left entirely to each family. Disputes among others would be rare; but if they occurred the whole community would mediate: 'The design of their intermeddling is to preserve the public quiet and the safety of individuals; they therefore endeavour to bring about a reconcilement betwixt the parties at variance.' Occasional individuals might be put to death for a heinous crime; 'but this is not in a judiciall way, but thro' the resentment or indignation the crime has raised in each individuall.' Finally, there was no legislative power.[90] The great leap that was represented by the age of shepherds, when the adventitious right of property came into existence, was what introduced government. Property meant inequality, and it was necessary to protect the property of the rich.[91] Furthermore, the introduction of property multiplied the causes of dispute: there would have been need for a judicial process. This would be met by gatherings of the people as a whole, though the rich would undoubtedly take the lead and influence others.[92] Legislation would not be met with in this age: 'Laws and regulations are the product of more refind [sic] manners and improved government, and are never found till it is considerably advanced.'[93] As society further developed, however, not only did cultivation of arts and manufactures make attendance at trials more difficult, but causes of dispute multiplied. Consequently, a number of men would be chosen by the people to deal with disputes. The leading men would be among them.[94] There was still little scope for the legislative power.[95]

How did these assemblies of the whole people, or subsequently of men delegated by the whole people, decide causes? Smith is not entirely clear on the issue. He pointed out that these assemblies and courts first interposed 'as a friend without any legall authority', but grew to have a power similar to that of arbiters in deciding causes brought before them and inflicting 'some gentle penalty'. They then came to punish atrocious crimes, and finally came to have the power 'of a free judiciall authority'. Crucial in this development from compensation to punishment was the punishment of treachery or treason by government as it grew in power, as the state first punished actions that most immediately affected it.[96] Smith again added that there was little legislation in this period.[97] But since this was a property-owning society, there had to be regulations -- indeed, Smith had shortly before told his class that: 'Settled laws therefore, or agreements concerning property, will soon be made after the commencement of the age of shepherds.'[98] Here he added that such law 'would be but very short and have few distinctions in it, so that every man would understand it without any written or regular law.'[99] Though Smith does not spell it out, he can only have envisaged such laws being created by the mechanism of spectatorial sympathy. And, as he had argued in *The Theory of Moral Sentiments*, general rules would have been created by sympathetic reaction to individual cases. In other words, it would have been a type of common law. The authority of these rules would derive from the decisions being made initially by the community as a whole or by those delegated by the community to be judges. Governments as yet did not have the authority to legislate.[100]

After this, Smith went on to describe to his class the rise of chieftains of tribes, and the rise of republican governments in Greece and Rome, which moved through an aristocratic to a democratic form. He discussed the fall of the Roman Republic and the rise of the Imperial military monarchy, and finally the fall of the Roman Empire and the erection on its ruins first of allodial, and then of feudal, government. He made some remarks on the administration of law in these discussions to which I shall return below, especially as regards England and Scotland. It is only after this very lengthy discussion that he returned to the judicial and legislative powers considered in the abstract. Smith now briefly recounted again the rise of the judicial power until it became absolute.[101] It was the growth of judicial power into an absolute power (a process which he did not specify in historical detail) that occasioned the appearance of legislation: 'The thing which has given occasion to the establishment of laws has always been the generall or partiall institution of judges. When any nation has retaind [sic] its liberty, and property has been established amongst them, judges must soon be appointed to determine the many disputes which must occurr concerning it. A judge will to such an early nation appear very terrible.'[102] He later continued:

What shall be done in this case? The only way is to establish laws and rules which may ascertain his conduct; ... for when it is known in what manner he is to proceed the terror will be in a great measure removed. Laws are in this manner posterior the establishment of judges. At the first establishment of judges there are no laws; every one trusts to the naturall feeling of justice he has in his own breast and expects to find in others. Were laws to be established in the beginnings of society prior to the judges, they would then be a restraint upon liberty, but when established after them they extend and secure it, as they do not ascertain or restrain the actions of private persons so much as the power and conduct of the judge over the people.[103]

While this may not be exactly consistent with what Smith told his class earlier, since it suggests legislation followed more swiftly on the establishment of courts than he there said, the basic idea is clear: in a people that had retained its liberty, the aim of laws was to restrain the arbitrary authority of judges.[104]

It is important here to consider some remarks in the *Lectures on Rhetoric and Belles Lettres*, the surviving notes from which come from the same session as the first set of notes on jurisprudence. There Smith gave an account of the rise of courts apparently somewhat different from that in the *Lectures on Jurisprudence*. While in the latter he had considered courts in the pastoral age as some sort of delegated assembly of the whole people, here he stated that the first judges were eminent men to whom others submitted their disputes. Judges such as the kings and consuls and other magistrates of Rome would have found their judicial office burdensome: 'They therefore were very bold in passing sentence. They would pay very little regard to the conduct of their predecessors as this was the least important part of their office.'[105] To ease the burdens of these great men, their judicial office was given to another set of magistrates, whose only office was judicial, and who 'would be at pains even to strengthen their conduct by the authority of their predecessors. ... Whatever therefore had been practised by other judges would obtain authority with them and be received in time as Law.'[106] This fills in the 'gap' in the *Lectures on Jurisprudence*, and explains why in the latter the treatment of the appointment of judges was separated by the account of the rise of chieftains and kings from Smith's discussion of courts in early pastoral society as delegated bodies of the people. Judges as such were appointed only after chieftains or other similar figures had emerged, the latter having inevitably been burdened with settling disputes, because of their authority. This understanding of the account in the *Lectures on Rhetoric and Belles Lettres* makes it reasonably compatible with those on jurisprudence and is supported by what Smith was to write in the *Wealth of Nations*.[107] Such judges, once appointed, tended to follow precedent. Smith next drew an important comparison:

This is the case in England. The Sentences of former Cases are greatly regarded and form what is called the common law, which is found to be much more equitable than that which is founded on Statute only, for the reason as what is founded on practise and experience must be better adapted to particular cases than that which is derived from theory only.[108]

Common law thus permitted the spectatorial mechanism to operate to recognise and enforce rights as they arose historically, rather than theoretically through legislation. Precedent prevented judges from acting arbitrarily. But Smith added that for this to be so, judges must be few in number: where they were numerous, responsibility was not easily laid on any individual judge if an inequitable decision were made. Furthermore, 'a great number of Judges naturally confirm each others prejudices and enflame each others Passions.'[109] In other words, the mechanism of mutual sympathy operated within the group of judges, rather than between the judge and litigants. What Smith had in mind here was numbers of judges deciding one case. He added that: 'We see accordingly that the Sentences of the Judges in England are greatly more equitable than those of the Parliament of Paris or other Courts which are secured from censure by their number.'[110]

We may then conclude that as rights developed in the various stages of society, courts became necessary to enforce them. At first courts decided on the basis of spectatorial sympathy creating common law, but in free nations judges came to be seen as having a potentially arbitrary power, and laws were made to restrain that power. The aim of such laws would presumably have been to inscribe into legislation rights as defined by the spectatorial test. What was important was that courts should continue to apply natural jurisprudence whether in the form of common law or that of legislation. Common law, however, was the best type of law as closest to justice because it arose directly from cases requiring the exercise of spectatorial sympathy, rather than from abstract speculation. But for common law to avoid arbitrariness it required a doctrine of precedent to avoid excessive judicial freedom. One prerequisite for this was that courts consist of few judges and not be like, for example, the Areopagus at Athens. Another was the separation of the judicial power from that of government, which was 'the great advantage which modern times have over ancient, and the foundation of that greater Security which we now enjoy both with regard to Liberty, property and Life.'[111]

4. THE SCOTTISH AND ENGLISH COURTS

The above will have indicated that Smith considered the English courts well adapted to securing liberty (through their lack of arbitrariness) and justice (through the common law). In this section of the paper I shall attempt to explain why he thought this was so. I shall then apply his analysis to the Scottish courts. Once more Smith approached the matter historically. I shall add in advance that the remarks made above about the English courts and precedent, though drawn from the *Lectures on Rhetoric and Belles Lettres*, will be shown to be quite consistent with what he told his class in those on jurisprudence.

Smith stated in his discussion of government that '[a]nother thing which tends to secure liberty is the form of the courts of justice.'[112] He was here considering England.[113] Smith explained this historically. He referred to the Chief Justiciary who became very powerful as both judge and collector of revenues under the early English kings. Edward I destroyed this power as it rivalled his own, and in the place of the Great Justiciary created four courts: Common Pleas, Kings Bench, Exchequer, and Chancery, (Smith added that this last 'was at first only an office of briefs').[114] Smith next stated that Edward appointed as judges men who 'were generally of the meanest sort of no fortune or rank, who had been bread [sic] to the knowledge of the law.'[115] Because they were 'all low men who depended on the will of the king, they would be very unwilling and afraid in any shape to go beyond the meaning of the law or any ways to alter it; and therefore in all cases brieves and writts were drawn out according to which they decided justice, and exact records of all proceedings were kept in the officina brevium.'[116] Smith suggested that the 'meanness' of the judges made them suspected by both king and people 'by the irregularity and injustice of their proceedings'. Accordingly:

> They were therefore orderd [sic] to judge by the strict law, and were to be tried in their proceedings by their own records, which were kept all along with great exactness, and no alteration, explanations, or amendments of any sort would be admitted, and any attempt of this sort would be punishable.[117]

Smith had already stated:

> I had observed another thing which greatly confirms the liberty of the subjects in England. – This was the little power of the judges in explaining, altering, or extending or correcting the meaning of the laws, and the great exactness with which they must be observed according to the literall meaning of the words, of which history affords us many instances.[118]

Smith may possibly have been referring here to the interpretation of statutes, but whether or not, the exact following of precedent or legislation avoided judicial arbitrariness. All this meant that the powers of the judges were small: brieves or writs had to be followed precisely, 'or if there be any particular statute with respect to any cause, the words of the statute are in like manner to be observ'd exactly.'[119] Smith further argued that the existence of three courts 'support[ed] the liberty of the people and render[ed] the proceedings ... very exact'. This was because Kings Bench, Common Pleas, and Exchequer all became rivals and started to compete for business. Kings Bench and Exchequer extended their jurisdiction by fictions, with the result that:

> As the whole profits of the courts thus depended on the numbers of civill causes which came before them, they would naturally endeavour to invite every one to lay his cause before their court, by the precision, accuracy, and expedition (where agreeable) of their proceedings, which emulation made a still greater care and exactness of the judges.[120]

This was a point Smith was to develop further in the *Wealth of Nations*:

> The present admirable constitution of the courts of justice in England was, perhaps, originally in a great measure, formed by this emulation, which antiently took place between their respective judges; each judge endeavouring to give, in his own court, the speediest and most effectual remedy, which the law would admit, for every sort of injustice.[121]

The competition made the courts not only more effective, it also made them promote justice. Smith next recounted in his lectures the rise of Chancery as a court and the growth of its jurisdiction.[122] The Chancellor, however, was 'as arbitrary a judge as most. But neither is he very dangerous to the liberty of the subject, as he can not try any causes besides those which have no remedy at common law. Nor can he in any case act directly contrary to any method of proceeding laid down by the courts of common law. And from this court as from all others appeals may be carried before the House of Lords.'[123] Smith next pointed to juries as curbing the power of judges, as they decided the facts in all causes.[124] English law ensured juries were impartial: this was 'a great security of the liberty of the subject.'[125] The one defect of the English jury was the requirement of unanimity: this made service disagreeable.[126] Smith finished his encomium to the English court system by commenting:

> There seems to be no country in which the courts are more under regulation and the authority of the judge more restricted. The form of proceedings as well as the accuracy of the courts depends greatly on their standing. Now the courts of England are by far more regular than those of other countries, as well as more ancient. ...
>
> New courts and new laws are ... great evills. Every court is bound only by its own practise. It takes time and repeated practise to ascertain the precise meaning of a law or to have precedents enough to determine the practise of a court. Its proceedings will be altogether loose and inaccurate[.][127]

This passage is important, and I shall return to it later; but it is worth noting that historical continuity in law was regarded by Smith as important in avoiding arbitrariness. It is another of his many arguments against innovative legislation. In an earlier lecture Smith had told his class:

The English law was ... formed into a system before the discovery of Justinians Pandects; and its courts established, and their methods of proceedings pretty much fixed, before the other courts in Europe were instituted, or the civil and cannon law came to be of any great weight. It is for this reason that it borrows less from those laws than the law of any other nation in Europe; and is for that reason more deserving of the attention of a speculative man than any other, as being more formed on the naturall sentiments of mankind.[128]

The meaning is plain. Because of its historical continuity, English law had been formed as a system of natural jurisprudence. This was because the judges were prevented from being arbitrary, for the reasons already canvassed. Smith gave at least one instance of English judges inscribing into law a community practice, thereby recognising a right. This was as regards the form of succession known as Borough-English. He told his class:

'The judges, who must regulate their sentence by the common practise, finding it to be in common use that the youngest son should succeed to all his father died possessed of, established this as the rule in the severall burrows and counties where they found this practise.'[129]

As well as these historical and structural reasons for the English courts not being arbitrary and thus being just, another reason for their securing liberty was the independence of judges from the king. Judges held their offices for life and were accountable for wrongdoing.[130]

In contrast with the attention devoted to the English courts, Smith said little on those of Scotland. This in itself may be of little significance, as his students would have been much more likely to be familiar with the Scottish than the English courts. There are some allusions to a number of Scottish courts,[131] but the only one that he discussed to any extent was the Court of Session. My remarks will accordingly be confined to his treatment of it.

I have mentioned above that Smith contrasted the English courts with the *Parlement de Paris*, arguing that the decisions of the former were more equitable than those of the latter because there were few judges. Smith also alluded to 'other Courts which are secured from censure by their number.'[132] A first point to be considered is whether the Court of Session was one of those other courts. The standard view in Smith's day was that the Court of Session had been modelled on the *Parlement de Paris*.[133] This is mistaken, and the two courts were really quite different in many ways, but it is worth reflecting on. The Court of Session was, however, a collegiate court of fifteen judges, and though interlocutory matters could be dealt with by a single judge, in all causes of significance final decrees were issued collectively. Did Smith consider fifteen to be a sufficiently large number that judges could feel secure from censure if they acted arbitrarily? It is important to examine the mentions made of the Court of Session by Smith.

Smith's first reference to the Court was in his discussion of contract. He noted the use of indentures in England and commented:

This method is in disuse in Scotland. We may observe that where courts are for a long time on the same footing there is much less difference in the manner of proceding from the old customs than where new courts are instituted. Now the constitution of England has long been much the same with regard to the courts as it is at present. The Court of Kings Bench is as old as Edward Ists time; that of the Exchequer much older; and also that of Common Pleas is very old: these accordingly adhere in a great measure to the old manner of proceedings. A new court, as that of the Star Chamber instituted by Henry 8th, would pay little attention to those of former courts, and we see accordingly that it proceeded very arbitrarily as long as it subsisted. The constitutions of Scotland are of very late establishment. The Court of Session in its present form was created by James the [fifth]. A new court, ispecially a supreme one as this is in many causes, would instead of adhering to the proceedings of the old alter them in many circumstances; as all new courts are supposed to be intended to correct some defects of the old ones.[134]

It is surely significant that Smith has here linked the Court of Session with Star Chamber, and has pointed out that, as a new court, it would not have following existing precedents, a practice he considered necessary to avoid judicial arbitrariness. Smith's next mention of the Court of Session came when he pointed out that in Scotland, as in most of Europe, *nuda pacta* sustained an action. This was because 'these courts, as the Parliament of Paris and the Court of Session, were established long after the civil and cannon law had been in great force in these countries, and consequently borrow considerably from both of these laws.'[135] It was after this comment that Smith drew a contrast with the English law's antiquity and its being 'more formed on the naturall sentiments of mankind', in the passage quoted above.[136] Again, the newness of the Court of Session is highlighted; a link is also made with the *Parlement de Paris*, and a contrast with the English law.

Smith's views on the forms of the courts of justice as a means of securing liberty have been discussed above, and they amounted to a general encomium on the English courts.[137] Smith made some remarks there on the Court of Session. First, after commenting on the strictness of procedure on writs (which restricted the power of English judges) he told his class: 'But there is this difference, that the Court of Session, being of late institution and formed in great part on the cannon and civil law, one may apply to it immediately.'[138] This meant, of course, that no one could go away from court without redress, as he had just pointed out could happen in England were there no chancery writ applicable; but since he was later to indicate that the Chancellor gave a remedy in these circumstances, one possible implication of his remarks was that the lack of the strict forms of action in Scotland made the Court of Session potentially arbitrary. Smith mentioned the Court of Session in discussing juries: 'The Court of Session in Scotland never use a jury. The reason seems to be that being 15 in number they considered themselves as a jury.'[139] One needs only recall his opinion that juries curbed the arbitrary power of the judge.[140] His final comment on the Court of Session in his discussion of the importance of the form of the courts of justice in securing liberty came in his remarks about the significance of the antiquity of the English courts. He told his class:

> The courts of England are much more ancient than those of France or Scotland. The Parliament of Paris was instituted by Francis the 1st who was contemporary with Henry the 8, and the Court of Session by James the 5th about the same time. As the authority of government is then strong and they have at first no precedents, we see that the courts at their first institution have allways taken great liberties. They are neither tied down by the brieves nor encumbered with a jury. These courts were also instituted after the civil law came to be known and to be a fashionable study; the new courts would disdain to follow the precedents of those courts on whose ruin they had been erected, but would rather follow the rules of the civill law. The Court of Session would pay little regard to the proceedings of the old Court of Justiciary, the Parliat. of Paris to those of the baillies, and the Star Chamber to those of other courts. The law of England is free from all such [illegible] and is therefore of a peculiar nature and well worth the study of a speculative man. ... Our courts are altogether regulated either by the feudal or civil law.[141]

This was immediately followed by Smith's remarks on the evils of new courts and new laws as causing uncertainty.[142] The Court of Session was once more linked with the *Parlement de Paris* and Star Chamber. Again the discontinuity in the development of the Scottish civil courts is stressed as productive of uncertainty in the law. Furthermore, instead of following precedents and deciding cases on the basis of sentiments and sympathy, the Court used civil and feudal law.

A final point is that the Court of Session was a court of equity as well as of law (Smith specifically described it as such),[143] and the relationship between equity and law was a matter of debate in Scotland when Smith delivered these lectures -- a debate to which the most notable contribution had been that of Lord Kames, who viewed the equitable jurisdiction as the appropriate way of developing and reforming the law.[144] Smith had commented that the Chancellor was an arbitrary judge, but that he was not a threat because of the limited nature of his jurisdiction. He told his class in 1763-64 that: 'In Scotland the office of the English Chancellor is lodged in the Court of Session.'[145] Even if this comment may perhaps be more directed at the initiation of actions rather than the operation of judges, the Court's equitable jurisdiction on Smith's opinion must potentially have led to arbitrariness. This suggests that exploration of the differences between Smith's and Kames's views of common law, equity, and legal development would be fruitful.

Smith has avoided direct criticism of the current practice of the Court of Session, and given his audience and the tight social circle within which he moved, it was obviously politic for him to do so. Yet some criticism must be implied. Not that it is necessary to suppose that he actually considered that the Court of Session in fact acted arbitrarily, but rather that its form was such that it could. It is useful here to summarise his arguments, and to introduce a few new points. First, by Smith's time, the judges of the Court were independent of the crown as they were appointed for life;[146] but it is as well to remember that still in Smith's day great nobles could sit as Extraordinary Lords of Session. This was the type of potential interference in the administration of justice by great men which Smith would have seen as a vestige of feudalism. The last Extraordinary Lord, the Marquess of Tweeddale, was appointed in 1721 (none could be created after 1723), but he lived until 1762.[147] Though essentially obsolete by the time Smith was lecturing in Glasgow, this institution, of which we can fairly assume he was aware, may well have colored his attitude to the Session. Secondly, Smith clearly linked the Court of Session with the *Parlement de Paris* which he had criticised as potentially arbitrary because of its multiplicity of judges. The collegiate structure of the Court of Session laid it open to the same criticism. Thirdly, the Court of Session, as a newly created court, had rejected old precedents and received civil law, thus causing Scots law to depart from law derived from the natural sentiments of mankind on the basis of the spectatorial test of justice in individual cases. Fourthly, the Court of Session used neither forms of action nor juries, two important controls on the arbitrary actions of courts. Fifthly, the Court of Session had a jurisdiction similar to that of the English Chancellor whom Smith regarded as an arbitrary judge. Sixthly, the Court of Session followed the doctrine that Scottish statutes could fall into desuetude (though Smith did not mention this).[148] Smith had argued that the English courts' strict following of the wording of statutes prevented them from being arbitrary. In contrast, Scottish courts could declare Scottish statutes obsolete. The argument, of course, cut two ways. By declaring statutes obsolete, the Court of Session could be seen as deciding justly on the basis of moral sentiments by the spectatorial test. Seventhly, when precedent was so important, the inadequacy of law reports in Scotland at this period must also have been a concern (although again Smith did not refer to this).[149] Eighthly and finally, there was no competition in Scotland between courts and judges to promote efficiency and the adoption of just and attractive remedies. (Though it is worth noting that Smith suggested in the *Wealth of Nations* a system of remuneration '[i]n courts which consisted of a considerable number of judges' that would promote competition among them.)[150] He obviously considered the lack of competition in the Scottish civil courts a disadvantage.

It would be easy to exaggerate this criticism; but it none the less must be significant that Smith's praise was entirely directed to the English courts. It is difficult to escape the conclusion that for Smith the Court of Session was one of those 'other courts' in which the multiplicity of judges promoted arbitrariness. Smith was to write in the *Wealth of Nations*:

> At Rome ... the principal courts of justice consisted either of a single judge, or of a small number of judges, whose characters, especially as they deliberated always in publick, could not fail to be very much affected by any rash or unjust decision. In doubtful cases, such courts, from their anxiety to avoid blame, would naturally endeavour to shelter themselves under the example, or precedent, of the judges who sat before them, either in the same, or in some other courts.[151]

The Scottish judges had safety in numbers. It is also worth noting that in the eighteenth century some commentators saw the Court of Session as acting arbitrarily. David Dalrymple, one of the counsel in *Millar v. Robertson* (1712) remarked: '*In cumulo* one of your Lordships is moved by one Reason, and another by another, which Reasons, if they were examined or determined separately, would be repelled by the Plurality, which also is the Case why in most Sovereign Courts, especially in England, the judges do resolve particular Points, which renders the Reason of the Decision clear, and makes the Precedent of greater Use in other Cases.'[152] This was possible because the judges decided cases by voting among themselves, without necessarily giving justifications for their voting one way or the other. David Hume commented to Smith in a letter of 21 July 1763 about the actions of the judges in the Douglas cause that '[t]heir partiality is palpable and astonishing'.[153] There was also much controversy over the Court's attitude to the legality of the creation of fictitious votes through the establishment of artificial superiorities. Some contemporaries at least saw the judges' behaviour as influenced by political aims.[154] It is worth stressing, however, that the multiplicity of judges might lead to arbitrariness, but it did not necessarily lead to corruption. Smith commented that the French *parlements* were perhaps 'not very convenient courts of justice, but he added that they had never been suspected or accused of corruption.[155]

Smith's views on the Court of Session were an early, perhaps the earliest, contribution to the debate over the structure of the Court of Session that was finally to result in reforms in the early nineteenth century, and Nicholas Phillipson has shown that already in the 1780s reduction in the size of the bench and the introduction of civil juries were being considered to make the Court of Session more efficient and reduce the possibility of corruption.[156] And these reforms did indeed resemble what Smith considered as ideal. The Court remained in theory collegiate, but it was first split into two divisions, and then formally divided into the Outer House where a single judge sat at first instance and could give a final determination of causes subject to a reclaiming motion to the Inner House, now primarily an appeal court.[157] The same period saw the introduction of a jury court which was eventually amalgamated into the Court of Session.[158] These Whig reforms of the Court turned it into an institution somewhat more resembling the English courts that Smith had considered such a bulwark of liberty.[159] The intellectual history of these reforms obviously stretches back into the middle of the eighteenth century, and merits further exploration, especially as some of the debates on reform focused on issues in a way suggesting that they may have had an ancestry in Smith's view of courts.[160] It may also be worth speculating if Smith developed his view of how courts ought to be structured and to operate against the backdrop of his knowledge of the criticisms that could be made of the contemporary Court of Session. His knowledge of the contemporary English courts and their history seems scarcely to have been profound; he may have projected onto them his vision of the ideal court system as different from that of Scotland.

5. CONCLUSION

Smith wrote to the Duc de la Rochefoucauld in 1785 stating that one of 'two ... great works [he had] upon the anvil' was 'a sort or theory and History of Law and Government'.[161] He famously never completed it, though he still optimistically referred to it in the year of his death.[162] This work must surely have contained a discussion of how courts ought to be constituted. In *The Theory of Moral Sentiments* Smith wrote that in some 'countries the unfortunate constitution of their courts of judicature hinders any regular system of jurisprudence from ever establishing itself among them, though the improved manners of the people may be such as would admit of the most accurate.'[163] I hope the above discussion has indicated what Smith would have said about this issue. The way courts operated and were constituted influenced whether or not they would be able to fulfil their role in securing justice and liberty. Duncan Forbes is undoubtedly correct that for Smith liberty largely meant absence of subjection to arbitrary action.[164] Courts thus had above all to be so constituted that they avoided arbitrariness. This required not only that judges be independent of the government, but also that they be few in number, answerable for their actions, and follow precedent. Judges had to be identifiable and open to censure. This promoted liberty. Furthermore, court decisions had to be based on the natural sentiments of humankind. The judges and jurors had to operate within a system that encouraged them to act as impartial spectators. This promoted justice. His description of the English court system indicated how this was to be brought about.

The technical form of courts promoted liberty in free governments, as well as justice; Smith, however, was well aware that the freedom of the government was significant for liberty. Though the French courts might generally be just, they could do nothing against a *lettre de cachet* which deprived an individual of the natural right of liberty.[165]

In Great Britain the courts were able to promote liberty because of institutions such as habeas corpus (which did not apply in Scotland) and the division of sovereignty between Parliament and King -- in short, because of 1688.[166] Smith considered that in the Roman Empire or in England under Cromwell the administration of justice remained regular and people's rights in their private affairs were upheld; while not subject to arbitrary actions by courts, however, the people were subject to such by the sovereign.[167] For the courts to be able to protect liberty completely, government itself had to be free.

One particularly obvious stress in Smith's discussion of courts is that on historical continuity. It is important to realize that for Smith historical continuity did not provide any form of validity or authority in itself. He was not at all a believer in the vulgar Whig ancient constitution. Yet historical continuity was vitally important. Courts should follow precedents, and should have a form which encouraged them to do so. New courts were prone to act arbitrarily because they had no precedents. Precedents, built up incrementally from case to case, were also the best type of law because judges and jurors had to react sympathetically to real situations and realise what was just. A system of precedent progressively created law formed on moral sentiments. Smith nowhere described judges as impartial observers forming moral judgements through the mechanism of sympathy, but that is undoubtedly what he conceived to be their role. The inverse comparison is certainly found. In one passage in *The Theory of Moral Sentiments* (inserted in the second edition), he described the spectator as a judge and the person whose conduct was being judged as the panel (a Scottish legal term for the accused in a criminal trial).[168] His description in the same work of the creation of general rules out of specific decisions is also a description of the creation of common law.[169] But for common law to work as a means both of avoiding arbitrariness and of ensuring law created on the basis of moral sentiments the courts had to have a structure similar to the English courts as he depicted them.

Smith described new laws as 'great evills' because '[i]t takes time and repeated practise to ascertain the precise meaning of a law.'[170] Furthermore, in the United Kingdom, as in most countries, legislation tended to be in the hands of 'that insidious and crafty animal, vulgarly called a statesman or politician' rather than in those 'of a legislator, whose deliberations ought to be governed by general principles'.[171] Smith was realistic about Hanoverian politics and willing to admit that 'the length of the Parliaments, and the great extend of the Civill List' might 'obtain the passing of bad laws.'[172] Moreover, he was also suspicious of those who approached legislation in an overly systematic way.[173] He was, however, by no means opposed to legislation. Common law could hinder justice as well as promote it. Smith pointed out in his discussion of contract that English law was 'more formed on the naturall sentiments of mankind'; he added that '[o]n this account also it is very imperfect with regard to contracts.'[174] Personal rights had developed beyond the provisions of English law. There are many instances in the *Lectures on Jurisprudence* where Smith called for reform,[175] and the *Wealth of Nations* is entirely devoted to doing so. He stated, for example, of primogeniture: 'Laws frequently continue in force long after the circumstances, which first gave occasion to them, and which alone could render them reasonable, are no more.'[176] Legislation, however, had to be carried out carefully, as when a sovereign decided to turn a duty of beneficence into one of law:

Of all the duties of a law-giver, however, this, perhaps, is that which it requires the greatest delicacy and reserve to execute with propriety and judgement. To neglect it altogether exposes the commonwealth to many gross disorders and shocking enormities, and to push it too far is destructive of all liberty, security, and justice.[177]

There was a place for legislation as common law, by its nature, was not always adequate for the task of ensuring the law reflected natural jurisprudence, as custom, after all, could pervert moral sentiments and sanction infanticide;[178] but Smith's general attitude to legislation indicates that he considered legislation should be piecemeal, and only where necessary. Swingeing Benthamite projects of codification would have been considered by him to be folly likely to be productive of judicial arbitrariness and general uncertainty in the law. Smith recognised that continuity and innovation were both necessary, but that there was a delicate tension between them, requiring reform sometimes to be left to common law and sometimes to the legislature.

Natural jurisprudence had the task of ensuring courts decided justly and legislators legislated appropriately. Courts had to administer justice properly, or 'civil society would become a scene of bloodshed and disorder, every man revenging himself at his own hand whenever he fancied he was injured.'[179] But the proper administration of justice did not merely require courts; those courts had to have a form and procedure which allowed them to enforce natural jurisprudence, by ensuring judges did not act arbitrarily, but rather decided on the basis of justice as indicated by the theory of moral sentiments.

NOTES

An early version of this paper was read to a seminar at the University of Sussex on 12 December 1990. I am grateful for the comments of those who attended. Roger Emerson, Knud

Haakonssen, Hector MacQueen, and Donald Winch kindly commented on an earlier draft: none of them would necessarily agree with all that I have written, nor have I always followed the advice given.

1. A. Smith, *An Inquiry into the Nature and Causes of the Wealth of Nations*, ed. by R.H. Campbell and A.S. Skinner [hereinafter cited as *WN* by book, chapter, section (where appropriate) and paragraph] (2 vols., Oxford 1976), V.i.b.1.
2. A. Smith, *Lectures on Jurisprudence*, ed. by R.L. Meek, D.D. Raphael, and P.G. Stein [hereinafter cited as *LJ(A)* (report of 1762-63) by volume and page of original manuscript and *LJ(B)* (report dated 1766) by page of original manuscript] (Oxford, 1978), *LJ(A)*, i.1.
3. *WN*, V.iii.7.
4. *WN*, II.i30; II.iii.36; III.iii.12; III.iv.4; IV.v.b.43; IV.vii.c.54.
5. K. Haakonssen, *The Science of a Legislator: The Natural Jurisprudence of David Hume and Adam Smith* (Cambridge, 1981), 188.
6. *WN*, I.x.c.59.
7. See, e.g., D. Forbes, '"Scientific" Whiggism: Adam Smith and John Millar' (1953-54) 7 *Cambridge Journal*, 643-70; D. Forbes, 'Sceptical Whiggism, Commerce, and Liberty', in A.S. Skinner and T. Wilson (edd.), *Essays on Adam Smith* (Oxford, 1975), 179-201; D. Winch, *Adam Smith's Politics: An Essay in historiographic Revision* (Cambridge, 1978), 70-102; and see generally I. Hont and M. Ignatieff (edd.), *Wealth and Virtue: The Shaping of Political Economy in the Scottish Enlightenment* (Cambridge, 1983).
8. *WN*, III.iv.4.
9. Haakonssen, op. cit. note 5 supra, 151-3.
10. See J.W. Cairns, 'The Influence of Smith's Jurisprudence on Legal Education in Scotland' in P. Jones and A.S. Skinner (edd.), *Adam Smith Reviewed* (Edinburgh, 1992), 168-89 at 177-88.
11. See, e.g., Winch, op. cit. note 7 supra; D. Winch, 'Science and the Legislator: Adam Smith and After' (1983) 93 *Economic Journal*, 501-20; Haakonssen, op. cit. note 5 supra; and (more generally) J.H. Burns, 'The Fabric of Felicity: The Legislator and the Human Condition', in P. King (ed.), *The Study of Politics: A Collection of Inaugural Lectures* (London, 1977), 207-24; and J.H. Burns, 'Scottish Philosophy and the Science of Legislation' (1985) 2-6 *Royal Society of Edinburgh Occasional Papers*, 11-29.
12. *WN*, IV.intro.1.
13. D. Stewart, *Account of the Life and Writings of Adam Smith, LL.D.*, in A. Smith, *Essays on Philosophical Subjects*, ed. by W.P.D. Wightman and J.C. Bryce [hereinafter cited as Stewart, *Account*, by section and paragraph] (Oxford, 1980), IV.1-IV.8.
14. A. Smith, *The Theory of Moral Sentiments*, ed. by D.D. Raphael and A.L. Macfie [hereinafter cited as *TMS* by part, section, chapter (where appropriate) and paragraph] (Oxford, 1976), VII.iv.37; see also *LJ(A)*, i.1; *LJ(B)*, 1 and 5.
15. *TMS*, III.5.6.
16. Haakonssen, op. cit. note 5 supra, 151-3.
17. *TMS*, VII.iv.36.
18. *TMS*, VI.ii.2.17 and 18.
19. Winch, op. cit. note 11 supra, 505.
20. Haakonssen, op. cit. note 5 supra, 135-53.
21. D. Lieberman, *The Province of Legislation Determined: Legal Theory in Eighteenth-Century Britain* (Cambridge, 1989), 1-28.
22. See, e.g., ibid., 99-121.
23. See, e.g., R.H. Campbell and A.S. Skinner, *Adam Smith* (London and Sydney, 1982), 29-30, and 144-7. Hailes and Smith corresponded about matters of mutual interest: see *The Correspondence of Adam Smith*, ed. by E.C. Mossner and I.S. Ross [hereinafter cited as *Corr.*

and by page and letter number] (Oxford, 1977), 139-55 (nos. 115-120).
24. See quotation in text at note 17 supra.
25. D. Winch, 'Adam Smith's "enduring particular result"; a political and cosmopolitan perspective' in Hont and Ignatieff (edd.), op. cit. note 7 supra, 253-69 at 268.
26. W.R. Scott, *Adam Smith as Student and Professor* (Glasgow, 1937), 137-8; *Corr.*, 4 (no. 8).
27. *Corr.* 4-5 (no. 9).
28. Scott, op. cit. note 26 supra, 139-40.
29. [A.F. Tytler], *Memoirs of the Life and Writings of the Honourable Henry Home of Kames, One of the Senators of the College of Justice, and one of the Lords Commissioners of Justiciary in Scotland: Containing Sketches of the Progress of Literature and General Improvement in Scotland During the Greater Part of the Eighteenth Century* (2 vols. Edinburgh, 1807), i, 190-1; Scott, op. cit. note 26 supra, 46-61; Campbell and Skinner, op. cit. note 23 supra, 28-39.
30. Stewart, *Account*, IV.25.
31. On the development of Smith's ideas, see D.D. Raphael, 'Adam Smith and "The Infection of David Hume's Society": New Light on an old Controversy, together with the Text of a hitherto unpublished Manuscript' (1969) 30 *Journal of the History of Ideas*, 225-48; and R.L. Meek, 'New Light on Adam Smith's Glasgow lectures on Jurisprudence' (1976) 8 *History of Political Economy*, 439-77.
32. Stewart, *Account*, I.18-20.
33. *LJ(A)*, i.8 (the relevant section does not survive); *LJ(B)*, 6 and 339-58.
34. Stewart, *Account*, III.1.
35. See, e.g., Cairns, op. cit. note 10 supra, 169.
36. Stewart, *Account*, I. 16-17; A. Smith, *Lectures on Rhetoric and Belles Lettres*, ed. by J.C. Bryce [hereinafter cited as *LRBL* by original volume and page] (Oxford, 1983).
37. N.T. Phillipson, 'Adam Smith as civic moralist', in Hont and Ignatieff (edd.), op. cit. note 7 supra, 179-202 at 179.
38. R.B. Sher, 'Professors of Virtue: The Social History of the Edinburgh Moral Philosophy Chair in the Eighteenth Century', in M.A. Stewart (ed.), *Studies in the Philosophy of the Scottish Enlightenment* (Oxford, 1990), 87-126.
39. P.B. Wood, 'Science and the Pursuit of Virtue in the Aberdeen Enlightenment', in Stewart (ed.) op. cit. note 38 supra, 127-49 at 148.
40. See, e.g. J.W. Cairns, 'John Spotswood, Professor of Law: a Preliminary Sketch', in W.M. Gordon (ed.), *Miscellany Three* (Stair Society: forthcoming).
41. J. Erskine to Lord Cardross, 24 Nov. 1762, Edinburgh University Library, MS La.II.238.
42. *TMS*, VII.iv.36.
43. Ibid.
44. *TMS*, VII.iv.37.
45. Ibid.
46. For fuller, illuminating discussions, see e.g., D.D. Raphael, 'The Impartial Spectator', in A.S. Skinner and T. Wilson (edd.), *Essays on Adam Smith* (Oxford, 1975), 83-99; V.M. Hope, *Virtue by Consensus: The Moral Philosophy of Hutcheson, Hume, and Adam Smith* (Oxford, 1989), 83-117; and T.D. Campbell, *Adam Smith's Science of Morals* (London, 1971), 87-126; A.S. Skinner, 'Adam Smith: Society and Government', in E. Attwooll (ed.), *Perspectives in Jurisprudence* (Glasgow, 1977), 195-220.
47. *TMS*, I.i.1-4.
48. *TMS*, I.i.5.1.
49. *TMS*, II.i.intro.2.
50. *TMS*, II.i.1.2 and 3.
51. *TMS*, II.i.2.4. and 5.
52. *TMS*, II.i.3.2 and 3.

53. *TMS*, II.i.5.2.
54. *TMS*, II.i.5.5.
55. *TMS*, II.ii.1.3.
56. *TMS*, II.i.1.6.
57. *TMS*, II.ii.1.4.
58. *TMS*, II.ii.1.5.
59. *TMS*, I.ii.1.2; II.ii.1.5; II.ii.2.3; see Haakonssen, op. cit. note 5 supra, 83-87.
60. *TMS*, II.ii.1.7.
61. *TMS*, II.ii.1.9.
62. *TMS*, II.ii.2.1.
63. *TMS*, II.ii.2.2.
64. *TMS*, II.ii.3.6 and 4.
65. *TMS*, II.ii.3.9-11.
66. *TMS*, III.4.8 (this passage placed differently in editions earlier than the sixth).
67. *TMS*, III.4.11 (this passage placed differently in editions earlier than the sixth).
68. *TMS*, III.6.10.
69. *TMS*, III.6.11; see also *TMS*, VII.iv.1.
70. *TMS*, VII.iv.37.
71. *TMS*, VI.ii.intro.2.
72. *TMS*, VII.iv.8.
73. *LJ(A)*, i.9.
74. *LJ(A)*, i.10; see also *LJ(B)*, 6-7.
75. *LJ(A)*, i.12-i.23; *LJ(B)*, 7-11.
76. *LJ(B)*, 3.
77. *LJ(A)*, i.25.
78. *LJ(B)*, 8.
79. *LJ(A)*, ii.93.
80. Ibid.
81. *LJ(B)*, 19.
82. *LJ(A)*, i.27-i.32; *LJ(B)*, 149-50. On this type of stadial theory of social development, see R.L. Meek, 'Smith, Turgot, and the "Four Stages" theory' (1971) 3 *History of Political Economy*, 9-27; R.L. Meek, *Social Science and the Ignoble Savage* (Cambridge, 1976); P. Stein, *Legal Evolution: The Story of an Idea* (Cambridge, 1980), 15-50; P. Stein, *The Character and Influence of the Roman Civil Law: Historical Essays* (London and Ronceverte, 1988), 395-409. On its significance in Smith, see Winch, op. cit. note 25 supra, 258-62.
83. *LJ(A)*, i.36-7; i.42-4.
84. *LJ(A)*, ii.94-5; *LJ(B)*, 181-4.
85. *LJ(A)*, i.64-5; *LJ(B)*, 152.
86. *LJ(A)*, i.65-6.
87. *LJ(A)*, i.77; i.93; i.150-1.
88. *LJ(A)*, ii.43.
89. *LJ(A)*, iv.1-3; *LJ(B)*, 18-19 and 22.
90. *LJ(A)*, iv.4-6; see also *LJ(B)* 19.
91. *LJ(A)*, iv.7; *LJ(B)*, 20. On this advance being the greatest progression, see *LJ(A)*, ii.97.
92. *LJ(A)*, iv. 9-11.
93. *LJ(A)*, iv.14-15.
94. *LJ(A)*, iv.15.
95. *LJ(A)*, iv.18.
96. *LJ(A)*, ii.152-153; iv.26-27; iv.34.
97. *LJ(A)*, iv.35.
98. *LJ(A)*, iv.24.

99. *LJ(A)*, iv.35.
100. Ibid.
101. *LJ(A)*, v.105-7.
102. *LJ(A)*, v.108.
103. *LJ(A)*, v.110-11 (reading 'extent' as 'extend', as suggested in footnote 69).
104. *LJ(A)*, v.112.
105. *LRBL*, ii.199-200.
106. *LRBL*, ii.200.
107. *WN*, V.i.b.11-15.
108. *LRBL*, ii.200.
109. *LRBL*, ii.201.
110. Ibid.
111. *LRBL*, ii.203.
112. *LJ(A)*, v.12.
113. This is obvious from the context and his comment about the courts in Scotland before 1745.
114. *LJ(A)*, v.13-15; v.20-1.
115. *LJ(A)*, v.21.
116. *LJ(A)*, v.22.
117. *LJ(A)*, v.23-4.
118. *LJ(A)*, v.15.
119. *LJ(A)*, v.24.
120. *LJ(A)*, v.25-7.
121. *WN*, V.i.b.21.
122. *LJ(A)*, v.27-31.
123. *LJ(A)*, v.31-2.
124. *LJ(A)*, v.32.
125. *LJ(A)*, v.35-6.
126. *LJ(A)*, v.37-40.
127. *LJ(A)*, v.42-3.
128. *LJ(A)*, ii.74-5.
129. *LJ(A)*, i.148.
130. *LJ(A)*, v.5.
131. He discussed juries in the High Court of Justiciary, the Scottish criminal court: *LJ(A)*, v.37-41. This court had as its head in his day a nobleman as the Lord-Justice General, who can be traced as still sometimes sitting on the bench well into the mid-eighteenth century; but he was now apparently a largely titular head. Smith, however, surely could not have approved. He alluded to the survival of the Regality Courts: *LJ(A)*, v.12-13. These were abolished in 1747. Smith cannot have approved of them as franchise courts -- a great landowner exercising jurisdiction, one of the functions of government. He also made a passing reference to the sheriffs: *LJ(A)* v.5.
132. *LRBL*, ii.201: see text at notes 108-10 supra.
133. See J. Erskine, *An Institute of the Law of Scotland in Four Books, in the Order of Sir George Mackenzie's Institutions of that Law* (Edinburgh, 1773), I.iii.12.
134. *LJ(A)*, ii.64-6.
135. *LJ(A)*, ii.74.
136. See text at note 128 supra.
137. See text at notes 112-27 supra.
138. *LJ(A)*, v.23.
139. *LJ(A)*, v.40.
140. *LJ(A)*, v.32.
141. *LJ(A)*, v.42-3 (correcting 'het' to 'the').

142. See quotation in text at note 127 supra.
143. *LJ(A)*, ii.168.
144. See [H. Home, Lord Kames], *Principles of Equity* (Edinburgh, 1760); see also I.S. Ross, *Lord Kames and the Scotland of his Day* (Oxford, 1972), 222-46.
145. *LJ(B)*, 67.
146. See P.G.B. McNeil, 'The Independence of the Scottish Judiciary' (1958) *Juridical Review*, 134-47.
147. 10 Geo. I, c.19 (1723) enacted that no future vacancies among the Extraordinary Lords should be filled. On Tweeddale, see Lord Cooper of Culross, 'The Central Courts after 1532', in [G.C.H. Paton (ed.)], *An Introduction to Scottish Legal History* (Stair Society, vol. 20, Edinburgh 1958), 341-9 at 342.
148. Erskine, op. cit. note 133 supra, I.i.45.
149. The history of law reporting in Scotland is still to be written; but see H. McKechnie, 'Practicks, 1469-1700' in [H. McKechnie (ed.)], *An Introductory Survey of the Sources and Literature of Scots Law* (Stair Society, vol. 1, Edinburgh, 1936), 25-41; J.S. Leadbetter, 'The Printed Law Reports 1540-1935', in ibid., 42-58; see also A.L. Murray, 'Sinclair's Practicks', in A. Harding (ed.), *Law-Making and Law-Makers in British History* (Royal Historical Society, vol. 22, London, 1980), 90-104. Throughout the eighteenth century, the Faculty of Advocates attempted to ensure better law reporting, see, e.g., *The Minute Book of the Faculty of Advocates Volume I 1661-1712*, ed. by J.M. Pinkerton (Stair Society, vol. 29, Edinburgh, 1976), 109 (16 Jan. 1692); but they encountered difficulties, see, e.g., *The Minute Book of the Faculty of Advocates Volume 2 1713-1750*, ed. by J.M. Pinkerton (Stair Society, vol. 32, Edinburgh, 1980), 68-9 (21 Dec. 1723), 71 (7 Jan. 1724), 124 (25 July 1730), 189-91 (4 Jan. 1743); and National Library of Scotland F.R.2, 'Minutes of the Faculty of Advocates 1751-1783', 252-3 (27 Feb. 1768). The Faculty's minutes regularly allude thoughout the eighteenth century to problems in collecting decisions adequately and promptly. (I am grateful for the permission of the Faculty to examine and cite their records.)
150. *WN*, V.i.b.20.
151. *WN*, V.i.f.44.
152. Found quoted in J.A. Inglis, 'Eighteenth Century Pleading' (1907-9) *Juridical Review*, 42-57 at 52.
153. *Corr.*, 90 (no. 72).
154. A. Murdoch, 'The Advocates, the Law and the Nation in Early Modern Scotland', in W. Prest (ed.), *Lawyers in Early Modern Europe and America* (London, 1981), 147-63 at 154-5; W. Ferguson, 'The Electoral System before 1832', in D. Sellar (ed.), *Miscellany Two* (Stair Society, vol. 35, Edinburgh, 1984), 261-94. See also N.T. Phillipson, 'Scottish Public Opinion and the Union in the Age of Association', in N.T. Phillipson and R. Mitchison (edd.), *Scotland in the Age of Improvement: Essays in Scottish History in the Eighteenth Century* (Edinburgh, 1970), 125-47, esp. at 127-9.
155. *WN*, V.i.b.20.
156. Phillipson, op. cit. note 154 supra, 127-9 and 135-40. In fact, reduction of the size of the bench had also been under consideration in 1743, see Marquess of Tweeddale to Lord Arniston, 8 Feb. 1743, Scottish Record Office microfilm of Dundas of Arniston MSS Vol. 3 RH 4/15/3.
157. Court of Session Acts 1808 (c.151) and 1825 (c.120).
158. Jury Trials (Scotland) Act 1815 (c.42). The merger with the Court of Session took place by the Court of Session Act 1830 (c.69).
159. A.J. MacLean, 'Jeremy Bentham and the Scottish Legal System' (1979) *Juridical Review*, 21-44; N.T. Phillipson, *The Scottish Whigs and the Reform of the Court of Session 1785-1832* (Stair Society, vol. 37, Edinburgh, 1991).
160. Phillipson, op. cit. note 159 supra, 85-110.
161. *Corr.*, 286-7 (no. 248).

162. *TMS*, Advertisement to 1790 edn.
163. *TMS*, *VII*.iv.36.
164. D. Forbes, 'Sceptical Whiggism, Commerce, and Liberty' in A.S. Skinner and T.W. Wilson (edd.), *Essays on Adam Smith* (Oxford, 1975), 179-201.
165. *LJ(A)*, ii.135.
166. *LJ(A)*, iv.178-9; v.i-8.
167. *LJ(A)*, iv. 97-9, 105-8.
168. *TMS*, III.1.6 (in the sixth edition he substituted 'person judged of' for 'panel').
169. See text at notes 64-66 supra.
170. *LJ(A)*, v.43.
171. *WN*, IV.ii.39 (I have quoted Smith quite out of context; but not, I hope, unfairly).
172. *LJ(A)*, v.12.
173. See quotation in text at note 18 supra.
174. *LJ(A)*, ii.75.
175. See, e.g., *LJ(A)*, i.164-ii.1 (entails); ii.38 (thirlage); ii.41 (corporations); ii.149-50 (capital punishment too severe for theft); v.65, 67, 71 and 73-4 (various aspects of the treason laws).
176. *WN*, III.ii.4.
177. *TMS*, II.ii.1.8.
178. *TMS*, V.2.15-16.
179. *TMS*, VII.iv.36.

The University of Edinburgh, Old College, Department of Scots Law

J. RALPH LINDGREN

ADAM SMITH'S TREATMENT OF CRIMINAL LAW

1. INTRODUCTION

During the century since Smith's *Lectures on Jurisprudence* first became available only one of Smith's commentators has given any consideration whatsoever to his views on criminal law, and that was a scant ten pages devoted mainly to Smith's 'theory of punishment.[1] By relying primarily upon Smith's strategic and programmatic remarks, Haakonssen understandably concluded that Smith supported basically a retributive approach to criminal law.[2]

Although this essay does not neglect Smith's more theoretical statements, it relies more heavily upon the detail of his treatment of criminal laws. The result is a strikingly different account. Smith's thinking about criminal law was in transition. He set out to represent it as a community's expression of righteous indignation, but in the process of collecting and organizing the legal materials found that the project had changed under his pen. What emerged was a picture of criminal law aimed primarily at crime prevention. What was perhaps even more disturbing was that his arguments relied increasingly upon considerations of utility. This must have left Smith in a quandary. His response was to have the papers containing these researches destroyed.[3]

What follows, then, is an essay of recovery. The first two sections develop two models of punishment that might be used to illuminate the criminal law. The first of these Smith endorsed, the second he opposed. The next two sections discuss the detail of Smith's treatment of criminal law, the one focusing upon criminalization of behaviors, the other on the gradation of penalties. Both disclose a picture of criminal law based largely on the model of punishment that Smith officially opposed. The final section comments briefly on Smith's view of the relative importance of the criminal law as a means of crime prevention.

R.P. Malloy and J. Evensky: Adam Smith and the Philosophy of Law and Economics, 63–81.

2. THE CRIMINAL LAW

Smith understood criminal law as one of the branches of law that redresses injuries that people suffer at the hands of one another.

The wisdom of every state or commonwealth endeavours, as well as it can, to employ the force of the society to restrain those who are subject to its authority, from hurting or disturbing the happiness of one another. The rules which it establishes for this purpose, constitute the civil and criminal law of each particular state or country. (*TMS* VI.ii.intro.2)

What distinguishes criminal from civil law is the sanction that it is authorized to impose. Although not stated directly, this point is brought out nicely in a contrast between breach of contract and fraud.

It is to be observed that the declining to fullfill a contract has never been considered a crime, tho a fraud always is. The judge sentences a person cited before him for having neglected to fullfill a contract, in the first place to fullfill it, and 2dly to make satisfaction to the other party for what damages the delay and suit may have occasioned him, but never inflicts any punishment for the intended evasion. But on the other hand one who fraudently would bring another under a contract is very severely punished. Thus one who forges a bill or bond is in this country punish'd with death. (*LJ(A)* ii.94)

The lesser frauds are generally obliged to be recompensed by the deceiver and are besides punished with a fine. (*LJ(A)* ii.157)

Breach of contract is not a crime because judges are not authorized to punish in those cases, but fraud is because punishment is authorized there. Unsuccessful defendants in both types of action, of course, are subject to coercive sanctions from courts. That is not what distinguishes a punishment from being required to make recompense. A punishment, here death or a fine, imposes a loss upon the perpetrator that goes beyond what is required to restore the victims to their *status quo ante*. The criminal law, then, is that arm of the law which is authorized to coercively impose penal sanctions.

Punishment, in Smith's view, is the characteristic feature of criminal law. This focus raised a number of questions about criminal law for Smith. As punishing goes beyond what is required by recompense, what is the point of punishing? how is it apportioned? what prompts us to punish? how is punishing justified? in what ways can the power to punish be abused and what protections can be afforded against those abuses? In addressing these and other questions about criminal law Smith drew heavily upon his more general analysis of punishment.

Smith saw punishing as a form of reciprocation, but one that is distinguishable from rewarding. 'To punish, too, is to recompense, to remunerate, though in a different manner; it is to return evil for evil that has been done.' (*TMS* II.i.1.4) Punishing, then, is a form of retaliation. From this initial characterization it is but a short step to what, for convenience, I will call his resentment analysis of punishment.

What prompts a person to punish is the sentiment of resentment. That sentiment, however, is not as simple and straight forward as it may at first seem. Resentment is not occasioned simply by suffering a loss as a consequence of what another person has done or failed to do. Were retaliation triggered by every disappointment life brings our way, society could not survive even the benign competition evident among merchants. Neither is resentment to be confused with hatred. We are said to hate those for whom we have formed long-standing disapproval based upon their past misbehavior, even to the point of taking some satisfaction when misfortune comes their way. But that is not yet resentment. Resentment prompts more than disapproval, it prompts us to take it upon ourselves to impose misfortune upon the villain and to do so in a very particular way.

Resentment would prompt us to desire, not only that he should be punished, but that he should be punished by our means, and upon account of that particular injury which he had done to us. Resentment cannot be fully gratified, unless the offender is not only made to grieve in his turn, but to grieve for that particular wrong which we have suffered from him. (*TMS* II.i.1.6)

Resentment, however, while it is a person's motive for punishing, is not the standard for deciding whether punishment is appropriate in a particular case. Like all our original sentiments, resentment can be too strong or too weak. An excess of resentment, Smith called it revenge in one place, retaliates where it is not due or to an extravagant extent. A deficiency of resentment, where a person has too little a sense of injury, does not retaliate where it is due or exacts too small a penalty upon the offender. (*TMS* II.i.5.8)

The test of whether the resentment experienced by victims is appropriate, the standard by which the proper objects of punishment are identified and the proper level of penalties measured, is the level of resentment that an impartial spectator could approve.[4] The impartial spectator, however, would approve a victim's resentment, would condemn the offender's behavior as punishable and sanction punishing the offender, only if both of two conditions are satisfied. Not only must the offender's behavior have harmed the victim, but the offender's behavior must have been improperly motivated.

But when to the hurtfulness of the action is joined the impropriety of the affection from whence it proceeds, when our heart rejects with abhorrence all fellow-feeling with the motives of the agent, ... such actions seem then to deserve, and, if I may say so, to call aloud for, a proportionable punishment .... (*TMS* II.i.4.3-4.)

Smith recognized that unless retaliation is premised upon something more than the hurtfulness of the offender's conduct, there would be no way of distinguishing punishment which is visited upon the offender from a simple return of one offense for another. Desert is what distinguishes the suffering of the victim from that of the punished offender. The latter deserves what he gets, the former did not.[5]

The disposition that prompts people to avoid becoming an object of proper resentment is called justice. Approached in this way justice is a negative virtue. It 'only hinders us from hurting our neighbour.' (*TMS* II.ii.1.10) Another way of saying the same thing is that there is a virtue which may be enforced.

> This virtue is justice: the violation of justice is injury: it does real and positive hurt to some particular persons, from motives which are naturally disapproved of. It is, therefore, the proper object of resentment, and of punishment, which is the natural consequence of resentment. (*TMS* II.ii.1.5)

The resentment analysis of punishment gives rise to strict limits upon what can properly be done in punishing.

> There can be no proper motive for hurting our neighbor, there can be no incitement to do evil to another, which mankind will go along with, except just indignation for evil which that other has done to us. (*TMS* II.ii.2.1)

We are not permitted to impose a penal sanction except in response to an improper and hurtful act on the part of an offender. Striking out against another cannot be justified in any other way. Were people, whether judges or ordinary citizens, to hurt one another for any other reason that would itself be an injury which is a proper object for resentment and punishment.[6]

The resentment analysis of punishment also establishes a standard for grading penal measures. Smith called for punishments to be proportionate to the offenses in the sense of a cardinal ordering. Not only are graver offenses to be treated more severely than less grave offenses and vice versa, but in each instance the severity of the penalty is to be proportionate to the gravity of the offense. The metric in each case is the extent of the victims' resentment that an impartial spectator can approve.

> As the greater and more irreparable the evil that is done, the resentment of the sufferer runs naturally the higher; so does likewise the sympathetic indignation of the spectator, as well as the sense of guilt in the agent. Death is the greatest evil which one man can inflict upon another, and excites the highest degree of resentment in those who are immediately connected with the slain. Murder, therefore, is the most atrocious of all crimes which affect individuals only .... To be deprived of that which we are possessed of, is a greater evil than to be disappointed of what we have only the expectation. Breach of property, therefore, theft and robbery ... are greater crimes than breach of contract .... The most sacred laws of justice, therefore, those whose violation seems to call loudest for vengeance and punishment, are the laws which guard

the life and person of our neighbour; the next are those which guard his property and possessions; and last of all come those which guard what are called his personal rights, or what is due to him from the promises of others. (*TMS* II.ii.2.2)

As these reflections suggest, Smith was convinced that were penal sanctions securely based upon proper resentment, a great deal of precision and accuracy could be introduced into discussions of justice and law. 'The rules of justice are accurate in the highest degree, and admit of no exceptions or modifications.' (*TMS* III.6.10) Before turning to Smith's treatment of criminal law within that context it will be useful to consider Smith's rejection of what he took to be the most plausible alternative to his resentment analysis of punishment.

3. UTILITY AND RESENTMENT ANALYSIS

Smith repeatedly considered and rejected what I will call the utility analysis of punishment. He attributed that analysis to Hume, Grotius and Pufendorf. On Smith's reading, they had noticed that the practice of punishing offenders tends to generate a number of socially useful consequences. Among these are 'the correction of the criminal and the example to the public' (*TMS* II.i.1.6) or what today is called the reform and deterrence effects. On the strength of that observation, Smith surmised, they concluded that people engage in punishment in order to further those ends. (*TMS* II.ii.3.6; LJ(A) ii.93)

Smith professed to reject that view, preferring instead his resentment analysis.[7] Care must be taken in interpreting this profession. Smith, after all, did not reject all appeals to the utility of punishing. He readily admitted two. Considerations of the necessity of punishment for maintaining a secure social fabric not infrequently are required to counteract any softening of resolve that would otherwise result in pardoning and forgiveness rather than in punishment. (*TMS* II.ii.3.7) Furthermore, appeals to utility also have an important rhetorical role to play. When our settled moral sentiments are called into question, such challenges can often be effectively quieted by reference to consideration of the disorder and confusion of society that would otherwise result. (*TMS* II.ii.3.8)[8]

What Smith was anxious to reject was the thesis that considerations of utility form the foundation of the rules of justice and so of law. By contrast, what he wished to assert was a two-pronged thesis.[9] One prong is factual. Punishing occurs spontaneously in the first instance, not as the result of any calculation of social advantage, even social necessity. The other is normative. Punishing is appropriate just in case an impartial spectator can go along with the resentment expressed by the victim. The propriety of punishing does not turn, in the final analysis, upon whether punishing advances the welfare of society. Although the arguments that Smith adduced in support of the resentment as opposed to the utility analysis are framed for the most part in terms of the factual prong, it is fair to say that the substantive issue at stake in the debate falls within the scope of the normative prong. By what standard, in the final analysis, are penal sanctions authorized and their severity justified? Is it to be the sense of indignation that wells in the breast of every righteous spectator or a perception of the social usefulness, even the necessity, of punishing?

Smith adduced a number of arguments which he declared demonstrates the superiority of the resentment over the utility analysis of punishment. Many of them are clearly crafted for the ears of the converted. Our concern for the welfare of society is dependent upon our concern for particular individuals and not the other way about. (*TMS* II.ii.3.10) It is absurd to think that moral approval is the same type of sentiment as aesthetic taste. (*TMS* IV.2.4) Many of those qualities of mind and character that we now value as socially useful were originally approved for quite different motives. (*TMS* IV.2.6-11)

Fortunately, he also proposed six more objective arguments in support of the resentment analysis. Each claims that the resentment analysis of punishment affords a better explanation of what is or ought to be a feature of the criminal law than does the utility analysis. The first two of these bear upon the persons and objects that are eligible for criminal sanctions. (1) 'Certain persons are not to be considered as objects of punishment, such as ideots, madmen, and children.' Criminal law incorporates these exclusions because 'we are not so much shocked by an action done by a madman [ideot or child] as one done by another person.' (*LJ(B)* 201) The utility analysis would not support these exclusions. 'The danger is no less great to the community, and the examples where there may be an opportunity of committing are no less frequent, and even more so, as they have less reason to restrain them.' (*LJ(A)* ii.178) Accordingly, the resentment analysis is superior because it can account for the exclusion of children, the insane and the mentally retarded from criminal liability, whereas the utility analysis cannot.

(2) The ancient law of deodand is another feature of criminal law that the resentment analysis can explain, but the utility analysis cannot. According to that law criminal liability extends not only to rational agents, but 'even the animate and inanimate things which have been the occasion of so great a misfortune as the death of a man ... as the sword or other instrument, or the ox that gored.' (*LJ(A)* ii.118) As is easily understandable, this law originated in the resentment of victims and victims' kin. Equally obvious is the disutility of the practice. 'This proceeds from a resentment blind and foolish indeed ....' (*LJ(A)* ii.177)

The next two arguments bear upon differences in the gradation of offenses. In both the resentment analysis can explain the differences, the utility analysis cannot. (3) '[T]here is no country where the attempt to commit a crime is punished with the same severity as the actuall committing it.' This is not what would be expected were considerations of utility to determine the gradation,

... for with regard to the guilt of the offender, there can be no difference .... The safety of the society also would require the removing of a dangerous person as well here .... It is evident also that there is the same reason for making an example of him to the deterring of others. (*LJ(A)* ii.175)

However, this is exactly the difference that would be predicted by the resentment analysis.

The resentment of the friends of one who had been attacked with a design to murder him and had made his escape is not near so great as if he had been actually murdered. In this case the grief for their friend blows up their resentment and makes them demand the greatest rigour of punishment. In the other case their joy on the escape of their friend sooths and lays asleep their indignation. (*LJ(A)* ii.175)

(4) The same point is made relative to the respective punishments levied in those cases in which reckless conduct, such as throwing a large stone over a wall into a public street without warning, does and does not result in injury to others. 'In the same manner one who, doing a thing in itself dangerous, if he happens to kill or hurt one, is punished much more severely than if no bad effect should follow.' (*LJ(A)* ii.176) Here again the utility analysis affords no way to distinguish these cases, but the resentment analysis does. 'Resentment never rises to any great pitch unless some injury be actualy done.' (*LJ(B)* 201)

The last two arguments bear upon the criminalization of conduct that can be explained on the utility, but not on the resentment analysis. 'Wool in England was conceived to be the source of public opulence, and it was made a capital crime to export that commodity.' (*LJ(B)* 182) The statute was initially adopted out of considerations of utility. But that was not the end of the matter. 'No one would consent to the punishment of a thing in itself so innocent by so high a penalty. They were therefore obliged to lessen the punishment to a confiscation of goods and vessel.' (*LJ(A)* ii. 92) This example of what today is called jury nullification can be explained only on the resentment analysis. 'This exportation was no crime at all, in naturall equity, and was very far from deserving so high a punishment in the eyes of the people; they therefore found that while this was the punishment they could get neither jury nor informers.' (*LJ(A)* ii.91)[10]

(6) Another example of a law enacted from considerations of utility but which is of doubtful merit comes from the laws of nations. 'A centinel, for example, who falls asleep upon his watch, suffers death by the laws of

war, because such carelessness might endanger the whole army.' Smith found this law to be a very troubling. 'The natural atrocity of the crime seems to be so little, and the punishment so great, that it is with great difficulty that our heart can reconcile itself to it.' (*TMS* II.ii.3.11) Smith's complaint here is that the sentinel's conduct should be considered reckless and so not punished so severely as it would were the worst to have happened and the enemy overwhelmed the encampment as a result of his lack of diligence.

For the purposes of this essay let us allow that the first four arguments establish the factual point, viz., that resentment is more likely than reflection on considerations of utility to have been the mechanism by which punishment came to be an established practice. Here the emphasis will be on the more substantive issue, the normative claim that sympathy with resentment rather than considerations of utility is the standard by which the appropriateness of punishment is to be assessed. What are we to make of this package of arguments in that connection?

In presenting these arguments Smith was not as candid as he might and perhaps should have been. On his own analysis, the contrast between the resentment and utility analyses along the normative dimension was not so great as these arguments pretend. When Smith came to consider the influence of fortune upon our moral sentiments he amended the resentment analysis so thoroughly as to blur the differences between it and the utility analysis. A brief review of that discussion is helpful at this point.

The considerations that led Smith to adopt the resentment analysis convinced him that only intentional wrong doing deserves punishment.

> Its self-evident justice is acknowledged by all the world, and there is not a dissenting voice among all mankind. Every body allows, that how different soever the accidental, the unintentional and unforeseen consequences of different actions, yet, if the intentions or affections from which they arose were on the one hand, equally proper and equally beneficent, or, on the other, equally improper and equally malevolent, the merit or demerit of the actions is still the same, and the agent equally the suitable object either of gratitude or resentment. (*TMS* II.iii.intro.4)

He went on to specify that in order for anything to be the proper object of punishment it must: (1) cause pain in the victim; (2) be capable of feeling pain itself; and (3) have caused the victim's pain from an improper design. (*TMS* II.iii.1.6) Were these qualifications honored by the criminal law, the law of deodand would never have been enacted, attempts would be as severely treated as accomplished crimes, and neither reckless nor negligent conduct would subject a person to criminal liability. (*TMS* II.iii.1-2)

That the law does not honor these qualifications presented Smith with a dilemma. He could have stuck by the requirement of 'self-evident justice' and joined those moral prophets who storm against the law asserting that, in these respects at least, it has lost its moral legitimacy. This 'has been in all ages the complaint, and is the great discouragement of virtue.' (*TMS* II.iii.3.1) To do that, however, would have encouraged the animosity of hostile factions and invited the very violence within society that Smith found most repugnant. (*TMS* III.3.43) On the other hand, he could have qualified the demands of the resentment analysis so that following it through would avoid faction and violence. To do that, however, would involve conceding that considerations of utility override those of propriety where the stakes are high enough. It would involve making a virtue of necessity. Smith chose the latter course, but did not do so openly. Instead he proposed that the divergence of law from the requirements of 'natural equity' is evidence of what he called 'an irregularity of sentiment', an irregularity that affects not only the actual, but also the impartial spectator. (*TMS* II.iii.intro.6)

> If the hurtfulness of the design, if the malevolence of the affection, were alone the causes which excited our resentment ... every court of judicature would become a real inquisition. There would be no safety for the most innocent and circumspect conduct. .... That necessary rule of justice, therefore, that men in this life are liable to punishment for their actions only, not for their designs and intentions, is founded upon this salutary and useful irregularity in human sentiments concerning merit or demerit, which at first sight appears so absurd and unaccountable. (*TMS* II.iii.3.2)

In view of the 'irregularity' amendment to the resentment analysis, the differences between it and the utility analysis, at least as regards the law of deodand, attempts and reckless conduct, evaporate. As we will see, the same thing happens with the last two of Smith's arguments.

The last two arguments differ from the first four in that they pull in the opposite direction. They assert that considerations of utility commend much more severe sanctions both as regards wool export and sentinel dereliction than would the resentment analysis. But, here again Smith himself undermines that claim. In *The Wealth of Nations* Smith opposed not only prohibitions on the export of wool, but of smuggling generally and indeed most restrictions on free trade. But the premise upon which that opposition was argued, his 'system of natural liberty', was itself supported in the main by arguments based firmly on considerations of utility. (*WN* V.ix.51)

As regards the laws of nations generally and those that bear upon military discipline in particular, Smith showed in the discussion of the sentinel case that 'a general view to the interest of society' requires more severe discipline than 'natural equity' permits and so the more severe penalty is accepted. 'This severity may, upon many occasions, appear necessary, and, for that reason, just and proper.' My point here is that although the 'man of humanity' finds it more difficult to go along with a severe punishment in the sentinel case than he does in those of 'an ungrateful murderer or parricide', he goes along nonetheless. (*TMS* II.ii.3.11) Once again utility overrides propriety.[11]

Upon examination, then, five of the six objective arguments fail to demonstrate the superiority of the resentment over the utility analysis of punishment. Only the first, excluding 'ideots, madmen, and children' altogether from criminal liability, survives. That this argument was not repeated in TMS may signal that Smith had developed doubts even about it when addressing audiences outside the college lecture room. Even so, that is a thin reed upon which to rest a case against the utility analysis of punishment.

4. NATURAL JURISPRUDENCE

Throughout his career Smith aspired to working out the detail of the rules of justice. He called that project 'natural jurisprudence', 'that science which inquires into the general principles which ought to be the foundation of the laws of all nations.' (*LJ(B)* 1) This was a traditionally philosophical project. Self-evident, universally accepted 'foundations' were to be identified and from these the basic elements of law inferred.[12]

Smith frequently represented the product of his researches in the form of histories.[13] These afford a convenient point of departure for a discussion of the detail of his treatment of the criminal law.

Smith regarded criminal law as a function of government and the central function of government as the prevention of crime, especially crimes against property. As we have seen, securing the minimum essentials of justice is necessary for the existence of society. Governments are required to provide for the administration of justice under some conditions, but not others. In the absence of property holdings, people would be in jeopardy of crimes only against their persons and reputations. The temptation to commit these crimes, however, is relatively slight because, although they harm their victims they yield no benefit to offenders. These crimes can be motivated only by envy, malice, or resentment, and these passions are commonly held in check by prudentially considering probable retaliation by the victims, their friends and kin. Absent conflicts that arise because of property holdings, people 'may live together in society with some tolerable degree of security, though there is no civil magistrate to protect them from the injustice of those passions.' (*WN* V.i.b.2)

When property holdings are introduced into the equation the matter changes dramatically. When some are possessed of large property holdings and others of little or none, 'the affluence of the rich excites the indignation of the poor, who are often both driven by want, and prompted by envy, to invade his possessions.' With crimes against property, unlike those against the person and reputation, the victims' loss can result in an equal benefit to the perpetrator. This is because property is alienable. As a result, those with more property are at continuing risk of being plundered at the hands of those who have less.[14] Because offenders stand to gain more from property crimes than from crimes against the persons or reputations of others, the likelihood of these crimes increases beyond what simple prudential considerations of possible reprisal can constrain. That, in turn, renews the prospect of every intensifying cycles of invasion followed by reprisals. It is the avoidance of such blood feuds that makes governments necessary.[15]

To prevent the confusion which would attend upon every man's doing justice to himself, the magistrate ... undertakes to do justice to all, and promises to hear and to redress every complaint of injury. In all well-governed states too, not only judges are appointed for determining the controversies of individuals, but rules are prescribed for regulating the decision of those judges; and these rules are, in general, intended to coincide with those of natural justice. (*TMS* VII. iv. 36)

The extent to which governments can perform this function depends upon their power. When governments are weak they cannot punish crimes, but only mediate between the antagonists, seeking at most a reconciliation by encouraging the offender to compensate the victim or the victim's kin. When governments are strong enough to coercively intervene into the affairs of its citizens, they can and typically do impose very severe criminal sanctions.

But when the society gathers greater strength, they not only exact a compensation but change it into a punishment. The punishments in this stage of society are always the most severe imaginable. It is not the injuries done to individuals that [it] ... will first take into its consideration. .... Those which immediately affect the state are those which will first be the object of punishments. (*LJ(A)* ii.152-3)

For these reasons crimes that strike at the capacity of governments to prevent crime, at what Smith called the administration of justice, rightly receive punishments that are among the most severe. Smith assigned very high priority to this because 'upon the impartial administration of justice depends the liberty of every individual, the sense he has of his own security.' (*WN* V.i.b.25)

The most important of the laws that secure the orderly administration of justice fall under the heading of treason. 'Treason is that crime which consists in attacking the being and existence of the government or sovereign power.' (*LJ(A)* v.61) Crimes of treason are divided into four grades, each with its distinctive punishment. Only his comments on its most extreme grade, viz., high treason, address the concerns of this essay. High treason is 'the greatest crime' (*LJ(B)* 79) and is accordingly given the most severe penalty. Those convicted of this crime are punished by a combination of sanctions. These include death by torture and 'besides this it is attended with forfeiture of goods and land estate, and the dower of the wife, and corruption of blood on the children, by which they are deprived not only of his estate but of every succession which would have fallen to them thro him.' Significantly, high treason is the most severely punished crime, 'the only one which in this country admits by law of any torture.' (*LJ(A)* v.74-5)

Five types of offenses qualify under the laws of England as high treason. Very generally, these are: (1) attempts on the person of the sovereign; (2) corruption of the king's companion; (3) levying war against the king; (4) counterfeiting the great or privy seal; and (5) counterfeiting the king's coin. Smith approved of the most severe punishment for all except the last of these offenses, which he preferred be treated as a felony, punishable simply by death. His approval rested entirely upon the observation that these offenses 'would intirely overturn the foundations and prevent the execution of government.' (*LJ(A)* v. 73)

Statutes prohibiting the crimes of false imprisonment and forced entry also protect the orderly administration of justice. Statutes forbidding false imprisonment provided substantial fines for judges who refuse offers of sufficient bail for bailable offenses or who detain accused parties without sufficient grounds and for witnesses who intentionally give false information that leads to detention or imprisonment. Statutes forbidding forced entry required anyone who was wrongly ejected from his property to abstain from forcibly retaking it, seeking instead restoration by establishing rightful title through a judicial process. Although both of these provisions were in tension with the requirements of natural equity, Smith approved them nonetheless from considerations of their utility. Consider forced entry first.

> For naturally any one who is turned out of what he justly possesses would think himself intitled to reinstate himself in the possession of his property by force. But this civil governments do not allow, as dissagreable to the peace and order of society. (*LJ(A)* ii.146)

Smith brought up the practice of pre-trial detention in connection with the crime of false imprisonment. From the standpoint of natural equity coercively detaining someone who is in fact innocent of any charge is every bit as much a miscarriage of justice whether it is done before or after a trial. 'No one ought in equity to be confined but a criminall....' (*LJ(A)* ii.127) But, once again, Smith insisted that equity give way to expediency.

> It must often happen that innocent persons accused of a crime will be either obliged to find bail for their appearance; or if the crime be very heinous or the bail necessary very high, even to suffer imprisonment. This indeed is not by the law looked upon as wrongous or false imprisonment, if he be committed on due evidence or information, but is at the same time a great incroachment on the liberty of the subject. It is however unnavoidable in all societies; for if no person could be put in prison or secured till the crime he was accursed of be proved against him, no criminall could ever be brought to justice. (*LJ(A)* ii.133)

Smith was never secure in his treatment of what he classified as domestic crimes. These include infidelity (adultery) on the part of the wife and polygamy. As to the latter, Smith observed that although polygamy does not violate natural equity, 'it must always be a very bad policy .... Polygamy excites the most violent jealously, by which domestic peace is destroyed.' (*LJ(B)* 112) The criminalization of polygamy was evidently approved in the interest of preventing the disruptions and violence that the practice is apt to encourage. Here again, it was crime prevention that was central to Smith's thinking.

On first reading, Smith's treatment of adultery appears in the opposite light. It looks to be based entirely on the resentment analysis. A breach of chastity on the part of a wife is not condemned out of concern about uncertainty over the parentage of possible children born to an illegitimate union. This 'real utility' is not the basis of the crime. 'The indignation of the public against the wife arises from their sympathy with the jealousy of the husband, and accordingly they are disposed to resent and punish it.' (*LJ(B)* 103) Looking into the jealousy of the husband, however, Smith describes him as outraged because 'he considers her infedility as an entire alienation of that preference to all other persons which she owes him.' (*LJ(B)* 103) Still, what was the ground of this duty of chastity that she owed him, but he did not owe her in return? A remark made in connection with another domestic crime is suggestive. If the wife kills her husband this 'is considered as a sort of petty treason, and the punishment by the English law is burning alive.' (*LJ(B)* 148) The magnitude of the punishment along with the label as a treason, is suggestive. The analogy with treason gives domestic crime a distinctly instrumental flavor. Just as treason laws are necessary to protect the institution of government against conduct that would undermine it, so also laws that prohibit domestic crimes are motivated by a concern to secure patriarchal marriage from inroads. If that is a fair reading, then the crime of adultery as well rests squarely, if indirectly, upon an interest in securing a traditional institution that is deemed essential to the maintenance of a just social order.

5. DIVISIONS OF LAW

As envisioned by Smith, natural jurisprudence was to be composed of five divisions of law, viz., justice, police, revenue, arms and the laws of nations.[16] Although most of the crimes that Smith discussed fall under one of the sub-divisions of the laws of justice, viz., delict, many fall under other headings. The last section showed that the crimes falling outside delict are governed entirely by considerations of utility.[17]

Upon some occasions, indeed, we both punish and approve of punishment, merely from a view to the general interest of society, which, we imagine, cannot otherwise be secured. Of this kind are all the punishments inflicted for breaches of what is called either civil police or military discipline. (*TMS* II.ii.3.11)

Smith's principal concern when discussing the crimes treated under the heading of delict was the grading of penalties. His main contention was that the severity of penalties for crimes is a function of a number of variables, the requirements of natural equity being but one of them. Furthermore, the salience of resentment is greater for some crimes, less for others. Of the crimes of homicide,

... the most attrocious of these is willfull murder. For this, to be sure, the only proper punishment is the death of the offender. The resentment of the injured persons can not be satisfied by a mere simple punishment, unless there be an equality at least betwixt the suffering of the injur'd person and the offender, (that is) unless the injury be in some measure retaliated. We find accordingly that in all civilized nations that the punishment has been the death of the murderer. (*LJ(A)* ii. 94-5)

The resentment analysis of punishment requires that punishments to be proportionate to the injuries they cause, proportionate in the sense of a cardinal ordering. The severity of the penalty must equal the extent of the injury. Otherwise the resentment of the victims and their kin will not be satisfied. Smith's discussion of affronts, i.e., actions that cast someone's character in disrepute, actions such as shaking a fist at him or spitting in his face, shows what happens if the severity of the penalty falls considerably short of this equality. The current practice was to categorize those actions as assaults and batteries, typically imposing relatively slight penalties. But such trivial penalties contributed to the spread of duelling, 'for when the law do not give satisfaction somewhat adequate to the injury, men will think themselves intitled to take it at their own hand.' (*LJ(A)* ii.139) What is risked when the penalties for crimes fall too far short of the proper resentment of victims is a resurgence of resort to self-help measures, even blood feuds.

Smith discussion of crimes that injure a person's reputation, including affronts, reveals another variable that determine the proper level of criminal sanctions. There he showed that the severity with which a crime ought to be punished varies with its institutional context. His reason was that the extent of the injury often varies with that context. He gave three examples of this. Affronts are one of them. What the law failed to notice when it assigned slight penalties for those actions was the special significance that they took on by virtue of the codes of honor that had prevailed from the middle ages. Under those codes such conduct as someone spitting in one's face, if unsatisfied, would expose a person either to a life-threatening duel or a life of disgrace. 'It is intirely from this new notion of honor that the injury of such affronts has arose.' (*LJ(A)* ii.137) That the victim was subject to special customs should have figured into the gradation of penalties.

Another example of an institutional variable occurs in Smith's discussion of rape and forced marriage, crimes that he classified both as domestic crimes and crimes that injure one's liberty. He reported with approval that death was the punishment for these crimes. When we examine the reasons given for that approval, it turns out that these crimes are analogized with affront.

A rape ... is by the law of all civilized nations punished with death, as that alone seems to be sufficient compensation for the injury done her. In the same way a marriage which is entered into by force is void; and besides, the party who forced the other is liable to a capitall punishment; for as it is generally the man who compells the woman, the same injury is done *to her reputation* as in the case of rape. (*LJ(A)* ii.131) (emphasis added)

Once again we see that the nature and extent of the injury is dependent upon the institutional context of the victim. Here that context is, as it was for the other domestic crimes, the patriarchal family.

Libel, a written attack upon one's reputation, affords a third example of how the harm suffered by a victim varies with institutional context.

The severity of the punishment of libells and the earnestness of their prosecution depends greatly on the form of government. In all aristocraticall governments ... they are punished with the greatest severity, and even more than in absolute governments. (*LJ(A)* ii.142)

The reason for this is that the influence of the nobles is more dependent upon fluctuations in reputation than is that of absolute monarchs. In democracies, this protection is provided by the self-discipline of the people themselves. 'In generall the freedom in this respect is a great test of the liberty of the people.' (*LJ(A)* ii.144) The penalty for libel, therefore, should vary depending upon the type of government a society supports.

Yet another variable was identified in Smith's discussions of murder and theft, viz., the relative weakness of government. As murder was currently a capital crime, Smith needed to cite no other variables either to explain or to justify those sanctions. 'But,' he continued, 'amongst barbarous nations the punishment has generally been much slighter, as a pecuniary fine.' The explanation given for this variation was 'the weakness of government.' (*LJ(A)* ii.95) Where governments are weak they cannot exact punishments at all, but can only moderate feuds by encouraging offenders to compensate their victims. Where governments are powerful, they exact very stern penalties, especially for treason and crimes against the government and other institutions deemed essential for any just regime. Accordingly, as the strength of governments increases the penal sanctions become more severe.

Smith's discussion of crimes against property reveals yet a fourth factor that determines the proper level of punishment of crimes. The grosser forms of theft, 'clandestinely taking away the property of another' (*LJ(B)*

194), and fraud, 'whereby one cheats another out his property' (*LJ(A)* ii.157) were capital crimes in Smith's day.[18] He went on to explain why that penalty was appropriate for those crimes. The reasoning is plainly aimed at crime prevention. As the likelihood of an offense increases so also should the severity of the penalty. 'For where ever the temptation and the opportunity are increased, the punishment must also be increased.' (*LJ(A)* ii.158) One of the examples Smith gave of a just penalty of death for the crime of fraud involved concealing assets during a bankruptcy proceeding. The death penalty in such cases is a 'great justice' because that offence is often highly lucrative and also very difficult to detect. (*LJ(A)* ii.157-8) Capital punishment for forgery was endorsed for the same reason. 'Whenever written obligations came to be binding, it became absolutely necessary that all frauds of this sort should be prohibited. For otherwise one by forging an obligation might extort any sum he pleased.' (*LJ(A)* ii.159)

Smith relied upon the likelihood of occurrence factor not only in justifying increased, but also decreased penal sanctions. Strong governments sometimes lower the punishment for crimes as they become less likely.

> When society made a still greater progress and the peace and good order of the community were provided for, and tranquillity firmly established, these punishments would again be mitigated and by degrees brought to bear a just proportion to the several crimes. (*LJ(A)* ii.153)

Four variables that determine the proper level of punishment have been identified. The severity of punishment for a particular crime varies with the proper resentment felt by the victim; with the institutional context of the action; with the weakness of government; and with the likelihood that the offense will be committed. Together, they reinforces the view that the overriding point of criminal law is crime prevention.

6. CONCLUSION

Based upon what has gone before and a few of Smith other remarks[19], one might infer that Smith commended heavy reliance upon the wisdom and rigorous enforcement of the criminal law. But, that would be a mistake. His investigation of the differences in the murder rates of Paris and London convinced him that they were not dependent upon the volume of regulations or the extent of home guards, or what we would call police, 'this is not the cause.' (*LJ(B)* 205)

Rather, 'In generall we may observe that the disorders in any country are more or less according to the number or retainers and dependents in it.' (*LJ(A)* vi.4) Those accustomed to having others care for their needs, who lack the skills of self-sufficiency, 'when turned out, had no other way of getting their subsistance but by committing robberies and living on plunder

....' 'Upon the whole it is the custom of having many retainers and dependents which is the great source of all the disorders and confusions in some cities...' That being so, investing in commerce and industry and reeducating the public in the habits of self-sufficiency, would yield greater security and at considerably less expense in treasure and lives than would an expansion of the criminal law and the administration of justice. '...[I]t is not so much the regulations of the police which preserves the security of a nation as the custom of having in it as few servants and dependents as possible.' (*LJ(A)* vi.6)

Nothing tends so much to corrupt mankind as dependencey, while independencey still encreases the honesty of the people. The establishment of commence and manufactures, which brings about this independencey, is the best police for preventing crimes. The common people have better wages in this way than in any other, and in consequence of this a greater probity of manners takes place thro' the whole country. No body will be so mad as to expose himself upon the highway, when he can make better bread in an honest and industrious manner. (*LJ(B)* 205)[20]

The criminal law together with the system of courts, prisons, executioners, etc. is one means that governments, as they become more powerful, may use to protect the liberties of citizens from injuries at the hands of one another, but it is not the most promising. Governments are best advised to depend in advancing that objective instead upon the fostering of commerce and manufacturing. Smith's hope was that as crime is caused principally by envy, so it can be prevented by enabling those who have little or no property to obtain more and to do so by honest labor. In retrospect this hope seems today to be perhaps not so naive as it might at first seem.

NOTES

1. Knud Haakonssen, *The Science of a Legislator: The Natural Jurisprudence of David Hume and Adam Smith*. Cambridge: Cambridge University Press, 1981. Pp. 114-23.
2. *Ibid*. p. 116.
3. John Rae, *Life of Adam Smith*. New York: Kelley, 1965. P. 434.
4. The 'General Introduction' to *WN* affords a short and accurate overview of Smith's philosophy. For a more detailed treatment of his moral theory, see: T. D. Campbell, *Adam Smith's Science of Morals*. London: Allen and Unwin, 1971 and my *The Social Philosophy of Adam Smith*. The Hague: Nijhoff, 1973.
5. 'When an inhumane murderer is brought to the scaffold, though we have some compassion for his misery, we can have no sort of fellow-feeling with his resentment.... The natural tendency of their just indignation against so vile a criminal is indeed the most fatal and ruinous to him. But it is impossible that we should be displeased with the tendency of a sentiment, which, when we bring the case home to ourselves, we feel that we cannot avoid adopting.' (*TMS* II.i.3.3)
6. See: Smith's discussion of the crimes of wrongful imprisonment (*LJ(A)* ii.128-9) and perjury (*LJ(A)* ii.160-1).
7. 'Nature, antecedent to all reflection upon the utility of punishment, has in this manner stamped upon the human heart, in the strongest and most indelible characters, an immediate and instinctive approbation of the sacred and necessary law of retaliation.' (*TMS* II.i.2.5)

8. Here, as most places, Smith showed no sign of accepting the possibility of real diversity in our moral sentiments. He did not consider responding to questioning of our own sentiments by inquiring into the grounds such challenges, but instead sought only to defend against them. Haakonssen caught this sense quite nicely when he mused: 'Why is it that on such occasions we do not rely on our real reason? It is simply because the fact that people can put forward such criticism shows that the natural value-community between them and us has broken down: they have lost their sense of propriety, as we see it.' (p. 88)

On one occasion, when discussing utility as a ground for political obedience, Smith did seem to concede the need to recognize diversity of opinion. 'It is the sense of public utility, rather than private, which influences men to obedience. It may sometimes be for my interest to dissobey, and to wish government overturned. But I am sensible that other men are of a different opinion from me and would not assist me in the enterprize. I therefore submit to it's decision for the good of the whole.' (*LJ(B)* 14)

9. This is not quite the same as the distinction between efficient and final cause sponsored by Campbell. (T. D. Campbell, 'Adam Smith and the Economic Analysis of Law,' in *Philosophers of the Scottish Enlightenment*, V. Hope (ed.), Edinburgh University Press, 1984, p. 150) The two prongs mentioned here rely on the distinction between explanatory mechanisms and justifying standards. The factual prong bears upon identifying the mechanism(s) that best account for the occurrence of a particular phenomenon. The normative prong bears upon the standard(s) by which we approve retaining or rejecting existing phenomenon.

10. Smith echoed this same view with respect to smuggling generally. (*WN* V.ii.k.64)

11. Raphael and Macfie concluded their discussion of the sentinel case with the following observation. 'The fact is that Smith found himself in a cleft stick on this issue and had not thought out his position consistently.' (*TMS* Appendix II at p. 394) I have argued that this dilemma affects Smith views on criminal law generally and that he did in fact seize one horn, although not openly.

12. Haakonssen concludes from this that Smith was working within the natural law tradition. (pp. 147-9) Of course, if subscribing to what is today called 'foundationalism' is all it takes to be a natural law theorist, this interpretation is true but trivial. On that usage it would be difficult to identify any but a very small handful of philosophers from Plato through Nietzsche who were not working within the natural law tradition.

13. His practice in this respect has occasioned some confusion. As his sources, though exceptionally complete for his day, were sketchy in many important details, Smith not infrequently exercised the option of speculating about details that were, it seemed to him, missing. This style has prompted apologies from sympathetic commentators from Dugald Stewart to Campbell and Skinner. Stewart calls that style 'theoretical or conjectural history' because it insinuated speculation in the accounts where "direct evidence" is wanting. "...[W]hen we cannot trace the process by which an event *has been* produced, it is often ofimportance to be able to show how it *may have been* produced by natural causes.' (*Account of the Life and Writings of Adam Smith, LL.D.* II.46-48) In their 'General Introduction' to *WN* Campbell and Skinner distinguish between Smith the 'orthodox historian' who chronicles events taking care to avoid 'distortion of historical evidence' and Smith the 'philosophicalhistorian' of whom Stewart spoke. (*WN* vol. I, pp. 50-60) I don't share the view that there is a distinction to be made here. Serious, orthodox historians are not clairvoyant as regards 'direct evidence.' They must speculate and seek out vindication just as 'philosophical historians' do. Worries about distorting the facts of history are premised upon the incredible conviction that there is independent access to that supposed realm of facts. In my view there is nothing about Smith's approach to history writing that requires an apology.

14. 'Civil government, so far as it is instituted for the security of property, is in reality instituted for the defence of the rich against the poor, or of those who have some property against those who have none at all.' (*WN* V.i.b.12)

15. 'The acquisition of valuable and extensive property, therefore, necessarily requires the establishment of civil government.' (*WN* V.i.b.2)
16. The laws of justice are addressed to securing citizens from injury from one another. Those of police are concerned with public health, safety and the cheapness of commodities. The laws of revenue which relate to the means of providing revenues for the government. Those of arms bear upon defense of the nation against foreign invasion. The Laws of Nations comprehend issues of war and peace as well as the rights of ambassadors and aliens. (*LJ(B)* 6) The only parts of the project that Smith ever completed to his own satisfaction were those relating to police, revenue and arms. These he presented in the form of *WN*. (*TMS* Advert. 2)
17. Haakonssen supported this conclusion at pp. 120-22.
18. In the cases of the other crimes against movable property, robbery and piracy, death is also regarded as an appropriate punishment. 'Though theft does not excite our resentment to any great pitch, yet robbery, which forcibly takes our goods from us, will step us our resentment very much.' (*LJ(A)* ii.155) This seems an odd assertion for two reasons. First, robbery was distinguished from theft by the presence of force. Evidently robbery excites greater resentment because it is seen as a form of battery as well as theft. But battery is not a capital crime.Indeed, Smith approved a relatively small penalty for battery, viz., a fine and imprisonment. (*LJ(B)* 191) Second, he also approved death for piracy, also a crime that forcibly deprives people of their property. But death was approved there for both of two reasons: 'not only from the resentment which all robberies excite in us but also from the great opportunities there are of committing it and the great loss which may be sustained by it ....' (*LJ(A)* ii.156)
19. 'In generall the best means of bringing about this desirable end is the rigorous, severe, and exemplary execution of laws properly formd for the prevention of crimes and establishing the peace of the state.' (*LJ(A)* vi.2)
20. In combination with education, this is also the key to a more peaceful world. 'But nothing seems more likely to establish this equality of force [between nations] than that mutual communication of knowledge and of all sorts of improvements which an extensive commerce from all countries to all countries naturally, or rather necessarily, carries along with it.' *WN* IV.vii.c80)

Lehigh University, Department of Philosophy

KENNETH A.B. MACKINNON

ADAM SMITH ON DELICTUAL LIABILITY

1. TORTS AND DELICT

For the majority of readers, more familiar with the Anglo-American system of common law than with Scots Law, the title of this chapter would have made greater sense if it were 'Adam Smith on Tort.' But, while there are many similarities between Tort(s) and Delict in modern law, it is important to distinguish the two systems when examining Smith's contribution to the area. Much of the Scots Law of Delict has its origins in the Roman Law 'lex Aquilia', and provides for a general liability for the wrongful invasion of a person's rights. Liability is based on a comprehensive principle of fault ('culpa') covering both intentional and negligent wrongdoing (though 'culpa' is sometimes used in a more restricted sense of 'negligence', in which circumstances 'dolus' or 'dole' is reserved for malicious intent). The Scots system is thus more unified, comprehensive and flexible than the Anglo-American equivalent.

On this topic (as on nearly every other) Scots Law was true to type by laying down, while the subject was still fluid and adaptable, a few cardinal principles from which a very wide range of consequences could be deduced.[1]

And what, a few sentences later, Lord President Cooper called "the rational simplicity of our law of delict" is demonstrated by the listing of those cardinal principles by the late Professor T.B. Smith:

First, the generality of the right of reparation for unlawful harm or loss (damnum) must be stressed. Secondly, the pursuer must establish fault on the part of the defender. Thirdly, there must be a causative link between the harm suffered and the fault of which the defender can be accused.[2]

One comparative writer commented on the approaches to Torts/Delict of the Anglo-American Common Law systems and the Continental Civil Law systems:

But the law is not commensurate with morality. It would be going too far to say that an immoral act which causes me damage is actionable. The transition from the rule of morality to

R.P. Malloy and J. Evensky: Adam Smith and the Philosophy of Law and Economics, 83–112.

the particular legal situation is too abrupt. The mind seeks a middle term in a rule of law. But it is the peculiar weakness of this branch of law that the middle terms are rather conspicuously wanting. In the common law their place was taken by the forms of action which have left their indelible impress on the substantive law; hence the queer irrational entanglements of the common law of slander, libel, malicious prosecution, etc. ... If the common law errs in one direction by particularization of causes of action, the civil law perhaps incurs the opposite reproach of failing in precision ... 'Every one is liable for the damage which he does, not only by his wilful acts but also by his negligence or imprudence' [Article 1383 of the Code Napoleon] ... The antidote for this unwholesome vagueness is the fact ... that every private wrong is the invasion of a private right. If the defendant is in fault, it must be because he has violated the plaintiff's right ... The real question, then, is not whether the defendant has acted badly (this is what we usually understand by being in fault) but whether he has violated any right of the plaintiff.[3]

While Scots Law is not a pure Civil Law system, it is against the more civilian Scottish legal background that the fragments which can be pieced together as amounting to Adam Smith's account of the principles of delictual (or tortious) liability must be set. Certainly in his treatment of delict he does not repeat, nor could he consistently do so, his stated preference[4] for pragmatic English law in relation to contract.

2. THE PLACE OF DELICT IN ADAM SMITH'S JURISPRUDENCE

Although some of Smith's most valuable thoughts on the jurisprudence of delictual liability are to be found in his *Theory of Moral Sentiments*,[5] it is only in his *Lectures on Jurisprudence* that he provides the structure into which these can be fitted. Both versions of the lectures have a similar introduction which identifies jurisprudence as the theory of the general principles of law and government. Law and government have four objects: justice, police, revenue and arms.

The first and chief design of all civil governments, is, as I observed, to preserve justice amongst the members of the state and prevent all incroachments on the individuals in it, from others of the same society. That is, to maintain each individual in his perfect rights. Justice is violated whenever one is deprived of what he had a right to and could justly demand from others, or rather, when we do him any injury or hurt without a cause.[6]

Thus, justice is not injuring others, or, put another way, it is the respecting of rights. These rights in justice, as opposed to moral rights, are designated 'perfect' in that they carry with them correlative duties (in others) to respect them. In identifying these rights, Smith took a broader view than David Hume (who restricted them virtually only to property rights) and admitted a variety of rights, both those which are fully 'natural' and those identified as 'adventitious' or rights acquired through one's actions.[7] What is to count as a right is to be determined through the famous device of the impartial spectator, which Smith developed in his *Theory of Moral Sentiments*, assessing the justifiability of resentment felt as a result of a harmful action. There is thus, importantly, an unbroken continuity between morals and law. Each individual has rights, through violation of which he may be injured, and which it is the first task of government to secure:

as a man, with regard to
- (i) his person,
- (ii) his reputation,
- (iii) his estate;

as a member of a family, with regard to
- (i) his wife,
- (ii) his offspring,
- (iii) his servants;

as a member of a state,

which can be dealt with under private law, domestic law and public law respectively. Most of what Smith has to say about delict is handled under the first sub-heading:

> I come now to consider the third species of personall rights or obligations, which is, those which arise from Delinquency. That is, the right one has to be repaid the damage he has sustained ex delicto, from the delinquency of another. Delinquency may be of two sorts. Either the damage may arise from the willfull injury *malice propense* of the person, or from a criminal or faulty negligence, or culpa.[8]

Smith then commits what was by then a prevalent error[9] by listing three classes of negligence, identified according to the degree of culpability required - culpa lata (gross negligence), culpa levis or culpa levissima - but these distinctions more properly have their antecedents in the Roman law of contract rather than of delict. After referring the student/reader to the *Theory of Moral Sentiments* for fuller treatment of negligence, Smith abandons negligence (never to return to it in the lectures) and turns instead to the various types of wilful wrongdoing, which covers both criminal acts and intentional torts.

As far as the modern reader is concerned, this section of the lectures is made unnecessarily complex by Smith's failure to differentiate between private delictual wrongs and remedies on the one hand and public criminal wrongs and punishments on the other. However in disentangling private remedy from public punishment (especially if they relate to the same injury), much can be gleaned about the rationale of delict, for it is not lack of sophistication which leads Smith to treat the two together, but a firm belief that there is a continuity between delict and crime, that their purposes are not divergent, and that both have as their focus the reactions of the impartial spectator to the resentment felt by a person who is hurt. Immediately after the classification of delicts Smith asserts that in all cases the measurement of the punishment to be inflicted on the delinquent is the concurrence of the impartial spectator with the resentment of the injured party.[10]

It is this concept of the impartial spectator (though in fact Smith employs a variety of terms, including the 'reasonable man', to cover the same concept) which is the key to any understanding of Adam Smith's account of delictual liability - and, it has to be said, the key to his entire account of law and justice. For it is through the impartial spectator that the individual rights of man are identified and their scope is defined. The impartial spectator determines what is to count as a wrongful invasion of these rights and what the appropriate response to that invasion or injury is.

3. THE IMPARTIAL SPECTATOR[11]

Although when it comes to delict the impartial spectator is being employed as equivalent to the reasonable man as a legal standard (and for much more besides), it is as a moral standard of propriety and merit that the device is first used by Smith and it is as such that its characteristics must initially be examined.

Smith was not the first writer of the Scottish Englightenment to use the term 'impartial spectator' in print: this honour should, I believe, go instead to the now forgotten James Balfour of Pilrig, who was appointed to the chair of Moral Philosophy at Edinburgh University which David Hume had, unsuccessfully, sought.[12] In *A Delineation of the Nature and Obligation of Morality* (1753), largely an attack on Hume, Balfour introduces the idea of 'an impartial spectator or an angel from heaven' to identify what is praiseworthy and just.[13] The clear aim is that by reference to this impartial spectator an objective, perhaps absolute, standard can be discovered. A modern equivalent might be Firth's 'Ideal Observer',[14] about whom Emmet wrote

> It is easy to point out that an Ideal Observer who knew all the facts and the consequences of all possible alternatives and was completely impartial could only be God.[15]

In contrast, Adam Smith's version of the impartial spectator in his *Theory of Moral Sentiments* (first published in 1759) provides an inter-subjective or conventional standard for morals and justice. Indeed the difference between these two writers' notions, between the 'ideal spectator' and the 'impartial spectator,' is an important one. For Smith's impartial spectator does not have the superhuman qualities of an angel. Rather the standard which it represents is very much a practical human one, and moreover one that may vary with time and place:

We are not at present examining upon what principles a perfect being would approve of the punishment of bad actions; but upon what principles so weak and imperfect a creature as man actually and in fact approves of it.[16]

The starting point of his inquiry is an account of the role of 'sympathy' in the formation of moral sentiments. In Smith's writing, sympathy is the natural capacity of one person to participate (in his imagination) in the sentiments of another, and it can relate to the sentiments of an agent or of a person acted upon. Thus we, as spectators, share the joy of a sporting achievement, are distressed by the suffering of a homeless refugee, and are angered by the injustice meted out to a loyal employee unfairly dismissed, as if we were that athlete, refugee or employee. But, of course, the sympathy which the spectator feels does not have the same intensity as the original feeling, whether it be the feeling of the agent or that of the person acted upon. Nevertheless it is open to the spectator to compare his own (sympathetic) reaction to a given situation with the sentiments of those principally involved. It is then that he may find that, as well as the shared sentiment, there arises a second feeling - that of the pleasure of the sharing of the sentiment, where the sympathetic sentiment matches the sentiment of the original participant. Where there is 'perfect coincidence' between the sympathetic reaction or passion and the original passion of the participant, the spectator has a sentiment of approbation towards the feelings of the participant: they are judged as right and proper.

...in the sentiment of approbation there are two things to be taken notice of; first, the sympathetic passion of the spectator; and, secondly, the emotion which arises from his observing the perfect coincidence between this sympathetic passion in himself, and the original passion in the person principally concerned. This last emotion, in which the sentiment of approbation properly consists, is always agreeable and delightful. The other may either be agreeable or disagreeable, according to the nature of the original passion.[17]

This pleasurable feeling of sharing sentiments is one which the participant too seeks, and in order to achieve such fellow-feeling, the participant may moderate his sentiments (of joy, distress, anger or whatever) so that they approximate to the spectator's reaction, while in turn the spectator may make an effort to heighten his feelings to match those of the participant:

These two sentiments, however, may, it is evident, have such a correspondence with one another, as is sufficient for the harmony of society. Though they will never be unisons, they may be concords, and this is all that is wanted or required.[18]

When an individual's conduct towards others is being evaluated, two aspects of his sentiments are relevant: the causal motives of his actions and their intentions or effects.

In the suitableness or unsuitableness, in the proportion or disproportion which the affection seems to bear to the cause or object which excites it, consists the propriety or impropriety, the decency or ungracefulness of the consequent action.

In the beneficial or hurtful nature of the effects which the affection aims at, or tends to produce, consists the merit or demerit of the action, the qualities by which it is entitled to reward, or is deserving of punishment.[19]

The morality of an action is assessed by the spectator by reference to both these aspects - by direct sympathy with the agent in relation to the propriety of its causes, and indirectly via sympathy with the degree of gratitude or resentment which the person acted upon should have. However in Smith's moral theory, the agent too can utilise that same device - of imaginative sympathy - to assess, in advance, the morality of his own actions.

If a moral agent who is about to act, seeks approval of the sentiments leading to the action (though Smith adds that more than the pleasure of actual approval or praise, it is the pleasurable state of being praiseworthy which the individual seeks[20]), he will need to bring about that 'perfect coincidence' between his sentiments and those of the spectator, by anticipating, and adapting to, the reaction of the spectator. This he can do by imagining himself as the spectator of his own behavior:

We either approve or disapprove of the conduct of another man according as we feel that, when we bring his case home to ourselves, we either can or cannot entirely sympathize with the sentiments and motives which directed it. And, in the same manner, we either approve or disapprove of our own conduct, according as we feel that, when we place ourselves in the situation of another man, and view it, as it were, with his eyes and from his station, we either can or cannot entirely enter into and sympathize with the sentiments and motives which influenced it.[21]

He can thus, in advance, adjust his behaviour to that with which he imagines the spectator would sympathise. However, there may be in fact no actual spectator observing his conduct and in any event a particular spectator may be prejudiced or idiosyncratic in his outlook, or may be unaware of some relevant circumstance. In other words, reference to an imagined actual spectator is unreliable. What is necessary is reference to an imagined uninvolved and standardised or representative spectator, i.e. the impartial spectator. Even he will not sympathise fully with the agent unless he has all the information about the situation which the agent has, and so Smith gives the impartial spectator the additional characteristic of being 'well-informed.' Having imagined the reaction of such an impartial spectator to the proposed action, the agent can assess whether his motives and his consequent action would receive sympathetic approval from the impartial spectator. That is, he can identify what he ought to do, his duty (a concept not well brought out by Francis Hutcheson or David Hume, who earlier made use of less sophisticated spectator ideas).[22] He can then take the appropriate steps to bring himself in line with the sentiments of the impartial spectator and enjoy the fellow-feeling and approval which result. This might legitimately be thought of as justified self-approbation.

The result of this process is that the agent seems to have a way of testing whether an action which he proposes is acceptable or not. And after the event the agent can look back and reassess his actions by the same test, the difference being, firstly, that by then it is likely that he "can more cooly enter into the sentiments of the indifferent spectator,"[23] and secondly, that the consequences of his action will be known and may affect its evaluation.

In turn, others - actual spectators - can evaluate the agent's actions using the standard of the impartial spectator, rather than their own subjective reactions.

While it is undeniable that, in this account, Smith has provided both significant insights into the psychology of moral behaviour and an original method of arriving at a code of acceptable conduct, this is not an exhaustive account of the origins of moral sentiments, a point that seems to have been first noticed by Thomas Reid, Smith's successor at Glasgow University:

> A very ingenious author has resolved our moral sentiments respecting the virtues of self-government, into a regard to the opinion of men. This I think is giving a great deal too much to the love of esteem, and putting the shadow of virtue in place of the substance; but that a regard to the opinion of others is, in most instances of our external behaviour, a great inducement to good conduct, cannot be doubted. For, whatever men may practise themselves, they will always approve of that in others which they think right.[24]

Put bluntly, what concerns Reid is that the fact that others (however impartial) agree with, sympathise with, or approve of, a sentiment (or action) says little about the inherent qualities of the sentiment. The criterion of acceptability is a formal, procedural one and not a substantive one, conventional, not absolute; one which does not objectively evaluate the original sentiments and may not even necessarily differentiate, for example, between selfish desires and benevolence. It is not always clear why a particular sentiment is felt in common and approved. This particular concern will re-emerge when the scope of negligence is discussed.

The situation is further complicated by Smith's admission that the impartial spectator sets a demanding standard and that there exists a second acceptable standard of conduct for exceptional situations when an agent is under extreme stress. In those difficult circumstances, no human conduct ever did, or ever can, achieve complete propriety and perfection, but there is an attainable standard which is what 'the greater part of men commonly arrive at,'[25] and if that is exceeded the effort deserves applause. It hardly needs to be added that this lower standard should not be viewed as a ready let-out for every occasion when following the higher standard of the impartial spectator would involve effort. There may be many times when an individual may be tempted to give in to his unbridled passions and when his power to summon up, far less go along with, the required impartiality is impaired. But then he has general rules of morality which have been inferred from individual moral judgments to fall back on.

Our continual observations upon the conduct of others, insensibly leads us to form to ourselves certain general rules concerning what is fit and proper either to be done or to be avoided... When these general rules, indeed, have been formed, when they are universally acknowledged and established, by the concurring sentiments of mankind, we frequently appeal to them as to the standards of judgment, in debating concerning the degree of praise or blame that is due to certain actions of a complicated and dubious nature.[26]

These exist in part because few people can always act with utmost propriety, but most are responsive to a sense of duty, a more specific notion and one more easily translated into stated rules.

The regard to those general rules of conduct, is what is properly called a sense of duty, a principle of the greatest consequence in human life, and the only principle by which the bulk of mankind are capable of directing their actions ... The coarse clay of which the bulk of mankind are formed, cannot be wrought up to such perfection [as propriety demands]. There is scarce a man, however, who by discipline, education, and example, may not be so impressed with regard to general rules, as to act upon almost every occasion with tolerable decency, and through the whole of his life to avoid any considerable degree of blame.[27]

Since these rules clearly cannot be sufficiently detailed as to cover every situation they are not a true substitute, in morals, for the well-informed impartial spectator. In law, however, while morality should always inform social practice and law, what is wanted is a statement, in general terms, of the minimum conduct required to satisfy justice, rather than ways of reaching for the higher virtues.[28] Emphasis is placed on duty rather than propriety, general rules rather than individualised prescriptions, consequences rather than motives.

4. THE IMPARTIAL SPECTATOR IN THE LAW OF DELICT

It seems that the impartial spectator device has, potentially, several functions in the law of delict. It can be used by the judiciary or even by the legislature to identify the rights which are to be protected by legal rules, the scope of the correlative duty of care and the requisite standard of care. Additionally it is available to the judge or jury when they are determining whether an action has fallen below the standard of care and is a breach of duty. Finally it may be of assistance in quantifying damages or setting a penalty.

5. ESTABLISHING THE DUTY OF CARE

Although Smith refers to various natural rights, these rights are not objective nor identified *a priori*; rather they are *a posteriori* 'inter-subjective' constructs in the sense that they only exist to the extent that they receive approval by the impartial spectator in a particular society at a particular time. Indeed Smith spends considerable parts of his lectures tracing the evolution of various rights. (While admittedly these are generally 'adventitious' or acquired rights, the two types run together, and in principle both are potentially variable.[29]) The purpose of positive law is to further define and to secure these rights.

Here, then, is a remarkably important role for the impartial spectator: the identification of the key concepts in jurisprudence - rights and duties. The impartial spectator's raw material is the sentiments of resentment felt and shared when a harm is suffered. The judgement (which results from consideration of the agent's perspective as well as that of the victim) that the resentment is justified turns the harm into a wrongful harm, that is, into an injury. Bound up with the concept of an injury is that of a right invaded (and a breached correlative duty). In respect of the intentional causing of harm, the impartial spectator's task is by and large straightforward. Both the resentment of the victim with which the spectator can sympathise, and, generally, the impropriety of the wrongdoer's motives with which he cannot, point the impartial spectator to a strong disapproval of the action. For example, assaults, fraud and abuse of legal process are invasions of rights relating to person, property and liberty (perhaps also reputation) respectively; they are injuries; and there is a duty not to so act.

As regards negligence and some other delicts, the situation is not so clear since there may not be a strong disapproval of the agent's sentiments and behaviour to reinforce the approval of the victim's resentment. Is the hurt simply a misfortune which must be quietly endured or is it an injury for which the agent has to take responsibility? Is it really appropriate to describe the situation as one where a right has been invaded? Did the agent have a duty of care towards the other party in respect of the hurt sustained in the way it was? Wearing the guise of the legislator or, more commonly, of the judge, the impartial spectator has to implement the values of the community in the form of answers to these questions. Smith's discussion of these issues is to be found in the *The Theory of Moral Sentiments* under the heading 'Of the Influence of Fortune upon the Sentiments of Mankind with regard to the Merit or Demerit of Actions.'[30]

Having asserted that the only two bases for evaluating an action can be the propriety of the agent's sentiments (ascertained through direct sympathy) and the merit of the effects the action tends to produce (assessed in terms of the appropriate reaction of the person acted upon), Smith has no doubt that, theoretically, praise or blame should disregard 'the accidental, the unintended and unforeseen consequences of different actions,'[31] concerning themselves only with the agent's intentions and affections. However, he admits that

... when we come to particular cases, the actual consequences which happen to proceed from any action, have a very great effect upon our sentiments concerning its merit or demerit.[32]

Although Smith does not spell it out, the reason for such a tendency is that an actual injury of another is much more readily brought home to us through sympathetic imagination than anything which might have happened but did not. Where an injury results from an action by someone who did not intend that result, the victim's and the impartial spectator's assessment of the perpetrator's motive is dominated by the fact of the injury. Despite having called this an 'irregularity of sentiment,'[33] Smith considers it to be natural and acceptable for even an impartial spectator to be particularly influenced by consequences in these circumstances.

Smith reinforces his argument by reference to the contrasting case where there has been a recklessness with regard to the safety of others but where no actual harm has ensued, for example,

...if a person should throw a large stone over a wall into a public street without giving warning to those who might be passing by, and without regarding where it was likely to fall, he would undoubtedly deserve some chastisement. A very accurate police would punish so absurd an action, even thought it had done no mischief. The person who has been guilty of it, shows an insolent contempt for the happiness and safety of others.'[34]

But, in fact, the impartial spectator is unable to feel the degree of resentment that would have arisen had there been a victim, and, while the perpetrator deserves punishment for wickedness on the retributive calculus, and requires as much deterrence as another whose stone does hit a passer-by, no penalty is imposed, because, it seems, of the lack of injury-caused resentment. Smith adds that since in any event the true sentiments, designs and affections of the wrongdoer are beyond human jurisdiction, the irregularity is salutary and useful in obviating errors which might arise in judging intentions; it would be dangerous to condemn someone for evil thoughts alone. This irregular human disposition fits well with the overall emphasis in delict, contrasted with the criminal law, on the harm to the injured party rather than on the wrongdoer's character.

Smith relates these few passing references to unintentional injuries to the traditional Roman law gradations of 'culpa': 'culpa lata' or gross negligence is almost equal to malicious design; 'culpa levis' - is carelessness -; and 'culpa levissima' - is 'a want of the most anxious timidity and circumspection'[35]. It is noteworthy that the latter two are not blameworthy unless damage to another is occasioned, so that in the law of negligence, the emphasis is on injuries before the conduct causing them is examined. Smith's cursory treatment of negligence concludes with a very instructive illustration which will serve as a focus for discussion of the role of the impartial spectator in the law of delict:

> Thus, by the Aquilian law, the man, who not being able to manage a horse that had accidentally taken fright, should happen to ride down his neighbour's slave, is obliged to compensate the damage. When an accident of this kind happens, we are apt to think that he ought not to have rode such a horse, and to regard his attempting it as an unpardonable levity; though without this accident we should not only have made no such reflection, but should have regarded his refusing it as the effect of timid weakness, and of an anxiety about merely possible events, which it is to no purpose to be aware of. The person himself, who by an accident even of this kind has involuntarily hurt another, seems to have some sense of his own ill desert, with regard to him ... [But] ... Why should he, since he was equally innocent with every other bystander, be thus singled out from among all mankind, to make up for the bad fortune of another? This task would surely never be imposed upon him, did not even the impartial spectator feel some indulgence for what may be regarded as the unjust resentment of that other.[36]

There can be little doubt that the victims of this accident (slave-owner and slave) will feel some resentment (even if only in passing) at the injury done. Smith points out[37] that this is an automatic response in man - even towards inanimate objects which have caused pain, such as a stone in the shoe. However, depending on the character of the victims, they are likely to feel less or perhaps no resentment when the accidental nature of the injury is ascertained. Smith's rather surprising description of the rider as 'equally innocent with every other bystander' and of the injured party's resentment as seemingly 'unjust' demonstrates his own reluctance to attribute blame in the case of unintentional injuries, and perhaps a desire to try to go beyond the 'irregularity of sentiment' to a more impartial and higher moral standard.

Presumably any actual spectators will, through sympathy, share in the resentment of the slave-owner (and perhaps even that of the slave himself!). This is done, Smith seems to believe, without regard to the actual reaction of real victims, a spectator merely imagining how he (the spectator) would feel in the victim's position.[38] But, again, they will assess the appropriateness of that resentment in the light of the motives and intentions they ascribe to the rider. Since the injury was not intentional, the resentment will be mollified: there will be some sympathy with the plight of the rider. However these spectator reactions are unpredictable: it may be that a spectator is biased in favour of one or other of the parties, or otherwise incapable of giving a fair assessment of the situation.

Someone judging the incident (beforehand and/or afterwards) - rimarily the rider, but also a lawmaker or judge - should evalulate the situation through the medium of the imagined reactions of an impartial and well-informed spectator. There is a series of acts of imaginative sympathy he must carry out in order to find out

i) whether an impartial spectator would go along with the victim in feeling some resentment [and the last line of the quotation suggests that Smith, at least, thinks he would];

ii) whether an impartial spectator would sympathise with the rider's motives and intentions [perhaps, generally approving of his innocent activities but condemning him for his over-confidence in taking on a horse which he could not be sure of controlling (impropriety), or condemning him for not adverting to potential risks to other persons (demerit)];

iii) where the overall balance of an impartial spectator's sympathies would lie, and thus the existxence and extent of a duty of care.

The rider may carry out a further act of imagination to determine whether he, in turn, sympathises fully with what he imagines the sentiments of an impartial spectator to be: if he fully sympathises with the disapprobation which he imagines an impartial spectator feels, then he judges his own conduct to have been blameworthy. If there is a dissonance, then he is unable to square his conscience with the prevailing social standards, but, of course, in the legal arena, these standards, or at least an interpretation of them, are now enforceable through the courts. The existence and adaptability of the spectator-based duty of care means that it is not necessary that the specific situation be "legislated for" in advance. Prospective riders are expected to imagine, in advance, the potential consequences (physical, moral and legal) of their intended actions.

A court, too, will reflect on the rider's conduct through the eyes of the impartial spectator (but in this case only as well-informed as the rules of evidence and the limitations of fact-finding allow). Considered charitably, the court is an impartial spectator in relation to a particular case, but it would be wise of judges and juries to go through the exercise of reference to the imaginary impartial spectator so as to neutralise any prejudice or idiosyncracy they might have. Their paramount question will be whether or not an impartial spectator - or his legal cousin, the 'reasonable man' - would have approved or gone along with the actions of the rider, rather than whether they themselves either approve or would have at the time approved of his actions.

Thus, although initially a device in a theory of morals, the notion of the impartial spectator looks to be well-suited to having a role in the law of delict. Additionally, although Smith does not draw attention to it, the details of the case he cites from the lex Aquilia can be used to bring home one of the more significant characteristics of the impartial spectator test (which it shares with delictual liability), namely its relativity. That it is not an absolute test will be proved by the imagined attitude of the impartial spectator to the injured slave; in classical times, the resentment of the slave per se, as opposed to that of his owner, was not significant in the calculations of the impartial spectator; whereas in more enlightened times, the assessment of any equally impartial spectator would be different.

6. SCOPE OF THE DUTY OF CARE

The impartial spectator device seems to lend itself to a delimitation of the scope of duties in negligence law based on neighbourhood or proximity, as famously set out by Lord Atkin in *Donoghue v. Stevenson*:

> You must take reasonable care to avoid acts or omissions which you can reasonably foresee would be likely to injure your neighbour. Who then in law is my neighbour? The answer seems to be - persons who are so closely and directly affected by my act that I ought reasonably to have them in contemplation as being so affected when I am directing my mind to the acts or omissions which are called into question.[39]

Smith (as Hume did before him[40]) notes that sympathy naturally reduces the further away the object of one's sympathy.

> Let us suppose that the great empire of China, with all its myriads of inhabitants, was suddenly swallowed up by an earthquake ... If [a man of humanity in Europe] was to lose his little finger to-morrow, he would not sleep to-night; but, provided he never saw them, he will snore with the most profound security over the ruin of a hundred millions of his brethren.[41]

Thus the impartial spectator, carrying - in a moderated form -this limitation on sympathy, will inevitably have greater difficulty in sympathising with, and approving the resentment of, an injured party remote from the agent than if the injured party is a close neighbour. Similarly, resentment reduces against injuries the further in the past they are: for this reason Smith argues for a prescriptive time limit on taking a court case[42]. For, as Stephen Hicks puts it,

> If it is our sympathy with the resentment of the injured that justifies the law of delicts, then one's neighbour is logically anyone into whose place one could put oneself.[43]

If an injured party was not sufficiently proximate or if the injury was not foreseeable or the damage was very remote, the impartial spectator's sympathies would preponderantly lie with the agent whose duty of care would as a result not be extended that far.

There is some evidence that other human dispositions, necessarily shared by the impartial spectator, must similarly impose limitations on the scope of the duty of care, for example, in relation both to economic loss and to 'acts of omission.'

7. ECONOMIC LOSS

It is not at all certain that Smith would be persuaded that there should be reparation for economic loss: although he makes no direct reference to the possibility, his treatment of breach of contract, a more immediate injury from the spectator perspective than a financial loss arising delictually, suggests that economic loss arouses little spectator resentment.

Breach of contract is naturaly the slightest of all injuries because we naturaly depend more on what we possess than what is in the hands of others. A man robbed of five pounds thinks himself much more injured than if he had lost five pounds by a contract.[44]

It is very true that the loss is as great, but we do not naturally [look] upon the injury as at all so heinous.[45]

However it is a feature of spectator reactions that they are conditioned by their setting rather than being universal. While Smith may well be reflecting the sentiments of the eighteenth century spectator, this seems to be an area where the spectator reaction has changed in the intervening two centuries so as to bring economic loss within the scope of the duty of care. The same can be said for acts of omission - although at first sight, and in Smith's own mind, they do give rise to issues which are more ones of principle.

8. ACTS OF OMISSION

It will be observed that Smith's way of deriving rights from injuries results in justice (the respecting of rights) being defined residually as non-injury, and indeed Smith himself declares:

Mere justice is, upon most occasions, but a negative virtue, and only hinders us from hurting our neighbour. The man who barely abstains from violating either the person, or the estate, or the reputation of his neighbours, has surely very little positive merit. He fulfils, however, all the rules of what is peculiarly called justice, and does every thing which his equals can with propriety force him to do, of which they can punish him for not doing. We may often fulfil all the rules of justice by sitting still and doing nothing.[46]

It seems clear from this where Smith would stand on one of the contentious issues in the modern law of delict or torts, namely, whether individuals should be liable for acts of omission as well as for acts of commission (leaving aside omissions made in the course of acting such that the act becomes a negligently performed one). Smith observes that, just as people are more affected by injuries done to their family and neighbours, and are little affected by economic loss, so they experience inappreciable resentment against someone who merely allows a harm to occur but is not the cause of that harm. He believes that these characteristics are necessarily shared by the impartial spectator and are so prevalent amongst mankind as to amount to a natural, universal human trait. Thus there is no right in an individual that another individual should carry out a positive action (such as a rescue): a positive action of assistance cannot be claimed as of right under justice, though it may be requested as a favour, as charity, as generosity -as an act of beneficence. The law is an appropriate way of securing justice but has no place in securing beneficence. This reflects the relative social importance of the two virtues:

> Society may subsist among different men, as among different merchants, from a sense of its utility, without any mutual love and affection... Society, however, cannot subsist among those who are at all times ready to hurt and injure one another. The moment that injury begins, the moment that mutual resentment and animosity take place, all the bands of it are broken asunder ... Beneficence, therefore, is less essential to the existence of society than justice. Society may subsist, though not in the most comfortable state, without beneficence; but the prevalence of injustice must utterly destroy it.[47]

The other factor working for the limitation of liability to acts of commission only is the preeminent place given to natural liberty in the writings of Smith. Natural liberty as one of the natural rights should be limited only if its free use is injuring another:

> In the race for wealth, and honours, and preferments, he may run as hard as he can, and strain every nerve and every muscle, in order to outstrip all his competitors. But if he should jostle, or throw down any of them the indulgence of the spectators is entirely at an end.[48]

- or where the public utility overwhelmingly requires it. But since these two qualifications show that natural liberty is not illimitable, and its scope is determined by the sympathetic approval of the impartial spectator, it does follow that if the impartial spectator, reflecting a shift in contemporary values, comes to treat a failure to act as an injury, then simultaneously a claim of the agent that it is his or her natural right to remain uninvolved loses validity.

Thus it does not seem to follow from Smith's basic principles that the law of delict should inevitably eschew liability for inaction, for the test of liability is not some immutable rational distinction between different types of acts. Rather the test is the reaction of the impartial spectator, and, as has been emphasised, that is not a permanently fixed standard. Part of its beauty is the flexibility it offers to societies as they develop and change. There is no reason why behaviour which was once condemned should not become acceptable to society as expressed through the impartial spectator standard, and vice versa. Specifically, there is no overwhelming reason why inaction which was not resented in times past should not now become a cause of justified resentment, the grounds for claiming that an injury has been done and that there has been a breach of a duty to act. It is precisely this which Lord Kames, Smith's mentor in several matters of law and philosophy, envisages in the introduction to his *Principles of Equity* when he writes:

Regulations to restrain individuals from doing mischief, and to enforce performance of covenants, composed originally the bulk of the common law; and these two branches, among our rude ancestors, seemed to comprehend every subject of law. The more refined duties of morality were, in that early period, little felt and less regarded. But law, in this simple form, cannot long continue stationary: for, in the social state, under regular discipline, law ripens gradually with the human faculties; and by ripeness of discernment, and delicacy of sentiment, many duties, formerly neglected, are found to be binding in conscience. Such duties can no longer be neglected by courts of justice; and as they made no part of the common law, they come naturally under the jurisdiction of a court of equity.[49]

He goes on to explain that these instances become formulated into rules of equity and that, especially in a legal system such as the Scottish one where common law and equitable jurisdictions have always been united in the one court, these become progessively part of the law of the land.

This is not to say that there is no significant difference between liability for omissions and that for commissions - simply that an assumed designation by an eighteenth century impartial spectator of justice as a purely negative virtue is not sufficient to ground it for all time. Interestingly, Smith himself does countenance the imposition through the legislative function of the sovereign of certain 'duties of beneficence' under the second concern of civil society, the improvement of society through 'police':

...he may prescribe rules, therefore, which not only prohibit mutual injuries among fellow-citizens, but command mutual good offices to a certain degree. When the sovereign commands what is merely indifferent, and what, antecedent to his orders, might have been omitted without any blame, it becomes not only blamable but punishable to disobey him.[50]

But he quickly adds that the police duty of the law-giver must be approached with delicacy since 'to push it too far is destructive of all liberty, security, and justice.'[51]

It is unnecessary for Smith to introduce a separate justification (i.e. police) for extending the scope of delict in this direction, since these instances where the individual has duties of positive action imposed by legislation could be brought under the same flexible principles as the traditional delicts, maintaining a unified system of delictual liability, especially since the examples he gives relate to specific relationships, the nature of which might mean there is more likely to be a resentment of a failure to prevent injury. On the other hand, it may be that there is a role for legislation which is being tacitly invoked here in not simply reflecting the current evaluations of the impartial spectator but going beyond them and stimulating a re-evaluation. The fact that something is regulated by the law affects the propriety of the individual's actions in doing or not doing it and this in turn has an impact on the reaction of the impartial spectator to the actions.

Certainly even if Smith were to accept in principle that a change in spectator reactions could give rise to general duties to act positively to render assistance, he would be quick to endorse the following objections to such a change in approach:

> Apart from causation problems there are, perhaps, four main lines of argument: a legal obligation to act as a good Samaritan is seen as an intrusion on individual freedom: there may be difficulty in identifying an appropriate defendant where many could have assisted; the imposition of affirmative duties may be particularly burdensome on the defendant; and generally the courts have been fearful of introducing a new and unpredictable area of responsibility.[52]

But, without exploring them thoroughly, it is safe to say that none of these objections is decisive or insurmountable; a change in public opinion could initiate a change in delictual liability, provided it happened gradually on a case by case basis. What does highlight a significant factor not brought out in the discussion so far is the third and fourth of these objections in so far as they suggest utilitarian or policy reasons for objecting to the expansion of delictual liability in that direction. Because spectator reactions are grounded in sentiments rather than reason, the impartial spectator is not required to state reasons for arriving at a particular judgement. It is not at all self-evident that the causes of the spectator sentiments are exclusively non-utilitarian.

9. THE ROLE OF POLICY[53]

What emerges from a consideration of the scope of the duty of care is that the impartial spectator test is more than merely flexible, it is indeterminate (though it is likely that the human characteristics which allow Smith to state, e.g., that resentment is less in cases of breach of contract than in relation to theft are sufficiently stable that at any particular stage in history such spectator reactions are fairly predictable). As a formal test of acceptability of judgements and conduct, it is opaque. Among the things hidden are the role, if any, of policy and utilitarian considerations in the impartial spectator's judgements of approval or disapproval, and changes in policy. Let us assume, for instance, that the impartial spectator does not extend the scope of liability to cover economic loss. That may well be because resentment is not strong enough to ground a claim. But it could equally be that for policy reasons (e.g. because giving a remedy would undermine the economic viability of a new type of enterprise or because there is a fear that the "floodgates" would be opened to a whole variety of less deserving cases which could clog up the courts), the impartial spectator feels stronger sympathy with the agent than with the wronged party.

Smith wants to give the impression that spectator reactions are 'natural', predominantly non-utilitarian. He denies that utility is the prime factor in moral and jurisprudential judgements:

But still I affirm, that it is not the view of this utility or hurtfulness which is either the first or pincipal source of our approbation and disapprobation.[54]

Nevertheless there is no reason to be found in his basic scheme why the impartial spectator should not take on board policy considerations when determining what is to be approved and what is not. And indeed it does look as if 'under cover' utilitarianism does penetrate into the impartial spectator judgements:

...a closer look reveals that Smith's analysis of moral sentiments is more consequentialist than it at first appears and is generally assumed to be. He allows, for instance, that considerations of 'utility' do have some effect on moral judgements, even if this is normally as an 'afterthought' which has the limited function of confirming rather than directing moral assessments.[55]

Smith suggests that resentment is strengthened where the motive for an unlawful act is financial gain (which he identifies as an attractive motive). What happens in such a case is the the impartial spectator takes into account the policy need to deter such conduct in his assessment of the level of justified resentment. Similarly Smith would be forced to admit that it was policy which identified the injured party in the 'negligent rider' case which he cited from Roman law as being the slave-owner instead of the slave. No doubt a Roman citizen or a Roman impartial spectator would have reacted in the way described, but that reaction is an acquired one; it has been learned, consciously or not, for utilitarian reasons. At one point Smith quite explicitly admits the dominance which utility can attain:

In our approbation of [the virtues of prudence, justice, and beneficence], our sense of their agreeable effects, of their utility, either to the person who exercises them, or to some other persons, joins with our sense of their propriety, and constitutes always a considerable, frequently the greater part of that approbation.[56]

This of course is quite consistent with the modern view of the law in this area.

...there is always a large element of judicial policy and social expediency involved in the determination of the duty-problem, however it may be obscured by the use of traditional formulae.[57]

But once it is acknowledged that spectator (dis)approval can be influenced by policy considerations, the impartial spectator device loses much of its value as a principled criterion of moral or jurisprudential judgement, as Thomas Reid suspected.[58] For Smith, as long as a policy is accepted sufficiently widely that it becomes an input into the judgements of the impartial spectator, its origins are of no account. The impartial spectator test is the only quality control necessary. Subject to that, delictual liability is infinitely variable. Policy considerations, such as the need not to discourage entrepreneurial risk-taking (of various kinds), may justify harmful conduct and be used to limit the scope of delictual liability. Although injured parties may appear to be thereby deprived of a remedy, their resentment will be assuaged by the realisation of the beneficial nature of the harmful conduct. While there is inadequate notice taken by Smith of this concession to the influence of utility, he would doubtless defend it by asserting that human nature is such that the public interest or policy issues do not seize the imagination of people (nor of the impartial spectator) as effectively as sympathy with more concrete or immediate sentiments:

> This beauty and deformity which characters appear to derive from their usefulness or inconveniency, are apt to strike, in a peculiar manner, those who consider, in an absract and philosophical light, the actions and conduct of mankind ... But ... it is only when particular examples are given that we perceive distinctly either the concord or disagreement between our own affections and those of the agent ... When we consider virtue and vice in an abstract and general manner, the qualities by which they excite these several sentiments seem in a great manner to disappear, and the sentiments themselves become less obvious and discernible.[59]

Smith does at one point[60] advocate distinguishing efficient from final causes in moral psychology, and what he is saying above could be interpreted as having the same moment. In the present context, that means that the sentiments of the impartial spectator are the efficient cause of moral judgement, the policy considerations being the (more remote) final cause. In practice, then, it may well be that an impartial spectator approach to the scope of delictual liability may not be significantly directly influenced by policy considerations. However, that the potential is there should be noted.

It is preferable that should the lawmaker (legislator or judge) wish matters of policy to have direct effect on the law, these ought to be introduced explicitly and separately - as part of the police function of the state, and, as such, as an exception to the principles of justice.

10. THE STANDARD OF CARE

The final and most obvious role for the impartial spectator device in delict is as the standard to be used to determine whether an individual's negligent conduct is in breach of the law - as an alternative to the reasonable man[61] -

though in the Scots Law of Delict, establishing the duty of care and identifying a breach of it cannot be fully divorced.

The impartial spectator is better at handling the problem of how subjective the test of acceptable conduct should be. The genius of Smith's system is that while the standard of the impartial spectator is not the universal absolute of the superhuman ideal spectator, neither does its relativity reduce it to the fickleness of actual spectators. The impartial spectator's attributes of impartiality and familiarity with the details ensure that. It is not a totally subjective test, since its standard is a shared community one. Yet, despite being external to the individual in the sense of not being entirely self-imposed, it is not a fully objective standard. Hence the term I have used to describe it is 'inter-subjective.' In cases of negligence, this intersubjectivity allows the impartial spectator to avoid the rigid harshness of a purely objective test of liability without losing its function as a means of identifying a minimum of socially accepted conduct. However one might question whether there is only one community standard of socially accepted conduct in the modern pluralistic society. Because the mechanics of the impartial spectator device involve imagining oneself as another person, it accommodates individual differences of circumstances and, to some extent, values (for example, racial or gender differences) more readily than the abstract but rather narrowly constructed reasonable man. In other words, it is a more relative standard. Nevertheless the degree of diversity which can be embraced by a single rule-circumscribed legal standard is limited.

Professor Raphael has some further doubts at the practical level:

> It seems to me that his concept of the impartial spectator is too complicated to be acceptable when one works it out fully in terms of his general theory of approval ... The process is not impossible but it seems too complicated to be a common occurrence.'[62]

Perhaps this is true, but then it need not happen commonly: Smith has explained that in the majority of cases the bulk of mankind can rely on general rules. The required level of acceptable behaviour may be achieved without conscious reference to the standard. As a standard of conduct, it is being presented as a means of identifying that which ought to be followed, not as a psychological description of what usually happens. Even so, perhaps Smith is correct in that people do go through a process of adjusting their behaviour to what they believe is expected - though without analysing it into the constituent parts which Smith identifies - and it is a process which the law is justified in encouraging. At its simplest ('Would I approve of what I am doing - e.g. riding a horse I cannot be sure of controlling - if I were a neutral observer of my behaviour?'), it requires less of the individual than asking him to identify the characteristics of a more abstract reasonable man - a task with which generations of eminent minds have struggled.

The impartial spectator test resolves most decisively the question of whether the required standard is what is commonly practised or what ought to be done. For the text concerns not the actions of an impartial spectator but the approval of that person. It is a normative standard. It may be that the level of conduct it requires is too demanding, since Smith at first seems to demand 'perfect coincidence' of sentiments if there is to be positive approval of the conduct. However, he realises that life is not as perfect nor as straightforward as that. Even before the weaknesses and irregularities of human nature are taken into account, Smith admits that sympathetic sentiments need only approximate to each other: when he starts to refer to the impartial spectator as 'going along with' someone's actions,[63] rather than having to fully approve of them, then the concept has at least the flexibility that would arise if the impartial spectator were being asked to judge their reasonableness. It has to be conceded that Smith is not entirely consistent here, and, if his theory of approval is to be taken strictly, then the standard of the impartial spectator is unreasonably high.

Generally attempting to look at our conduct from a perspective outside of ourselves is a useful way of testing its reasonableness. The significant advantage of the impartial spectator is that it takes a more concrete and comprehensible form than the reasonable man, and thus is of greater practical guidance to 'the man in the street.' It is ironical, then, that, as Smith notes,[64] there were no juries in civil cases in Scotland in Smith's time. Most of Smith's references to juries are at the descriptive level,[65] but it is clear that he supports such an institution as reflective of community values - often more so than Parliament.[66]

In theory the impartial spectator should be able to absorb policy considerations at this level as readily (or reluctantly, if Smith is correct) as when setting the scope of the duty of care, but it may be that there is greater resistance to incorporating policy issues into individual cases.[67]

But that still leaves a very real problem unanswered: how is an individual, making reference to the impartial spectator in advance of acting, to know whether it is even permissible to include in the evaluation of the act a weighing of the usefulness of the act against the risk of injury, or a balancing of the cost of precautions against the risk? Thus the agent simply may not know whether to go ahead or not. In delict, it is this, rather than the mechanics of the impartial spectator device itself, which is the chief obstacle to the effective use of the impartial spectator in practice.

These drawbacks aside, the impartial spectator is, I believe, sufficiently convincing as a standard of acceptable conduct in negligence and some other areas of law to serve as an instructive point of contrast or reference when applying the existing standard, that of the reasonable man. The courts, too, may be assisted at times by thinking of 'the reasonable man' as an impartial spectator. Indeed, perhaps they sometimes do:

The test is not what the negligent party himself could reasonably have foreseen, for he rarely has time to foresee anything. The test is what a 'hypothetical reasonable observer could reasonably have foreseen.'"[68] The matter has to be looked at from the point of view of the reasonable spectator as well as the reasonable participant ... because what a reasonable spectator would expect a participant to do without regarding it as blameworthy is as relevant to what is reasonable care as what a reasonable participant would think was blameworthy conduct in himself.[69]

11. QUANTIFICATION OF DAMAGES

Smith says very little about reparation and the calculation of damages, but in an account of the history of punishment - very derivative of Kames' *Tract on the Criminal Law* in the *Historical Law Tracts* - he refers to the early notion of compositions (effectively private criminal penalties) paid by the perpetrator to those injured by his crime.[70] In this way the perpetrator "bought off" the threat of retaliation.

Kames had suggested that compositions were initially permitted by government, then an offer of composition was required prior to retaliatory actions, and later, injured parties were required to accept a composition in lieu of retaliation. Exploring the history of criminal law, Kames too had identified resentment and the desire for revenge as the motive for criminal sanctions against the wrongdoer. In primitive societies where a strong state is absent, revenge lies in the hands of the victim; but as the state emerges, it assumes initially co-responsibility and later exclusive responsibility for punishment (partly because of the excesses of private revenge) leaving the victim with civil law remedies of reparation only. In this removal of the criminal sanction from the realm of private to public law, the justification for, and measurement of, it changes too - from a retributivist one to one based on public utility.

Smith, who was very familiar with Kames' work, was reluctant to acknowledge such a conclusion, since he did not wish to promote a utilitarian thesis - and, though there can be no doubt that in the area of the criminal law he was ultimately unsuccessful in excluding utility as the justification of certain laws and punishments, he could consistently claim that, on most occasions, there is no need for people to consider utility directly, since utility is often a by-product of spectator-modified resentment.[71] Tackling first the case of murder, Smith's historical account took a slightly different slant:

The government therefore at first interposed only in the way of mediator, to prevent the ill consequences which might arise from those crimes in the resentment of the friends of the slain,[72]

in a manner reminiscent of the impartial spectator acting as a check on excessive partiality. But then,

[a]s the governments of Europe gain'd more and more in strength, they thought themselves intitled to some gratuity for their trouble in interposing ... to some gratification for this protection ... By degrees the sovereigns came to consider, at least in practise [sic], themselves as the persons chiefly injured. ... This composition due to the king, in Scotland especially, so far exceeded that which was paid to the friends of the deceased that the criminal came to be considered as punished, not as the murtherer of the relation of such persons, but as the murtherer of the free subject of the king. The sovereigns however in time found it more to their advantage, in order to keep peace and harmony amongst their subjects, to substitute a capitall punishment in the room of that frankguild [composition] which was due them.[73]

A similar pattern for other offences is described. While compositions are not the same as compensation or reparation, Smith is insistent that they have the same basis - the resentment of the injured party - and that compositions would generally comprise compensation to the value of damage done plus an element to assuage any residual 'sense of injustice' felt by the injured party. When compositions were done away with in favour of public criminal punishment, the core damages element of compensation might still be due to the injured party. Thus were delictual civil remedies separated from criminal punishment.

Whatever the period of history, the degree of punishment and the quantification of damages are both properly measured by the level of justifiable resentment provoked by the injury.

Injury naturally excites the resentment of the spectator, and the punishment of the offender is reasonable as far as the indifferent spectator can go along with it.[74]

Smith explicitly rejects as primary various other principles of punishment such as those

...on which Grotius and most other writers on this subject have founded it. These are, the correction of the offender and the bringing him to a sense of his duty; 2dly, the deterring of others by making him an example to them; or 3dly, the safety of the community by taking away an unworthy and dangerous member.[75]

(it may be that these aims will be achieved incidentally, as might both deterrence of the offender himself from future offences and compensation.[76]) That compensation *per se* is not the prime justification for the delictual remedy is important to note. It is not only the amount of the physical loss incurred by the delict which determines the degree of resentment and the quantity of damages. The propriety of the actions of the wrongdoer is relevant (amongst other things, allowing the court to distinguish between intentional and accidental wrongdoings), but is not decisive.[77] More unusually, Smith holds that the injured party requires to be additionally compensated for the fact of invasion.

Ex delicto. Whatever reason there is for ones restoring what he has come by, that was the property of another, taking it to be his own [which he has just discussed under 'Quasi ex contractu'], there is as strong if not stronger reasons for his being bound to make up any damage another has received from him. The injury is here more sensibly felt and affects us more as the wilfull transgression of criminall negligence of the person who has injured us adds greatly to the uneasiness for the damage sustained. We think one has injured us more who wilfully did us an injury than one who only did not perform some promise.[78]

What chiefly enrages us against the man who injures or insults us, is the little account which he seems to make of us, the unreasonable preference which he gives to himself above us, and that absurd self-love, by which he seems to imagine, that other people may be sacrificed at any time, to his conveniency or his humour. The glaring impropriety of this conduct, the gross insolence and injustice which it seems to involve in it, often shock and exasperate us more than all the mischief which we have suffered.[79]

Smith backs this view up with specific examples. He claims that resentment is greater when a thief is caught red-handed than if he were apprehended long after the theft; similarly robbery is resented much more than mere theft. In both cases there is aggravated resentment where the invasion of the victim's rights is more immediately felt, though the material loss is the same. Hence if the wronged party is to have all resentment assuaged, more compensation than that which equals the material amount lost is required.[80] There may be a need for exemplary or punitive damages. And it is arguable that the appeasement of resentment necessitates there being an opportunity for the wronged party to take public legal action against the person who has wronged him or her. A payment, particularly in modern times one from an insurance company, may not be sufficient to restore the *status quo ante.*

All trials in early times were carried on by the whole people assembled together; and this was not so much to inflict a punishment as to bring about a reconciliation and some recompense for the damage the injured party may have sustained. Even in the case of murther the chief business was to procure some concessions from the murtherer in order to atone for the injury done the friends of the deceased, and on the other part to mitigate the resentment of the friends of the murthered person.[81]

What the public or the court, to the extent they are acting in the character of the impartial spectator, are doing is evaluating not only the original act causing the injury, but also looking at the appropriateness of a remedy or punishment as a separate, if related, act, potentially giving rise to resentment too. Any resentment which the wrongdoer may feel in response to his punishment is not justified so long as the impartial spectator would go along with that degree of retaliation as an appropriate response to the original act. On the other hand people do find it difficult on occasion not to sympathise with the recipient of the 'punishment' (especially - though this does not apply in delict where there is inevitably a party injured by the original act - where the motive for the punishment is as remote as mere public utility).[82] This sympathy may offer a response to a concern that it is hardly fair that a poor man may be forced into a life of begging merely to give pecuniary 'satisfaction' to a millionaire he has wronged:[83] for indeed the impartial spectator is likely in such a case to feel that the hardship being done to the poor man demands sympathy more than the propriety of the millionaire's action, and may adjust the damages accordingly.

Where the victim has helped to bring about his or her own injury or has failed to take the appropriate steps to avoid it, the resentment that he or she can justly feel (determined through the spectator device) is reduced. The sense of injustice is lessened even though the damage suffered is not. Smith would have approved of contributory negligence going to the level of damages, but not of the earlier rule whereby it defeated the claim entirely.

It appears that the impartial spectator could function well as a quantifier of damages by approving sufficient reparation to assuage justified resentment, and that it may simultaneously but unintentionally promote other social goals of the legal system.

12. RATIONALE OF DELICT

The rationale of the law of delictual liability is much disputed. It is sometimes viewed as the provision of compensation to victims; sometimes as deterrence; sometimes as punishment; and sometimes as a combination of two or more of these. The more cynical might want to argue that the law of delict, in emphasising the restoration of the status quo, serves only the utilitarian goal of maintaining (a particular) order to which appeasing victims is merely incidental. It has to be admitted that there are passages in Smith's writings which could be used to lend weight to claims for each of these to be considered as supported by Smith, but none seems to adequately describe his overall approach. Equally there is no evidence of Smith being concerned with delict simply as a system of allocating loss, especially by means of strict liability, nor that he would endorse a view of the law of delict as a mechanism for distributing or regulating risk. Again, such ideas are not entirely incompatible with Smith's thinking, but to place any emphasis on them would distort the focus of his express claims about the nature of delict.

Coming much closer to Adam Smith's ideas, Steven D. Smith has, in a recent article,[84] made out a strong case for viewing tort law as primarily a dispute resolution system. He identifies the sense of having been wronged as an unquestionably real and important aspect of a victim's injury, pointing out that, otherwise, victims fully compensated for their 'actual loss' should feel satisfied, even with no finding of wrongdoing and no sanction imposed against their injurers. But experience shows that a wronged party often wants to proceed with a case just for the 'principle' at stake. He suggests that this is because

A victim's sense of injustice does not amount simply to an irrational need to strike back at a wrongdoer; rather it represents the victim's consciousness that the normative order upon which the victim has relied has been threatened, and that if the norms constituting that order can be breached with impunity then they will lose their meaning and force. Therefore, when a tortfeasor compromises the normative order, punishment is not merely vindictive, but also serves a positive, restorative purpose.[85]

The victim's sense of having been wronged generates a dispute, and the law must offer a means of resolving the dispute, which necessitates assuaging the resentment (and when it does so it also reinforces the norms of conduct attacked by the wrongdoer). There are strong resonances between this view of tort as presented by Steven Smith and Adam Smith's interpretation of the basis of the delictual remedy:

The object, on the contrary, which resentment is chiefly intent upon, is not so much to make our enemy feel pain in his turn, as to make him conscious that he feels it upon account of his past conduct, to make him repent of that conduct, and to make him sensible, that the person whom he injured did not deserve to be treated in that manner. What chiefly enrages us against the man who injures or insults us, is the little account which he seems to make of us, the unreasonable preference which he gives to himself above us, and that absurd self-love, by which he seems to imagine, that other people may be sacrificed at any time, to his conveniency or his humour. The glaring impropriety of this conduct, the gross insolence and injustice which it seems to involve in it, often shock and exasperate us more than all the mischief which we have suffered. To bring him back to a more just sense of what is due to other people, to make him sensible of what he owes us, and of the wrong he has done us, is frequently the principal end proposed in our revenge, which is always imperfect when it cannot accomplish this.[86]

Delict, in "offering socially accepted methods for retribution and ventilation of feelings of indignation and resentment,"[87] has a distinct function and has attributes which other areas of legal regulation do not. Probably insurance schemes, private or social, offer a better way of compensation for victims; criminal sanctions deter and punish more effectively. However, both of these destroy the personal factor in the relations between the wrongdoer and the injured party, and so do not adequately allow for the assuaging of the resentment. There is a need, then, to retain in some form the law of delict.

Stephen Hicks points out that the impartial spectator concept is less impersonal and reinforces more adequately the mutuality of relations necessary for appeasing the injured party than the reasonable man in modern delict.[88] It may be that this is a feature of Adam Smith's approach that should receive even greater emphasis now at a time when impersonal insurance coverage is dehumansising the relationship between the parties. Urbanised society made up of isolated individuals might benefit from a return to something akin to the cohesiveness of relations of reciprocity and the ritualised (and hence contained and functional) retaliation of more 'primitive' peoples.[89]

Adam Smith understood well the fact of legal evolution, and it may be that the time is right for the state to assume responsibility for compensation, at least in relation to personal injury, as previously it did for punishment. This would be funded out of compulsory insurance, state or private, but could still leave open to the injured party who can prove fault the option of suing in the courts for 'satisfaction' of the sense of injustice and for damages above the standard allowed under the insurance scheme. It is suggested here that that scheme of delictual remedy, or any other, would benefit from being more closely attuned to the impartial spectator than are current systems.

This is not to say, however, that adoption of the impartial spectator device, as envisaged by Smith, would make for a thoroughly fair system of delictual liability. Formal impartiality is not synonymous with genuine justice. For as long as Smith is thirled to a narrow conception of justice (justice as a purely negative virtue), whereby the status quo is assumed to be both fair and desirable, he denies and camouflages the reality of significant disparities in the sharing out of the burdens of society such as susceptibility to risk and hazards in everyday life.[90] And to the extent that the impartial spectator shares uncritically Smith's misplaced complacency, he is not a well-informed and impartial spectator, but instead perpetuates social injustice.

NOTES

1. Lord Cooper: *The Scottish Legal Tradition* (Edinburgh: The Saltire Society 1949).
2. Smith, T.B.: *A Short Commentary on the Law of Scotland*. (Edinburgh: Green & Sons 1962).
3. Lee: (1917-18) 27 YLJ 721 at 727-9.
4. Smith, Adam: *Lectures on Jurisprudence*, edited by Meek, R.L., Raphael, D.D. and Stein, P.G. (Oxford 1978). Report of 1762-3 hereafter cited as *LJ(A)*; report dated 1766 hereafter cited as *LJ(B)*. *LJ(A)* ii. 74-5.
5. Smith, Adam: *The Theory of Moral Sentiments* (1st edition 1759). This and all further references to the Glasgow Edition' edited by Raphael, D.D. and Macfie, A.L. (Oxford 1976), hereafter cited as *TMS*.
6. *LJ(A)* i.9, omitting some editorial notation.
7. This distinction is ultimately unsustainable, but is unimportant for present purposes.
8. *LJ(A)* ii.88.
9. See Guthrie Smith, J.: *A Treatise on the Law of Reparation*. (Edinburgh 1864) at pp. 60-1.
10. *LJ(A)* ii. 89.
11. This section is based on a paper delivered at the Fourteenth World Congress in Philosophy of Law and Social Philosophy at Edinburgh in August 1989, published in Campbell, T.D. (ed.): *Law and Englightenment in Britain*. (Aberdeen 1990) (Hereafter *Law and Englightenment*). On Smith's impartial spectator theory generally, see Macfie, A.L.: *The Individual in Society*. (London 1967) at ch. 5; Campbell, T.D.: *Adam Smith's Science of Morals*. (London 1971) (Hereafter Campbell) at ch.6; Raphael, D.D.: 'The Impartial Spectator', in Skinner A.S. and Wilson, T. (eds.): *Essays on Adam Smith*. (Oxford 1975).

12. Of course, the term 'impartial spectator' was previously used in the first edition of *The Spectator*.
13. Balfour, J.: *A Delineation of the Nature and Obligation of Morality*. (Edinburgh 1753):

If we suppose an impartial spectator, or an angel from heaven, to take a view of human affairs; he might indeed see one prince or state lay hold of a favourable opportunity unjustly to seize the territory of another. But what would his sentiments be of such conduct, with regard to the interest of mankind in general? It would plainly appear, that one state just lost as much as another gained; and, in this respect, the general interest would remain the same as it was before. But our disinterested spectator would further observe, a right violated, a treaty broke, and such distrust and resentment, thence arising, as must weaken the common tye, and disturb the peace and tranquility of the public. at pp. 73-4.
14. Firth, R.: 'Ethical Absolutism and the Ideal Observer' (1952) 12 Phil. and Phenom. Research 317. See Campbell, supra at note 11, at pp. 128-34.
15. Emmet, D.: 'Universalisability and Moral Judgement' (1963) 13 Phil.Q. 214 at 223, cited by Campbell.
16. *TMS* II.i.5.10.
17. *TMS* I.iii.1.9. For criticisms of this theory of approbation, see Farrer, J.A.: Adam Smith (London 1881, Reprinted by J. Martin Stafford, Altrincham 1988), Morice, G.: 'Opinion, Sentiment and Approval in Adam Smith' in Hope, V.: *Philosophers of the Scottish Englightenment*. (Edinburgh 1984), Campbell, supra at note 11, at ch.5, and Macfie, supra at note 11.
18. *TMS* I.i.4.7.
19. *TMS* I.i.3.5-7.
20. *TMS* III.1.5.
21. *TMS* III.1.2.
22. See Raphael, supra at note 11, at p. 87.
23. *TMS* III.4.4.
24. Reid, Thomas: *Essays on the Active Powers of the Human Mind* in *Works*, ed. Hamilton (Edinburgh 1863) Essay III Part II Section ii at p. 557.
25. *TMS* I.i.5.8-10 and see also III.3.28.
26. *TMS* III.4.7, 11.
27. *TMS* III.5.1.
28. See Haakonssen, K.: *The Science of a Legislator* (Cambridge 1981) pp. 54-61 for a discussion of social and the higher moral approval.
29. A point noted by Haakonssen, who writes that the right to reputation, 'provides yet another illustration of the looseness of Smith's distinction between natural and acquired rights. For although he counts the right to protection of one's reputation as one of the natural rights, it should be fairly obvious that it is almost as changeable as many acquired rights, since it is determined by something as changeable as the standards of 'the common sort of men' and of professions.' [supra at note 28, at p. 103].
30. *TMS* II.iii. See Campbell, T.D.: 'Adam Smith and the Economic Analysis of Law' in Hope, supra at note 17, at p. 150.
31. *TMS* II.iii.intro.4.
32. *TMS* II.iii.intro.5.
33. *TMS* II.iii.2.2.
34. *TMS* II.iii.2.8. Cf. LJ(B) 201:

The reason is plain. Resentment never arises to any great pitch unless some injury be actually done. Some things that are in themselves criminal are not punished unless some bad consequences follow. A man meets with little resentment for riding an unruly horse in the

market place, but if he kill any body resentment is very high.
35. *TMS* II.iii.2.10.
36. *TMS* II.iii.2.10. Cf. *Holmes v. Mather* (1875) L.R. 10 Ex. 261.
37. *TMS* II.iii.1.1.
38. *TMS* II.i.5.11. This would allow for the protection of those who are not natural persons, such as incorporations and the unborn.
39. 1932 S.C.(H.L.) 31 at p. 44.
40. See, e.g., Hume, David: *A Treatise of Human Nature*, ed. Selby-Bigge (Oxford 1978) Book II, Part I Section xi at p. 318.
41. *TMS* III.3.4.
42. *LJ(A)* ii. 168-74, *LJ(B)* 199-200.
43. Hicks, S.C.: 'The Revolution in Social Theory in the Early Nineteenth Century: from Sympathy to Disinterestedness with an afterword on the Origin of the Tort of Negligence' in *Law and Enlightenment*, supra at note 11.
44. *LJ(B)* 176.
45. *LJ(A)* ii. 44-5.
46. *TMS* II.ii.1.10.
47. *TMS* II.ii.3.2-3.
48. *TMS* II.ii.2.1.
49. Lord Kames: *Principles of Equity*. (Edinburgh 1760), at p.5 of 1825 edition.
50. *TMS* II.ii.1.8.
51. Ibid.
52. Todd: (1986) 102 LQR 370 at 383.
53. On the principle/policy distinction see Dworkin, R.: *Taking Rights Seriously* (Duckworth 1978 (revised edit.) at pp. 90-100, 294-330. Cf. Greenawalt: (1977) 11 Ga.L.R. 991.
54. *TMS* IV.2.3. See also *TMS* IV.2.5 and II.ii.3.10.
55. Campbell: (1977) 25 Political Studies 523 at 530, referring esp. to *TMS* I.i.4.4.
56. *TMS* VI. Conclusion 6.
57. *Nova Mink Ltd. v Trans-Canada Airlines* [1951] 2 D.L.R. 241 at 256 (per MacDonald J.), quoted with approval in *McLoughlin v. O'Brian* [1983] 1 A.C. 410 at 426 (per Lord Edmund-Davies).
58. See text accompanying footnote 24 supra.
59. *TMS* IV.2.2.
60. *TMS* II.ii.3.5. See also II.i.5.10 where this is implicit.
61. I have discussed this elsewhere (Mackinnon, K.A.B.: 'The Reasonable Man as an Impartial Spectator' in *Law and Enlightenment*, supra at note 12). See also Hicks, supra at note 43.
62. Raphael, supra at note 11, at p. 99.
63. E.g. *TMS* II.ii.2.1, *LJ(A)* ii.90 and *LJ(B)* 181.
64. *LJ(A)* v. 39.
65. E.g. *LJ(A)* v. 17; v. 24; v. 32-41.
66. E.g. *LJ(A)* ii. 92; *LJ(B)* 72.
67. Bohlen believed jurors cling to the idea that an injury should be paid for by whoever caused it, irrespective of the moral or social quality of his conduct. Therefore, though he was aware of the danger of thus entrenching in precedent what should be a flexible standard, he maintained that

It is quite clear that due consideration can only be given to the social utility of an act ... by the court's taking the decision into its own hands. And it is immaterial whether it does so by definitely asserting the right to fix the standard, or by saying that the jury would be acting unreasonably if they fixed a standard which regarded as wrongful, conduct which the court believes to be justified by economic necessity. Bohlen: (1924) 72 U.Pa.L.R. 111 at 119.

though he was aware of the danger of thus entrenching in precedent what should be a flexible standard.

68. Denning, L.J. in *King v. Phillips* [1953] 1 Q.B. 429 at p. 441.

69. Diplock, L.J. in *Woolridge v. Sumner* (C.A.) [1962] 2 All E.R. 978. My use of this quotation, I have to admit, is slightly fraudulent, since the case involved a spectator at a horse show being knocked down by a competing horse. Thus the spectator was the victim, and hence not impartial. The general approach of Diplock L.J. is nevertheless in point.

70. *LJ(A)* ii. 96-102.

71. On the efficient and final causes of punishment, see Norrie: (1989) 2 Ratio Juris 227 at 235. Also footnote 59 supra and accompanying text.

72. *LJ(A)* ii. 95.

73. *LJ(A)* ii. 99-101.

74. *LJ(B)* 181. Cf. *LJ(A)* ii. 90.

75. *LJ(A)* ii. 169. Cf. *LJ(A)* ii. 90 ('the publick good'), *LJ(A)* ii. 176-7 ('correction,' 'safety of society,' 'deterrence'), *TMS* II.i.1.6 ('all the political ends of punishment; the correction of the criminal, and the example to the public').

76. *LJ(A)* ii. 92-3.

77. As the example of the 'reckless stone-thrower' and the advocacy of a time limit on remedies, where the culpability of the wrongdoer is no different to that of other offenders who are held liable, demonstrate.

78. *LJ(A)* i.23.

79. *TMS* II.iii.1.5.

80. The 'extra' element beyond the physical damage demonstrates that Norrie's conclusion in relation to criminal punishment applies also to delictual reparation:

There is no attempt to achieve the strict proportionality between crime and punishment sought by the classical retributivists.

Norrie, supra at note 70, at 230.

81. *LJ(A)* ii.45.

82. *TMS* II.ii.3.7. See Raphael's Appendix II to *TMS*, Haakonssen, supra at note 29, at pp. 114-23, and Norrie, supra at note 70.

83. Williams: (1951) Current Legal Problems 137 at 145.

84. Smith: (1987) 72 Cornell L.R. 765.

85. Ibid., at 792.

86. *TMS* II. iii.1.5.

87. Ingber: (1985) 73 Calif.L.R. 722 at 789.

88. Hicks, supra at note 43.

89. E.g. the practices of 'utu' and 'muru' of the Maori of New Zealand/Aotearoa. See Firth, R.: *Economics of the New Zealand Maori* (Wellington 1973) at pp. 400-1.

90. Abel, R.L.: 'Torts' in Kairys, D. (ed): *The Politics of Law* (New York: Pantheon Books 1990) at p. 334.

University of Waikato, School of Law

ROBIN PAUL MALLOY

ADAM SMITH AND THE MODERN DISCOURSE OF LAW AND ECONOMICS

1. INTRODUCTION

In one way or another Adam Smith remains a central figure in the law and economics movement. More than 200 years after the publication of the *Wealth of Nations* he remains the key philosophical reference point from which most economists seek validation or distinguishment.[1] Nowhere is this more true than in the evolution in legal theory brought on by the emergence of law and economics as a legitimized subdiscipline. For within the realm of discourse and disputes concerning the allocation of scarce resources and political power there are a number of influential scholars that invoke Smith or his ideas as reference points for their own work. People such as myself, Judge Richard Posner, and Professor Richard Epstein all borrow in a positive sense from Smith although we may have dramatically different interpretations of his views. At the same time liberal economist Professor Bruce Ackerman makes reference to Smith in the sense of an outdated relic; law and society have advanced far beyond the point of seeing usefulness in the work of Adam Smith. Likewise, some in critical legal theory (CLS) such as Professor Duncan Kennedy portray Smithian ideas as the foundation principals of certain political and philosophical views that should be rejected because of their self centered and alienating antisocial characteristics.

Understanding Smith's contribution to modern day debates concerning the relationship between law and economics is complex because he is invoked in so many different ways. Adam Smith remains an important social icon and there is still intellectual force and fascination behind using his metaphor of the 'invisible hand' to describe market activity and the social dynamics of spontaneous social order. But the meaning of Adam Smith as social icon and the 'invisible hand' as metaphor are in dispute; a dispute most notable in these current debates addressing the relationship between law and economics.[2] To more clearly understand the philosophical background of these modern debates one needs to examine Adam Smith's work regarding his views on both law and economics.[3] In so doing it must be remembered that Smith operated within the conceptual framework of political economy rather than in today's world where economics has taken on a distinct manner

R.P. Malloy and J. Evensky: Adam Smith and the Philosophy of Law and Economics, 113–150.

of inquiry and through complex mathematical and computer modeling has rendered itself more 'scientific'. The advancement of 'science' in economics over the past two hundred years, however, has not diminished the importance of the underlying *philosophical* issues raised and articulated by Smith.

In this chapter Smith's philosophical understanding of liberty; of the relationship between the individual, the community and the state will be explored for the connection he saw between these concepts and the development and function of law and legal institutions. It will be argued that Smith offered a dynamic and contextual understanding of the relationship between law and economics. Likewise, Smith's concern for morality and the individual led him to promote a system of social and economic organization that sought individual liberty as the end to be achieved rather than wealth maximization or economic efficiency. To this end capitalism and free markets were seen as useful means. As a consequence Adam Smith's work presented a philosophical foundation not only for explaining the relationship between law and economics but also for establishing a classical liberal philosophy that made individuals the key referential sign while acknowledging that we live not alone but in community with others.

In explaining Smith's work for its relevance and importance to the current discourse of law and economics I will first consider his approach to social contract theory as a way of understanding his view on how society might be constructed. Next I will present a brief discussion of the dynamic and contextual stages of development that Smith imagined for both law and economics. Then I will examine his understanding of liberty under the rule of law. Finally, I will attempt to put Smith's work into the context of current debates in law and economics by outlining the way in which Smith is treated by various participants in the discourse.

2. SMITH AND SOCIAL CONTRACT THEORY

The foundational interpretation of how a society or community is constituted or constructed is important for the way in which that interpretation affects one's understanding of law and legal institutions. If one believes John Locke's theory of the social contract for instance than one must commence a discursive inquiry into the nature and terms of the agreement. Who are the parties to the social contract, how does a newcomer opt into the deal and how do current participants opt out? These are familiar philosophical questions regarding social contract theory. Such a theory also presents a particular problem for legal interpretation. If society is constructed on the basis of some real or hypothetical contract of voluntary submission than we need a means for developing clarity in the process of defining and interpreting this agreement. The matter of 'original intentions' becomes very relevant in such a theory for contract law asks one to determine what the parties meant at the time they entered into their bargain. Likewise, one's views or criticisms of such a society should be shaped by reference to the agreement itself since this is the basis upon which the parties have agreed to interact.

Adam Smith rejected the social contract theory as overly problematic and unrealistic.[4] Social cooperation and social dynamics were not properly understood as emerging from a voluntary agreement in the sense of a legal contract between all of the current and future members of a community. Smith argued that social contract theory neglected the practical inability of people to opt out of such an allegedly voluntary undertaking.[5] The poor in particular were unable to have meaningful choice in the matter for their limited resources left them very much committed to a particular geographical location.[6] To assume, as social contract theory does, that one's remaining in a locality amounts to acceptance of the terms of legal, social, political, and economic participation in that community ignores the hardship realities and sociological impediments to moving. Modern critics might add to Smith's pragmatic concerns by noting that the governing structures of communities at the time of Locke and Smith were imposed from above by a limited hierarchy and failed to reflect any sense of law bargaining or participation on the part of the common people even if they appreciated the consequences of such a contract and might have the means to disagree.

In place of social contract theory Adam Smith offered an understanding of social organization based on the concepts of *authority* and *utility*.[7] To understand this one must remember that Smith was not an advocate of unfettered laissez faire. He was not an anarchist and anarchy was not the basis of spontaneous social order.[8] Smith always postulated a framework for social cooperation in which the rule of law was understood.[9] The general rules of law and social cooperation were seen as positive attempts to articulate the governing standards of morality, and social norms within the community.[10] They were not, therefore, elements of a legally constructed social contract but rather a contingent and dynamic pronouncement of an evidentiary process. The development of moral and social norms evolved over time as a result of experience.[11] Positive law attempted to articulate these guiding principles.[12] In this manner Smith saw society constructed around the need for authority where authority operated as a necessary part of difficult decision making and dispute resolution. Societies needed a source of authority so that decisions could be made and anarchy avoided. Likewise, the ability to make decisions and to decide disputes in an orderly manner presented the community with a certain necessary utility. Thus authority and utility worked together as the necessary cornerstones in Smith's consideration of the social construct of a community. Such a construct did not require the functional explanations of bargaining and agreement, inclusions and exclusion, as was required under Locke's social contract theory. Smith's conception was more pragmatic.

It is important to remember that Smith's conception of the role of authority and utility are presented within the context of his various works on protecting the individual and promoting dynamic systems of free exchange. Thus Smith, while acknowledging the role and utility of authority, was able to criticize unsavory and unresponsive hierarchy. Smith's dynamic and evidentiary theory of norm creation, by way of experience, provided a way for directing the need for authority towards the ends of greater individual liberty. At the same time, by rejecting the legal construct of contract law, Smith was able to present a theory that allowed one to criticize government not merely by reference to a mythical social agreement but rather by reference to a continually evolving set of morals and norms that revealed themselves through the ongoing experiences of the individuals constituting the society.[13] Thus, Smith's view on the construction of society leads one to consider and discuss legal and economic issues in a manner quite different from that fostered under social contract theory. This distinction is of continuing importance today where, for instance, we have ongoing and heated debates in American jurisprudence regarding the original understandings with respect to the U.S. Constitution. Under a social contract theory the relevance of original intentions for legal interpretation is far more important than it would be for a jurist adopting a Smithian rejection of Locke's social contract theory. Smith's dynamic approach to the construction of society is more in line with the metaphor of the 'living constitution' rather than that of a strict interpretation of the original constitutional understanding.

3. STAGES OF LEGAL AND ECONOMIC DEVELOPMENT

Smith's conception of the dynamic and evolutionary construction of a society based on authority and utility was consistent with his similarly situated theory concerning the evolution of legal and economic development. Development was not to be seen as the product of some ill conceived social contract or plan but rather was an evolutionary process resulting from the numerous interrelated activities of countless individuals pursuing their own self interest. Self interest in Adam Smith's terms was not merely another way of describing selfish greed. Smith understood that these concepts were different and that self interest embodied a concern for fairness, respect for others, and a sense of one's existence and participation in a broader social community.

According to Smith, human history could be understood by way of major identifiable stages of economic development.[14] Corresponding to each stage of economic change would be a corresponding development in the nature of law and legal institutions.[15] The distinct stages that Smith identified included the age of hunters, the age of shepherds and agriculture, and the age of commerce.[16] Each stage or time period had its own distinct social, political, economic and moral arrangements. Smith refers to these stages not only in *The Wealth of Nations* but also throughout his *Lectures on Jurisprudence*.[17] In a similar manner Smith discusses the formation of languages in his work on *Rhetoric*.[18] Thus, Smith posits an evolutionary system of historical development that has implications far beyond mere economic arrangements. His theory gives meaning to language, law and a wide variety of social practices.

In considering the relationship between the various stages of development, Smith demonstrated that each stage progressed in a natural order from the lowest stage, being the age of hunters, to the highest stage, being the age of commerce. He also suggested that each higher stage of development opened the door to a greater realization of individual liberty. The key driving force that made progress possible from one stage to the next was Smith's identification of the central role of the division of labor and each individual's natural desire to enhance his or her own self interest.[19] The division of labor was not the result of social planning rather it was a natural and spontaneous result of human nature. Humans naturally pursued a division of labor as a consequence of seeing its ability to improve productivity and well-being. While some people might be directly benefitted more than others from particular advances in the division of labor, Smith considered that everyone, even the poorest members of society, were made better off by this evolutionary process.

As a society progressed through these various stages of development there would be a shift in the power structure of the community.[20] There would also be a corresponding change in the conception of property and in the legal regime. In outlining this transformation process Smith observed:

> The more improved any society is and the greater length the several [sic] means of supporting the inhabitants are carried, the greater will be the number of their laws and regulations necessary to maintain justice, and prevent infringements of the right of property.[21]

The advancement of society brought out new types of property. This created a need for new definitions of property and the establishment of rights of control and ownership. Advances in economic relationships also affected the distribution of wealth and power within a community. Smith gave some examples to illustrate this point. In the age of hunters power and social status was attached to the successful skills of hunting--bravery, speed, strength, and tracking. A hunting society was one in which there were few long-term assets. Food perished quickly and capital goods consisted of simple beads, crude tools and hunting equipment. Power and wealth were generally possessed by the individual for so long as they were superior in the essential skills of a hunting society.

As a society progressed into the age of shepherds and agriculture the nature of property and wealth changed. There were animal herds and planted fields that established themselves as new types of important assets. Livestock were controlled and provided young to add to the herd. Ownership of the livestock could be controlled and passed on from one generation to the next. The livestock provided food and oftentimes materials for clothing and useful social implements. Likewise, an agricultural society witnessed the importance of land identification as a valuable asset. Particular lands were controlled by identified parties so that crops could be planted, maintained and harvested over time. Again, the crops like the livestock, provided new forms of wealth. This wealth, in the form of control over fertile lands, was something that could be passed on from one generation to the next. The skills needed in dealing with livestock and agriculture were different from hunting and thus power shifted in these societies at the same time as it became possible to establish longer term conceptions of power by way of intergenerational control of wealth. Eventually the control of land dominated the definition of power and wealth in these societies and land became the key input for both agricultural and livestock production.[22] Land also proved to be an easy demarcation for establishing relationships between different communities as well as within communities by addressing one's relationship to a particular non movable piece of the earth.

The most advanced stage identified by Smith was the age of commerce. In the age of commerce creativity and mobility became the central focus of wealth and power and capital replaced land as the identifying force behind social organizations. Capital presented a fluid source of wealth in the sense that it was not tied to any particular location. Money, ideas, inventions, and other capital resources could travel freely beyond the bounds of a feudal Lord's control and thus dramatically transferred the distribution of wealth and power. This concept has become increasingly powerful in modern society as we witness instantaneous transfers of billions of dollars in capital by electronic impulses carried over satellites in global markets. Today's 'war lords' own and control capital. In modern society, therefore, one need not own millions of acres of land to live like a King or Queen. In the age of commerce the capitalists take over as the major socio-political as well as economic power brokers. At the same time more liberating possibilities emerge for individual members of these communities as contract relationships give power and choice to individuals of merit and creativity without regard to their social status. Power and wealth are diffused more broadly throughout such a society and the resulting multiplicity of power sources creates an environment more conducive to individual liberty than that which is possible under the earlier stages of development. In essence, the age of commerce gives rise to an environment in which a monopoly of power by a 'war lord,' 'landlord,' or 'religious lord' is much more difficult. The weakening of lordly power creates the possibility for greater freedom to be enjoyed by many more people in the community. This was seen as progress by Adam Smith.

Smith also observed that power brokers in any stage of development enjoy their power and prefer to prohibit competition as much as possible. Thus even in the age of commerce there is always an effort by some capitalists to recapture monopoly power in an attempt to control and exploit the general public. This was usually aided by the coercive interference of government. Smith identified and discussed many examples of regulations, restrictions and trade practices that demonstrated the efforts of capitalists to dominate and exploit the general public.[23] Smith argued that '[p]eople of the same trade seldom meet together, even for merriment and diversion, that the conversation ends in a conspiracy against the public, or in some contrivance to raise prices.'[24] Likewise he warned his readers not to be taken in by regulatory pleas of the capitalist made upon their own request in an effort to better serve the public. Smith advised that such request came 'from an order of men, whose interest is never exactly the same with that of the public, who have generally an interest to deceive and even oppress the public, and who accordingly have, upon many occasions, both deceived and oppressed it.'[25]

Smith went on to expand his observations on capitalists to include commentary on law and legal institutions. Smith wrote:

> But here when....some have great wealth and others nothing, it is necessary that the arm of authority should be continually stretched forth, and permanent laws or regulations made which may ascertain the property of the rich from the inroads of the poor, who would otherwise continually make incroachments upon it .... Law and government may be considered in this and indeed in every case as a combination of the rich to oppress the poor, and preserve to themselves the inequality of the goods which would otherwise be soon destroyed by the attacks of the poor...[26]

> Civil government, so far as it is instituted for the security of property, is in reality instituted for the defense of the rich against the poor, or of those who have some property against those who have none at all.[27]

Accordingly, Smith was no apologist for the capitalist class nor was he blind to the problems and abuses of power and wealth in the age of commerce.

In addition to recognizing that the power of government was frequently used to benefit the rich and powerful at the expense of others, Smith also observed the detrimental consequences of the division of labor in the age of commerce. Smith believed that the division of labor in an advancing age of commerce could lead to worker alienation.[28] The division of labor was generally considered beneficial by Smith because it allowed for increased productivity, greater personal and social wealth, and a generally high standard of living. At the same time the division of labor also resulted in diminishing the individual's identification with the finished products they helped to produce. By continually focusing a worker's attention on smaller and simpler component parts and tasks, the worker lost touch with the overall project in which he participated. The more focused and more simple the task the less thought and contemplation required from each worker.[29] While this allowed the worker more detailed concentration it also eliminated major opportunities and reasons for thinking about one's job as an important part of the social fabric of the greater community.[30] Since work consumed a major portion of a person's life, this concentrated attention to smaller and simpler tasks created a numbness of the mind that carried over into the rest of everyday life.[31] The worker in such a setting became increasingly unable to contemplate life, society, and government and consequently became further alienated from their fellow workers and from their own community.[32]

Smith explained the problem of alienation in *The Wealth of Nations* where he wrote:

> In the progress of the division of labour, the employment of the far greater part of those who live by labour, that is, of the great body of the people, comes to be confined to a few very simple operations; frequently to one or two. But the understanding of the greater part of men are necessarily formed by their ordinary employments. The man whose whole life is spent in performing a few simple operations, of which the effects too are, perhaps, always the same, or very nearly the same, has no occasion to exert his understanding, or to exercise his invention in finding out expedients for removing difficulties which never occur. He naturally loses, therefore, the habit of such exertion, and generally becomes as stupid and ignorant as it is possible for a human creature to become. The torpor of his mind renders him, not only incapable of relishing or bearing a part in any rational conversation, but of conceiving any generous, noble, or tender sentiment, and consequently of forming any just judgment concerning many even of the ordinary duties of private life.... [I]n every improved and civilized society that is the state into which the labouring poor, that is, the great body of the people, must necessarily fall, unless government takes some pains to prevent it.[33]

Smith argued that government had a major role to play in trying to counteract some of the most negative consequences of the division of labor in the age of commerce.[34] In the context of his above quoted discussion from *The Wealth of Nations* Smith addressed the need for a free and public education.[35] He was of the view that a basic education would help offset the 'numbness of the mind' and consequent alienation that would occur to the many laboring poor. He notes in his argument that the poor should be given such an education precisely because they cannot afford it and even if the sole beneficiaries of the education were the individuals themselves. There was no need to show a benefit to society that would outweigh the cost of such a program. Smith's concern was not one of utilitarianism or wealth maximization. He was concerned with the individual. To appreciate Smith's point one must consider it in light of his work on *The Theory of Moral Sentiments* and his *Lectures on Jurisprudence*. Adam Smith did not advocate a completely unfettered laissez faire society nor did he believe that capitalism and free markets should be pursued for their own sakes--they were *not ends* in themselves.[36] To the contrary, Smith was most concerned with maximizing individual liberty within a context of community. He understood humans to be social animals and he sought to articulate a process or *means* of social organization that would maximize individual liberty and well-being.[37] A market society and the advent of capitalism in the age of commerce were *means* for social organization not ends. As he saw it they generally resulted in beneficial consequences if not corrupted by the government or powerful special interests. At the same time there were negative consequences such as those described above. These negative implications were not disfavored by Smith because they diminished economic productivity or wealth accumulation, they were disfavored because they diminished the humanistic quality of life for the individual. The distinction here is important because it reveals the moral, ethical and humanistic aspects of Smith's philosophy of economics. Unlike some modern day legal economists, such as Judge Richard Posner, Smith envisioned liberty and human dignity as the ultimate values rather than efficiency or the maximization of wealth.

In acting to assure educational opportunities for the poor, the government, according to Smith, would be constrained here, as elsewhere, by a preference for limited government acting by general rules. In Smith's view the paramount purpose of civil government was to protect individuals.[38] Civil government in this respect was seen as a means for checking the coercive power of private individuals and yet it could not be forgotten that government too could be a part of a coercive enterprise against the public. At various points in his *Wealth of Nations*, *Theory of Moral Sentiments*, and *Lectures on Jurisprudence*, Smith observes that the power of government is frequently used to benefit the wealthy and powerful members of the community.[39] For this reason it is easy to conclude from Smith's work that he envisioned a strong and competitive marketplace as an essential check on governmental abuse. In essence the government, if properly constituted, could help protect individuals from the coercive abuse of private parties while a free and open market system provided significant sources of independent power capable of protecting the general public from an overreaching exercise of state authority.[40] In his various considerations of these points Smith was generally careful to always assess the position of law, government and private power within the context of his ever evolving stages of development. Historical development was an essential contextual footing for Smith's appreciation of economic relationships and their resulting implications for legal, political, and social organization.

4. LIBERTY UNDER LAW

In modern disputes concerning the philosophy of law and economics much is said about rights. Do individuals have rights? If they have rights are they natural rights or political rights? Can these rights be abridged by government and if so to what extent? What mechanism best protects rights while advancing a free society? In his various works Adam Smith offered some insights on these questions that were relevant to his time just as they continue to be relevant to us.

To begin with Smith observed that individuals can subsist only in the context of community. Smith wrote:

It is thus that man, who can subsist only in society, was fitted by nature to that situation for which he was made. All the members of human society stand in need of each other's assistance, and are likewise exposed to mutual injuries.[41]

Man it has been said, has a natural love of society, and desires that the union of mankind should be preserved for its own sake, and though he himself was to derive no benefit from it.[42]

Thus, Smith identified a fundamental tension between the individual and the community. While Smith's work generally advanced the reference point of the individual it was also apparent that Smith's individual was not an atomistic and isolated economic player. Rather, Smith presented the difficulty of many individuals existing in community with each other. From this starting point one can begin to appreciate the complexity that follows in Smith's work on self interest and the invisible hand. When examined in the context of society, self interest must be understood as something other than selfishness and the invisible hand becomes more than a simple justification for brutish indifference to one's fellow citizens.

In discussing an individual's responsibility to others Smith declared that 'One individual must never prefer himself so much even to any other individual as to hurt or injure that other in order to benefit himself, though the benefit to the one should be much greater than the hurt or injury to the other.'[43] Considered in light of recent law and economics debates over the role of Kaldor-Hicks efficiency and wealth maximization, Smith's words seem to be in opposition to the work of people like Judge Richard Posner.[44] Smith said the individual may not prefer himself even though the benefit would be far greater than the loss to another. Modern day advocates of wealth maximization seem to argue for the opposite conclusion and defend it on grounds of Kaldor-Hicks efficiency. They say that if the gains to the one person are greater than the loss to the other, then society will have a net social increase in its wealth. Adam Smith, however, was concerned with more than mere material accumulation. Smith was concerned with liberty and happiness. While material well-being was relevant to these concerns, wealth maximization was not his primary focus. He observed for instance that even the most ambitious of people:

find that wealth and greatness are mere trinkets of frivolous utility, no more adapted for procuring ease of body or tranquility of mind, than the tweezer-cases of the lover of toys; and like them, too, more troublesome to the person who carries them about with him than all the advantages they can afford him.[45]

In what constitutes the real happiness of human life ... In ease of body and peace of mind all the different ranks of life are nearly upon a level, and the beggar, who suns himself by the side of the highway, possesses the security which Kings are fighting for.[46]

Instead of selfishly pursuing wealth, Smith's individual is a self-interested yet fair and responsibly connected participant in society.

Smith explained the delicate balance required between the individual and society with reference to the metaphor of a competitive race. He wrote:

[I]n the race for wealth, and honours, and preferments, he may run as hard as he can, and strain every nerve and every muscle, in order to outstrip all his competitors. But if he should jostle, or throw down any of them, the indulgence of the spectators is entirely at an end. It is a violation of fair play, which they cannot admit of.[47]

The spectators referred to by Smith in the above quote are the metaphorically *impartial spectators* that pass judgment on our individual conduct. These impartial spectators impose a social standard or norm upon our conduct and judge our every act and deed by our adherence. In this setting individuals are naturally drawn to seek the praise and praise-worthiness of the spectators while avoiding blame. In this setting the individual does not possess a selfish survival of the fittest attitude but rather acts to maximize his or her own well-being within the guise and constraint of socially imposed mores and norms.

As Smith explained it, we each judge the conduct of others from our own perspective. To the extent that we agree or concur in the conduct of another we sympathise with them. Such sympathy is similar to an altruistic compassion for what the other party is experiencing. In a similar way we judge our own action by reference to how we think other impartial spectators will view us. In this respect we develop a subjective approach to considering a hypothetically objective criterion by which we should judge and by which we are also judged. As a consequence '[w]e endeavour to examine our own conduct as we imagine any other fair and impartial spectator would examine it.'[48] Likewise '[w]e soon become sensible, however, that others exercise the same criticism upon us.'[49] As such we come to see that our own merit and praiseworthiness is dependent and contingent upon the happiness and merit of others.

Developing a sense of what is acceptable conduct is a social process based on experience. It is from social interaction that we both learn of community norms and at the same time create new experiences that transfer and reshape such norms. Smith, therefore, argued that social morality or acceptable social norms were not part of an ordained truth but were instead part of an evolutionary process based on the experience of individuals acting in community with others. In his own words, Smith wrote that general standards of social morality:

> are ultimately founded upon experience of what, in particular instances, our moral faculties, our natural sense of merit and propriety, approve or disapprove of. We do not originally approve or condemn particular actions, because, upon examination, they appear to be agreeable or inconsistent with a certain general rule. The general rule, on the contrary, is formed by finding from experience that all actions of a certain kind or circumstanced in a certain manner, are approved or disapproved of.[50]

As a result of this introspective process individuals do not always act to pursue their own personal gain but rather find that their own self interest must be constrained and pursued within the confines of community values. Furthermore, these values are shaped by experience and the value structures or social preferences by which a society conducts itself and judges its members may change over time. In such a setting one may wonder what rights Smith ascribed to individuals within society and to what extent his invisible hand metaphor helps us understand his theory of interpersonal interaction.

Smith's work reveals a rather complex approach to individual rights. With general references to natural rights Smith seems to map out a system of rights based on both relative and nonrelative understandings. In essence his approach to natural rights is consistent with the theoretical conception of rights used in the American Declaration of Independence where each individual is described as possessing certain 'natural and inalienable rights.'

Smith argued that individual rights were in one sense relative as they related to material well-being.[51] Depending upon the historical context and stage of development, social norms may vary as to what material possessions and comforts would be considered necessary or essential. He argues that a linen shirt, for instance, was not a necessary of life nor was it ever available to the Greeks and Romans yet by the mid 1700's such a linen shirt was considered essential.[52] He extends this illustration to include the availability of leather shoes at different times in history as well.[53] The point being that the necessaries of life are dynamic and relative to their context. Although many things may not be strictly essential to sustaining human life they may become, according to Smith, standards by which a given society judges itself and thus, an individual's material rights and expectations within a given community are dynamic and in that regard relative to their context.

In contrast to this material relativism Smith considered certain notions of individual liberty to be natural rights which would seemingly be nonrelative.[54] He said that '[t]he system of government now supposes a system of liberty as a foundation.'[55] He went on to argue that both economic and social activity were grounded in an understanding of the general rule of law.[56] As such Smith understood individual freedom as a foundation for social interaction but this meant freedom under law and not the absence of government intervention.[57] In discussing this freedom under law Smith put great emphasis on fair process and on an independent judiciary.[58] His concern for individual liberty was one that focused on this fairness of process and on the attempt to 'neutralize' legal institutions by making them independent and thus not beholding to the Crown or other coercive power.[59] In this regard, even though the requirements of material well-being might be contextually relative, the fairness by which people should be treated might be judged by some other less relative means.

Social evolution and social interaction were complex phenomena under the Smithian conception of political economy. Smith, like the modern day Austrian Economists did not feel that individuals could master or control all of the independent variables of social organization.[60] Social progress would occur as a result of surprise, experimentation, and by the experiences of countless individuals acting not according to some general plan but in accordance with their own self interest. From this theoretical juncture Smith hypothesized the metaphorical symbolism of an 'invisible hand' which assisted social order and guided social evolution. The 'invisible hand' allowed society to advance cohesively through a process of spontaneous social order. It guided individuals along a path of cooperative and mutual benefit while protecting against outright anarchy and the dysfunctional collapse of beneficial exchange and interaction. While there were always private and governmental sources of power seeking to corrupt markets and destroy liberty, Smith suggested that a society based on his vision of moral sentiments and constrained self interest could proceed apace without central planning and control. Progress would occur on its own.

While Smith's most famous passage referring to an 'invisible hand' comes from *The Wealth of Nations* his first invocation of this metaphor occurred years earlier in his *Theory of Moral Sentiments*. In *The Wealth of Nations* Smith writes about those engaged in enterprise and says:

> by directing that industry in such a manner as its produce may be of the greatest value, he intends only his own gain, and he is in this, as in many other cases, led by an invisible hand to promote an end which was no part of his intention. Nor is it the worse for society that it was no part of it. By pursuing his own interest he frequently promotes that of the society more effectually than when he really intends to promote it.[61]

In *The Theory of Moral Sentiments* Smith mentions the invisible hand in the context of a discussion concerning rich landlords. This passage has a similar theme as that of the one just quoted. Smith wrote that:

The rich only select from the heap what is most precious and agreeable ... in spite of their natural selfishness and rapacity, though they mean only their own conveniency, though the sole end which they propose from the labours of all the thousands whom they employ be the gratification of their own vain and insatiable desires, they divide with the poor the produce of all their improvements. They are led by an invisible hand to make nearly the same distribution of the necessaries of life which would have been made had the earth been divided into equal portions among all its inhabitants; and thus, without intending it, without knowing it, advance the interest of the society.[62]

Thus, Smith was consistent in both of his major works despite the different focus in each. His rhetorical and philosophical critique of national wealth must be read in light of his earlier work on moral sentiments in order to fully appreciate the constraints that Smith imposed upon his economic actors.

Smith the moral and political philosopher cannot be separated and isolated from Smith the economist. He understood the moral and value laden aspects of individual action within the context of community. He expresses the dichotomy between individual action and community best when he writes:

Every man is, no doubt, by nature first and principally recommended to his own care; and as he is fitter to take care of himself, than of any other person, it is fit and right that it should be so. Everyman, therefore, is much more deeply interested in whatever immediately concerns himself, than in what concerns any other man ... Though every man may according to the proverb, be the whole world to himself, to the rest of mankind he is a most insignificant part of it. Though his own happiness may be of more importance to him than that of all the world besides, to every other person it is of no more consequence than that of any other man ... When he views himself in the light of which he is conscious that others will view him, he sees that to them he is but one of the multitude, in no respect better than any other in it ... [H]e must upon this, as upon all other occasions, humble the arrogance of his self-love, and bring it down to something which other men can go along with.[63]

Throughout Smith's work there is evidence of a strong moral philosophy that governed his views on economic conduct. His theory of self interest and wealth accumulation are complex. He held a notion of natural liberty and of individual autonomy but did so in the context of society. People were by their very nature social animals and thus constrained by the constantly evolving norms of social values. The selfish brute that did everything possible to create and accumulate wealth was not the Smithian ideal. Smith's homo-economicus was a socially connected and responsible individual. Furthermore Smith's conception of the individual had him or her playing a vital role in the shaping and creating of new social values over time. The Smithian ideal was not value free, was not amoral in a scientific sense, but rather was explicitly value centered and subjectively grounded in experience--experience of the individual within the broader context of the experience of the entire community.

With this basic overview and grounding in Smith's conception of the individual in relationship to his views of law, economics, values, and community, I will next turn to a discussion of Smith's central role in a number of foundational matters concerning the modern day field of Law and Economics. References to Smith have found their way into the work of many modern day scholars. This is not surprising since a standard rhetorical device in legal argument is one of grounding a current position in historical precedent. Smith's work is an exceptionally good source for historical precedent since he continues to cast such a powerful shadow over the entire field of economics and of political economy. Smith has become an iconic symbol of western and capitalist style economics and of the legal institutions that promote such economies.[64] It therefore becomes both interesting and at the same time vitally important to examine how this icon of the modern western economic tradition is currently understood.

5. SMITH AND THE MODERN DISCOURSE OF LAW AND ECONOMICS

In examining some of the current law and economics literature referencing Adam Smith's philosophical work or the relationship between law and economics I will look at a few key sources. I will not attempt to catalogue every citation made to Smith nor will I present an exhaustive critique of the way in which Smith's work gets manipulated in framing alternative positions in law and economics. Instead, my efforts will be directed at giving the reader a flavor for the way in which Adam Smith's philosophical work remains relevant to current debates in law and economics. The science of economics may have made dramatic progress over the past two hundred years but Smith's philosophic foundations are still essential. The relevance of Smith to law and economics today is the philosophical framework which Smith created for understanding the complex interrelationship between the individual and society. The fact that economic science may now reject Smith's early views on a labor theory of value or other 'scientific' issues does not mean that Smith's philosophical insights are not important or unhelpful. Adam Smith remains vital and relevant today in the same way in which Karl Marx continues to be a source of study and debate. Marx also held a labor theory of value which has since been rejected. Yet Marx has always seemed to have a philosophical following that went beyond his 'scientific conclusions.' Smith's followers, on the other hand, seem to have less concern for his insightful philosophical contributions and focus more on his early contributions to the science of economics. These followers of Smith generally seek, for themselves, an image as highly trained technical scientists. As 'neutral' scientific observers and reporters many such modern-day economists have cleansed themselves of the memory that philosophy and moral and political discourse played a major role in shaping their discipline.[65]

In an effort to recapture the philosophical tradition which indeed shapes the 'scientific' debate in law and economics we must return to and appreciate the work of Adam Smith. Having outlined, in this brief chapter, many of Smith's important observations and insights I will now look at how Smith's views are used by specific authors in modern debates concerning law and economics. Specifically, I will explain the role of Smith's work in my own school of Classical Liberal thought on the subject matter and then I will address the relevance of Smith in the work of Judge Richard Posner, Professor Richard Epstein, Professor Bruce Ackerman, and indirectly in the work of critical theorist, Professor Duncan Kennedy.

(A) SMITH AND THE WORK OF PROFESSOR MALLOY

In my own work I have borrowed extensively from the philosophical work of Adam Smith.[66] I have argued for a humanistic approach to law and economics that stresses the importance of values and of individual liberty in a social context.[67] Unlike the work of other legal economists, such as Judge Richard Posner, I argue that a capitalist free-market economy is a means of social organization meant to facilitate an end that promotes a Smithian conception of individual liberty. Posner's work on the contrary seems to advance a theory of the marketplace as an end in itself. By closely examining Smith's various writings I have concluded that Smith would not be supportive of the cold amoral cost and benefit calculations advocated by Judge Posner. I believe Adam Smith would not simply write off the poor, the homeless, the uneducated, the feeble minded, the minorities, or the slaves of society as Judge Posner does when it is arguably wealth maximizing to do so.[68]

My own work focuses on law and economics as a study of the discourse of social relationships and cultural evolution.[69] I argue that all discussions concerning the allocation of scarce resources and political power are by their very nature law and economics.[70] In this sense my approach to the subject matter is unique in its embracing of such things as feminist theory and critical theory as part of the same subject matter as law and economics. When one understands the subject matter in a philosophical context, as did Smith, one begins to see the metatheoretical connection between a vast array of ideological viewpoints. Restricting the conception of law and economics to only those forms of discourse that employ the scientific equations of economics to problems of law and society limits one at the outset to a narrow range of alternative perspectives. In addition it generally leaves one with a sanitized or amoral approach to important issues of law and social policy in an attempt to unrealistically mimic the approach of the natural sciences. The study of people, of law and of society is not at all like the study of rocks or of chemical reactions.[71] While modern-day economists and followers of Judge Posner's brand of law and economics may pretend otherwise, the study of who gets what and why is a very subjective and indeterminate undertaking.[72] I argue that Smith understood this and that his subjective orientation of the individual's relationship to society by way of the impartial spectator embodied such a conception. Likewise, his notion of evolving social norms through the complex interaction of individual and collective experience recognized the tentative nature of many social customs and practices and consequently of situational outcomes.[73] He stressed the importance of context in understanding the relative nature of well-being. In all of this he is describing a dynamic process of spontaneous social evolution in the tradition of the Austrian School of Economics.

While Smith recognizes the role and function of positive law he is less of a positivist than many modern economists or lawyers. He views positive law as an attempt to capture in writing the current established understanding of the community but he saw all of this as somewhat tentative and speculative.[74] The important point was to grasp the dynamic nature of social organization and evolution and to see this as furthered through a metaphorical appeal to a marketplace of exchange. In this marketplace people were guided by self interest but this was a constrained self interest and not the equivalent of selfishness or a brutish pursuit of one's own material self gain.[75] This leads me to conclude that Smith was a free market philosopher that nonetheless knew the difficulty that past history and prior distributions imposed on the workings of a fair and just society and its political, economic and legal institutions. In this manner Smith's work is receptive to many critiques of law and economics which are based on challenges to the prior distribution of wealth and resources or which are tainted by a history of coercion. Consequently, I have argued that law and economics must be open to re-evaluating the rights and claims of the poor as well as such other disenfranchised groups as women and minorities. A purely 'scientific' approach to issues involving women or minorities may not adequately account for the historical context in which certain distributions have become fixed. Borrowing from Smith, one can properly question numerous laws and financial arrangements as being biased despite the ability to otherwise rationalize them as economically efficient.

Smith's rejection of the social contract theory also plays a key role in my own work on law and economics.[76] The rejection of this contractual metaphor provides much needed flexibility in doing critical reviews of law and social policy. Freeing oneself from the metaphor of contract allows one to push legislative history and original intentions debates into the background of legal economic analysis. In their place we can spend more time on what the law ought to be accomplishing at the present time. This rejection of social contract theory is compatible with the evolutionary notion of changing social norms by way of experience and the role of positive law in attempting to reflect these changes. Legal interpretation in this sense is dynamic in the same way that experience and market transactions are dynamic rather than static. Smith's philosophic positions allow one to pursue a very dynamic and flexible approach to law and economics constrained primarily by a focus on individual rights and liberty. It is reasonable to conclude that Smith's major focus in all his writing is the liberty of the individual--of an individual that lives in community with others and not as an isolated or atomized and alienated being. All of Smith's elaborate theories and insights on moral sentiments and economic relationships return to the same concern for identifying a proper form of social organization that would allow individuals to attain the greatest degree of freedom and liberty while advancing their own well-being. While he acknowledged that individuals lived in community with others he was not talking about communitarian group rights or collectivism, Smith was clearly an individualist.

I borrow from Smith's individualist work and his concern for natural liberty. I argue in much of my work that Smith's views have, in modern times, been best advanced by such classical liberal economists as Fredrich Hayek and Milton Friedman. Extending these arguments into law, I have elaborated on a number of Smithian and classical liberal principles that should govern law and economics.[77] In synthesizing a vast array of philosophical viewpoints in this tradition I have developed three key principles to govern my own approach in this area. All three principles, as I have argued elsewhere, are derivable from Smith and taken together they provide a discursive framework different from that offered by other legal economic scholars. In sticking with a dynamic framework that places the individual at the center of its purpose I have argued for the necessity for mandatory counterbalancing forces by and between the private and public sectors of our society.[78] I thereby acknowledge both the need for government regulation and intervention and at the same time the need for extensive elements of private property and private capital. The subset mechanisms of each sector create a dynamic within each of them while each sector serves as a counterbalance to the other.[79] The entire idea is that the social structure of society can be envisioned as a dynamic and metaphorical marketplace in which the give and take and competition by and between the different elements of the public and private sectors leads to beneficial results for individuals and society in a manner similar to the benefits consumers derive from competition in the commercial marketplace.

My work on law and economics assumes an active role for government and rejects the so called laissez faire approach in a way that I believe Smith would have rejected it. Given this, I then have to deal with the manner in which we might limit government intrusion into the private sphere.[80] This is where my three key principles come into play and where there is a marked distinction between my approach and that of others such as Posner, Epstein and Ackerman. In my approach there are no set boundaries beyond which the government cannot go. Instead there is a discursive framework established to shape social preferences in the way that Smith imagined that experience transformed social norms.[81] This discursive framework assumes that the way in which a society discusses and shapes the discourse of its pressing social problems has a substantive impact on its actual outcome.[82] In other words, the form of discourse is in fact substantive and of consequence. Thus, I start from a presumption in favor of individual autonomy and against government intrusion into the activities of private life. This presumption holds to the extent that we can be persuaded that the activity is indeed primarily private. From this starting point I then require that a persuasive argument for government intervention must be constructed with reference to three key principles. First, there must be evidence of a market failure.[83] This means a persuasive argument must be made that the private sector fails to address, in a proper manner, an important issue of social policy. For example we might consider the problem of homelessness and the seeming inability of the private market to make housing or shelter affordable enough for everyone. In looking at such market failures we would of course consider possible reasons for the lack of a private response including externalities and free rider effects as well as considering problems of past inequalities and any history of inappropriate discrimination or exclusion. The second principle requires that any proposed government action must be defendable as a means of protecting some fundamental aspect of human dignity or as Smith might say natural liberty.[84] Again there is no set list of what this might include but there is a notion of what such an argument might embrace. For instance one might argue for government intervention in the urban marketplace in an effort to provide housing opportunities to the homeless inasmuch as people without resources are unlikely to attract the attention of developer/sellers. Likewise, in the relative sense that Adam Smith used to address material well-being, I would suggest that one's persuasive argument would need to explain how the given context, the given wealth and historical position of the society, might render at least some form of minimal shelter necessary. As with Smith's arguments for a free education one need not show an efficient benefit to society from providing such a government program, but rather must show that the intervention fulfills an essential element of human dignity of value to the individual. While arguments concerning minimal shelter for the poor may make sense here, it is unlikely that arguments in favor of subsidies to large corporations or shopping center developers will be persuasive. Third and finally, any government intervention must proceed by general rules rather than outcome specific legislation.[85] For this principle I borrow heavily from Hayek who asserts its origination in the understandings of Adam Smith.[86] The requirement for general rules is one that greatly limits the methods of government intervention so as to preserve a continuing vitality for private sector counterbalancing.[87] General rules are ones that would apply to a broad category of individuals and groups and would preserve many elements of private choice. As an example, general rules are like those of most card games. The rules are established and known before the individual players are selected and players are free to enter or exit or try various strategies within the context of the game. Likewise the winners and losers are not known in advance. To apply this to our example of housing the homeless, a general rule approach might favor establishing a system of housing vouchers whereby the homeless are given government sponsored subsidies to shop for housing within an otherwise private marketplace. This general rules approach to the problem would be different than an outcome specific approach. An outcome specific program, to be avoided in my system, might have government pre-select favored private developers to build specific housing in which the poor would be sheltered. Such an approach clearly reduces choice for the home seeker but also establishes clear advantages for special interest politics between private sector actors and the government. This is likely to destroy the counterbalancing aspects of competition and instill a cooperative effort which in most cases is likely to work against the public.[88]

The ultimate import of my discursive restraints is that they establish no absolutes but rather create a *process* for understanding and discussing pressing social problems.[89] This process is geared towards preference shaping and is dynamic. It considers context and responds to individual and social experience. Furthermore it favors the fulfillment of the individual within a community setting and relies on a vision of constrained self interest that is very different from selfishness or wealth maximization. Systematically the process I envision as a classical liberal approach to law and economics is metaphorically consistent with the dynamic and interactive structure of Smith's philosophical outlook on the subject.

(B) SMITH AND JUDGE POSNER

Judge Richard Posner is probably the most well known of the various practitioners of the economic analysis of law. He has provided us with a wealth of scholarship on his views regarding the relationship between law and economics and continues to publish and lecture on the subject.[90] Judge Posner was one of the early writers involved in expanding the use of economics in addressing law and social policy beyond the bounds of its traditional venue in the field of antitrust law. Posner's economic analysis of law is rooted in the 'science' of economics more than in the discourse or rhetoric of economics and political economy.

Posner's approach to the subject places central attention on a concept he refers to as wealth maximization.[91] This concept is really an application of Kaldor-Hicks efficiency. In his work Posner asserts that a proper understanding of the common law reveals that it, in fact, is wealth maximizing (his descriptive claim) and he further argues that the goal of the law *ought* to be one of promoting such wealth maximization (his normative claim). In so doing he focuses attention on material well-being and wealth generation as the ultimate goals of society. Individual rights and complex issues of morality and values are, in his view, too amorphous to be useful and thus take a back seat to protecting and promoting wealth accumulation.[92] This seems to put him immediately at odds with Smith's work where it is evident that society should be organized in such a way as to serve more than the interests of the wealthy. Interestingly enough, however, Posner asserted that his theory of wealth maximization was directly derivable from and resembled the morality present in Adam Smith's philosophy.[93]

In Posner's approach to law and economics an attempt is made to avoid indeterminacy and to promote objective truth through scientific inquiry.[94] An implicit assertion is that there are true and correct answers to pressing social problems and legal economic scientists can help us uncover them.[95] The primary tools used in this quest for answers are the assumptions of neoclassical economics and some simplified econometric formulas and models. Posner presents, therefore, a discourse not of values and morals (the soft stuff of the liberal arts), but formulas, equations and the mystifying powers of scientific investigation (the concrete stuff of the hard sciences). Rather than merely arguing about the legal meaning of fairness or justice in a given situation the Posnerian approach is one that seeks a quantitative investigation of the costs and benefits to the various parties involved. The fair and just result in such a situation would be, according to a Posnerian, the wealth maximizing solution to the equation. As many lawyers and public policy makers are averse to math, the symbolic representation of a problem with a mathematically determined conclusion makes for a very strong rhetorical style of argument. It's difficult to argue with science some might say. This method of argument also appeals to those among us that take some comfort in imagining that there are objective and determinate truths that can be uncovered and used to solve our many problems. The fallacy of the entire approach, however, is that the assumptions of neoclassical economics are hopelessly subjective in their embracing of prior distributions of wealth and resources and their avoidance of difficult contextual problems of exclusion and discrimination.[96] Equally troubling is the gap between concerns for fairness and justice when cost and benefit numbers are assumed in situations of no reliable market evidence as to their real values.

By stressing the scientific aspects of his approach Judge Posner offers up a brand of law and economics that appeals to the modernist in all of us. He seemly puts many of us into a trance as we forget the subjective nature of his assumptions and embrace the certainty and comfort of his conclusions. More importantly for this discussion is the way in which Adam Smith is summoned up by Posner for a brief mention of validation of his own theories, while very little is done to demonstrate any real connection between the two. Posner's rendition of Smith is one dimensional like the one's frequently found in undergraduate textbooks where a paragraph is devoted to Smith's place in the history of economics. The paragraph generally describes Smith's fame and importance as emerging exclusively from his work on *The Wealth of Nations* and portrays him as a proponent of allowing the self interested pursuit of wealth in an laissez-faire society free of government regulation. Such a depiction of Smith is one that rings with the rhetoric of Herbert Spencer's notion of "the survival of the fittest" and all but ignores Smith's extensive work in *The Theory of Moral Sentiments* and in his various *lectures*. Following this narrow and erroneous view of Smith, Posner is able to make all sorts of claims that would seem completely out of step with Adam Smith's actual moral philosophy. Posner is able to endorse slavery; justify racial, ethnic and religious discrimination; and, to suggest that the poor and feeble minded should have no legal claim to any social resources.[97] It is difficult to see how any of this would be compatible with Smith's work on *The Theory of Moral Sentiments*. How might the impartial spectator respond to such harsh conclusions which are justified by Posner when and where they are wealth maximizing - that is when they promote the accumulation of wealth or reflect the preferences of those with wealth. Such a view seemingly confuses selfishness with self interest in the Smithian sense and avoids a great deal of what Smith has to offer us as warnings about the activities and preferences of those with wealth and power.[98] Most certainly such a view also ignores such matters as Smith's powerful argument in defense of a free education for the poor because their own liberty and dignity rather than some conception of wealth maximization makes such an activity the proper ends of social organization.[99] For Judge Posner the rhetorical formulation for demarcating the boundary lines of limited government are justifications based on Kaldor-Hicks efficiency. Although the outcomes in such a model may be manipulated by means of varying assumptions it is nonetheless an appeal to this criteria of wealth maximization which is the cornerstone of Posner's theory. While much more could be said about Judge Posner's views on the subject I will leave further inquiry for the Chapter reprinting the debate between myself and the Judge regarding the issue of the morality of law and economics.

(C) SMITH AND PROFESSOR EPSTEIN

While Richard Epstein does not rely heavily on the work of Adam Smith, he presents an interesting approach to law and economics which is distinctly libertarian in its philosophical outlook. Epstein's important and controversial book *Takings: Private Property and the Power of Eminent Domain* appeared in 1985 and is still the object of scholarly debate.[100] He has followed this up with an equally controversial book attacking affirmative action and antidiscrimination laws in employment.[101] In both he is true to his libertarian grounding as he supports market mechanisms and freedom of contract. His libertarian perspective in many ways compliments and intersects with key elements of classical liberalism. At the same time there are important distinctions between Epstein's libertarianism and the classical liberalism of Adam Smith.[102]

As a libertarian, Epstein seeks to ensure a limited form of government in which autonomous individuals will be able to engage in freely negotiated contractual exchanges and relationships.[103] In order for such a form of social organization to exist there would be a need for a minimal state or governmental apparatus.[104] Laws relating to contract enforceability and damages for breach for instance would need to be established in order to facilitate voluntary bargaining. His concern for the maintenance of the minimal state is consistent with libertarian theory in general. In his book, *Takings*, Epstein presents an interesting way of ensuring the limited nature of government as a way of maintaining the minimal state. He argues, for instance, that the American founders considered the need to restrain government in order to preserve natural liberty. Thus, he supports his libertarian perspective by rhetorical reference to historical precedent. The key instrument by which the Founders accomplished this end was, according to Epstein, adoption of the Fifth Amendment to the U.S. Constitution which prohibited a taking of private property without just compensation.[105] From this humble starting point Epstein manages to construct a philosophical framework that requires a governmental payment as just compensation for almost any action the government might take including the outright confiscation of real property and the more limited passage of an economic regulation or restrictive zoning code that merely interfered with the use of private property. In essence the government would pay people whenever any limitation was imposed on the current distribution of rights and resources. By virtue of some apparent limit to uncontrollable government spending the state would have to take a more planned and limited course of action than is possible when no such compensation needs to be paid.[106] Consequently, government intervention into the private sphere would necessarily be reduced and the size of government would be restricted. Epstein uses his analysis to assert the unconstitutionality and undesirability of most of the 'New Deal' and the 'Welfare State' legislation of the 20th century.[107] These programs all represent wealth transfers made for the benefit of some without just compensation to those that saw their wealth and power diminished. Such transfers were and are therefore, according to Epstein, unlawful takings of private property.

In many ways Epstein's basic beliefs in market mechanisms, individual autonomy, and limited government are compatible with Adam Smith's work and with classical liberalism. On the other hand there are some essential differences that separate Epstein's work in law and economics from a philosophical ground in the work of Adam Smith. Central among these are (1) his views on social contract theory and (2) his seeming acceptance of the prior distribution of resources and political power.

Epstein in his reliance on John Locke is a social contract theorists in opposition to Smith's outright rejection of such a metaphor. By advancing a social contract theory Epstein becomes committed to a determination of the original contract itself and must seek to uncover the original intentions of the parties along with the particular means by which the parties agreed that their contract could be modified, if at all, in the future.[108] Epstein's *Takings* and *Forbidden Grounds* reflect this in their rhetorical style. Epstein's style typically relies on extensive references to specific cases, to legislation and to historical understandings. His inquiry and his discourse form are essentially within the contractarian metaphor. This leaves Epstein in a slightly different position than a Smithian. Smith, as will be recalled, rejected the social contract theory in lieu of a more pragmatic understanding that favored the notions of utility and authority.[109] As explained earlier in this chapter, such a view leads to a different discourse form and creates more flexibility for enhancing what many have called a 'living Constitution'. By rejecting a contractarian metaphor Smith opened the door to a more fluid and dynamic form of interpretation which was entirely compatible with his evolutionary notion of social norms changing over time as a result of individual and collective experience. Smith's interpretive reference point relative to Epstein's seems more permissive of change and more suitable for raising challenges against the original distribution.

Epstein seemingly accepts the original distribution of resources and political power.[110] He takes the original position as a starting point and assumes that transactions will lead to appropriate readjustments and opportunities for late comers or those poorly positioned in the first instance. This view can be derived from his sweeping analysis in *Takings* with its blanket condemnation of New Deal and Welfare State legislation. With little if any serious concern for problems associated with the original distribution he makes bold declarations against almost all modern wealth transfer systems. Possibly this is a pragmatic choice based on a determination that little can be done to correct the past so we should focus on transactions that can help ameliorate any problems in the future. Certainly this would be an important consideration in trying to assess the practicalities of public policy making. At the same time his views seem to seriously discount the importance that Smith's work would have given to historical context and the development of law and legal institutions within the various stages of economic development.[111]

The validity of law and of particular transactional exchanges is dependent upon one's understanding of the context in which they arose. If experience has transformed a community's social norms over time so that new conceptions of fairness and justice or of equality and opportunity or of participation and exclusion become relevant then law and legal institutions must also advance dynamically to this new understanding. As a result, understanding prior distributional inequalities becomes important as a means of understanding prior law. Likewise, understanding the contextual nature of law helps one to better critique and assess the validity of new directions in the law. It is, for instance, unclear that a Smithian would disapprove of all the New Deal and Welfare State legislation of the 20th century. I think Adam Smith's express concern for providing a free education to people that could not afford it demonstrates clear support for some forms of wealth transfer. Such wealth transfers can be easily understood in today's world as part of a wealth transfer system consistent with some of the underlying conceptions of the New Deal and the Welfare state. This interpretation is consistent with Smith's overriding concern for individual liberty and his recognition of the dignity of the human person as the ultimate end purpose of society. Smith was not opposed to wealth transfers per se, but Smith was concerned with the process by which such transfers might occur. There is nothing in Smith's work that would lead me to believe he would have opposed certain minimal protection and services for the poor or disadvantaged even if they required government intervention and the transfer of wealth. As I have argued elsewhere, it is more likely that one could conclude Smith would have supported such transfers provided they were done for appropriate purposes, in accordance with general rules, and consistent with prevailing social norms reflected by the community at large and not imposed as part of a coercive conspiracy against the public interest.[112] Epstein, however, sees the takings clause of the Constitution as the key mechanism for limiting government. In contrast Adam Smith did not have a takings clause to contend with and therefore relied on a more dynamic and interactive process for evolving and maintaining the appropriate limits to government.

(D) SMITH AND PROFESSOR ACKERMAN

Bruce Ackerman has long been an important voice in law and economics. He is an interesting character in this discourse because he clearly combines economic and political analysis with his legal work. In this respect he is very much the political economist rather than merely the economists giving attention to matters of law and social policy. Politically and ideologically Ackerman is a New Deal liberal and he approaches law and economics from this point of view.[113] Among his many works one gains great insight on Ackerman's view of Adam Smith from his short but insightful book *Reconstructing American Law*.[114] It is with reference to this book that I will make my observations.

In *Reconstructing American Law* Ackerman examines the transformation of law and legal institution through the era of the New Deal and thereafter. He is very much interested in the discourse of law or what he refers to as 'law talk'. He studies the underlying shift in normative and ideological values that suggested the New Deal and at the same time addresses the law's attempt to incorporate and respond to this new environment or context. In many ways Ackerman's project is an attempt at Smith's exploration of an evolutionary change in societal values as a result of individual and community experiences. The New Deal and its aftermath reveal a reaction to the experience of despair and hopelessness during the depression and of the law's inability to deal with changing technology, markets, social problems, and popular demands for more government involvement in the daily operations of the economy.[115]

Ackerman is no friend of Adam Smith and in his book he makes numerous references to the 'invisible hand' and related ideas. Ackerman envisions much of America's pre New Deal problems as the result of such Smithian conceptions and asserts that their wholesale rejection is the mark of activist lawyering in the new age of American Law which followed.[116] Early in his book, for instance, he writes:

> Nowadays, it seems obvious to all well-trained lawyers that the Old Court was wrong in contesting the constitutional legitimacy of the New Deal, that its precipitous retreat before Roosevelt in 1937 served, at best, as belated expiation for its half-century of sinful opposition to the triumphant activist state. The laissez-faire era increasingly seems a closed chapter of legal history, disconnected from the realities of present-day legal experience...Is it not time to move beyond Realist slogans and do the hard analytical work required if we are to use law to make good its activist promise - and help our fellow citizens build a world that is more just and more free than one ruled by the invisible hand?[117]

Ackerman associates the invisible hand and the quest for a rational or spontaneous social order with 'reactive lawyering'.[118] According to Ackerman such a type of lawyering is not activist and is out of touch with the reality of our current situation. He asserts it is no longer viable to look for social justice in the marketplace or in the 'millions-of-free-decisions-made-each-day-by-countless-Americans.'[119] Instead he asks us to consider 'what legal values are endangered by the uncontrolled operation of the invisible-hand.'[120] He further states that

> rather than presuming the sanctity of the distribution of power generated by the basic institutions - contract, property, family, market - thrown up by the invisible hand, the activist lawyer recognizes that any citizen disadvantaged by the status quo may appropriately question the legitimacy of existing arrangements.[121]

After making this statement he then goes on to talk about a need for due process. From the totality of his book and from these brief excerpts it is evident that Ackerman has a very different view of the 'invisible hand' than would most Adam Smith scholars. His is an almost villainous notion of a mechanism designed to protect the wealthy at the expense of the poor and to justify unfairness and injustice in a system apparently lacking in procedural standards.

Ackerman's views seem uninformed as to the content of Smith's work. As was set out in the first part of this chapter, Smith was greatly concerned with fair process for all people and argued for market dynamics as a means of protecting the individual rather than leading to his or her exploitation. Smith noted problems with the division of labor and the rise of capitalism.[122] He also observed that the exercise of caution was needed when requests for expanding government power came from people of means for their objectives were seldom in the best interest of society.[123] Smith's conception of the invisible hand in no way related to the evil consequences that Ackerman seems to presuppose. Smith's invisible hand was instead a way of endorsing market mechanisms as a method for diminishing unfairness and inequality of opportunity. Smith cautioned against the corruption of the marketplace by people of means seeking to protect their wealth and position from those with lesser resources. The evils Ackerman speaks of are related to the corruption of Smith's ideas. Smith did not endorse exploitation but rather sought to identify it as something contrary to the marketplace.

Ackerman's attack on the invisible hand is much less an attack on Smith's conception than it is an attack on the late 20th century understanding of what Smith's work was about. Most American law students and unfortunately most American economists have little or no real education regarding the philosophical foundations of the capitalists free market system in which they live. They probably have a much stronger education in the various criticisms of that system than they have in the system itself. Such a situation makes the critic seem all the more persuasive. In any event, it is clear that Ackerman's renditions of the invisible hand are of the sort often used by vocal critics. Where there is social injustice or economic inequity the invisible hand is said to be the cause.[124] Likewise, a belief in the invisible hand, according to Ackerman, supports the continuation of such injustice and inequality and must therefore be a belief perpetrated by those that are benefitted by such a system.[125] This is both simplistic and erroneous as applied to the work of Adam Smith and leads to a misunderstanding of the fundamental grounding of much individualist philosophy in law and economics.

While Ackerman would concur with Smith in rejecting the theory of social contract he is a supporter of government intervention on a large scale.[126] In place of the market validation of 'millions-of-free-decisions-made-each-day-by-countless-Americans,'[127] Ackerman would substitute decisions made in the political sphere. Like a Keynesian economist Ackerman fears the free marketplace and seeks to manage and regulate society through the political process. In this manner highly trained experts in given areas of public policy can address and correct (manage) various aspects of social life to ensure a more just and more fair distribution of society's resources.[128] The net result of Ackerman's theories are that major policy decisions become the province of political actors rather than economic actors. While this shifts the focus of power and decision making in society it is hard to see how our political process can be described as any less biased or subject to less manipulation and inequality of access than our market system.

In Smith's conception of market based decision making, as in that of modern day classical liberals, there is a very egalitarian favoring of the individual - the average person. Ackerman's shift to the political arena favors a different type of decision making. Ackerman's political arena favors highly educated and credentialized actors. In this regard it is less egalitarian and less just. One way to understand the consequences of this shift is with a simple example. In a society where a market model dominates, an individual can be a grade-school drop-out with no appreciation of the ballet or the symphony, and no knowledge of the great books, yet this individual might invent a gadget or have a musical talent that millions of consumers want to enjoy. As a consequence of providing something demanded by the public the individual becomes rich and in a market economy, where dollars act as votes in directing and redirecting scare resources, this individual will have a lot of clout. This individual may even have more clout in casting votes in the marketplace than a very well bred and highly educated person with advanced degrees from the finest Ivy League Universities. In a market system it is the wants and desires of the average person buying in the marketplace that determine which individuals will be more successful. If the brilliantly educated person offers nothing desirable to the public then the talented but 'uneducated' person is in a sense given more clout. For educated academics who think they have the answers to many of our pressing social problems the only conclusion to be drawn from this example is that the market system is a failure because it undervalues 'good' ideas by experts trained to address important matters of public policy. Shifting to a political process that relies on and values experts automatically raises the value of 'credentials' and shifts decision making power to a different group of people. Ackerman's model promotes those people trained to know what is 'best' rather than allowing countless individual decision makers to move us to any particular conclusion. Ackerman's model can be easily understood from a Smithian framework. Smith would likely have supported some of the same social welfare programs that Ackerman would promote for the same reasons that I previously suggested he might have disagreed with Richard Epstein's attack on the New Deal. Ackerman's arguments, while interesting, in no way undercut Smith's general observations about the invisible hand, self interest and the social development of a community. Ackerman's attack on the invisible hand is really a rhetorical device designed to enhance the validity of a shift in decision making power that is more favorable to himself and the people that share a similar political and economic agenda.

E. SMITH AND PROFESSOR KENNEDY

Professor Duncan Kennedy is a leader in the anti-market oriented Critical Legal Studies (CLS) movement.[129] From the point of view of law and economics CLS is of import primarily because of its attack on the marketplace and because it purports to offer an alternative method for allocating scarce resources and political power.[130] In essence the CLS approach to resource and power allocation is borrowed from marxist and socialist philosophy. Looked at from the perspective of resource and power allocation, CLS is therefore merely another form of law and economics discourse.

One of Duncan Kennedy's clearest attacks on the invisible hand and classical liberal philosophy came in an early article titled 'Form and Substance in Private Law Adjudication.'[131] In that article he attacked individualist theory and sought to replace it in law with a theory of altruism. Kennedy derided individualist philosophy as self interested and standing in opposition to a concern for others. He said, for instance, that individualist theory promotes the view that 'I am entitled to enjoy the benefits of my efforts without an obligation to share or sacrifice them to the interests of others.'[132] This of course is in opposition to what Adam Smith had to say about the impartial spectator and the obligation that we each have to one another. For example, in *The Theory of Moral Sentiments* Smith said: '[a]nd hence it is, that to feel much for others, and little for ourselves, that to restrain our selfish, and to indulge our benevolent, affections, constitutes the perfection of human nature.'[133] Thus, it is unclear what type of individualist theory Kennedy seeks to attack. His views clearly do not reflect Smith's work on individualist philosophy.

From the vantage point of disagreement Kennedy asserts that philosophical individualism is flawed because '[l]iberty or freedom or autonomy is conceived as a good in itself, because it is synonymous with the ability to pursue one's own conception of the good to the best of one's ability.'[134] He then suggests that this self absorbed view of the world is legitimized by 'the notion of the invisible hand transforming apparent selfishness into public benefit.'[135] In opposition to this view Kennedy offers altruist philosophy for which he says '[t]he essence of altruism is the belief that one ought *not* to indulge a sharp preference for one's own interest over those of others.'[136] But here as elsewhere Kennedy is mistaken as to the position of Adam Smith whose philosophical grounding is indirectly challenged by reference to the workings of the invisible hand. Smith repeatedly asserted that self interest and selfishness were not the same thing.[137] Furthermore as evidenced in some of the quoted passages of Smith's work in this chapter we see that he argued for controlling and restraining self interest. He acknowledged that individuals had to live in community with others and constructed the impartial spectator as a rhetorical device for illustrating the need to avoid the kind of unrestrained selfishness to which Kennedy refers.

At various places in his article Kennedy refers to classical individualism in the legal theories of such people as Pond, Llewellyn, Gillmore and Holmes.[138] To a large extent these people were not Smithians but were more in tune with the utilitarian conceptions that stemmed from Benthem's work. By using the metaphor of the invisible hand Kennedy summons up the ghost of Adam Smith but he fails to directly analyze Smith's work as he proceeds to attack the individualist philosophy that he seemingly believes is grounded in the work of Smith. I would indeed argue that Adam Smith's philosophical outlook would not differ so sharply from that of Kennedy at least on matters of identifying systemic problems with injustice and institutionalization of biased criteria in social process. Where Smith's position is likely to be different however is in the conditions associated with giving rise to the undesirable situations in question and consequently in the recommendations that would be forthcoming to correct such problems. Smith's work cannot properly be viewed as a tract in socialist or marxist thought - Smith offered a different vision for understanding the human experience. The view offered by Kennedy, however, is simply incorrect when it suggests that the classical tradition rooted in the work of Smith is based on a selfish pursuit of one's own interest without due consideration for others.

Kennedy revealed further differences from Smith when he said:

Stripped to essentials, the altruist substantive and formal arguments are identical. Legislative, administrative and judicial action based on a detailed knowledge of particular situations can achieve paternalist and regulatory objectives without paralyzing private economic energies. The state should move directly to implement "the public interest" rather than relying on the combination of property and contract rules with private activity to produce a social maximum.[139]

From this passage we learn that Kennedy appeals, as does Ackerman, to extensive government regulation based on the advice and knowledge of experts. Kennedy's experts may not be the same ones that Ackerman has in mind for Kennedy's experts must possess the quality of altruism so that the state can act to correct the prior and entrenched misdeeds of individualism. No matter how one defines the experts, however, it is clear once again that a shift is being made away from the legitimization principles of Smith's market based allocation process and being delivered to a state apparatus that will function at the hands of 'enlightened altruists.' Altruists that seemingly know people's needs better than the individual's themselves. Altruists that purport to work together with government for the enhancement of the public good. To this Smith might have responded with his warning that such convictions come 'from an order of men, whose interest is never exactly the same with that of the public, who have generally an interest to deceive and even oppress the public, and who accordingly have, upon many occasions, both deceived and oppressed it.'[140]

6. SUMMARY COMMENTS ON SMITH AND THE MODERN DISCOURSE OF LAW AND ECONOMICS

In this chapter I attempted to provide a brief overview of Adam Smith's work as it bears upon a philosophical understanding of the relationship between law and economics.[141] Basically, I have suggested that law and economics can be understood by references to competing forms of discourse concerning the allocation of scarce resources and of political power. After reviewing Smith's general foundational principles I then demonstrated the way in which leading authors in law and economics use Smith as a ground for theoretical support or criticism. In either situation it is clear that Adam Smith's work remains at the center of law and economics theory. Supporters and opponents of Smith's work in a modern context must nonetheless confront the imposing shadow of his philosophical legacy.

NOTES

1. A. Smith, *An Inquiry Into the Nature and Causes of The Wealth of Nations* (E. Cannon ed., University of Chicago Press, Chicago, 1976) [hereinafter *TWN*] (first published in 1776; now in two volumes).
2. See generally Robin Paul Malloy, 'Of Icons, Metaphors, and Private Property - The Recognition of "Welfare" Claims in the Philosophy of Adam Smith', in *III Law and Semiotics* (R. Kevelson ed., Plenum Publishers, New York, 1990) [hereinafter Malloy, 'Icons'].
3. See generally, Robin Paul Malloy, *Planning for Serfdom: Legal Economic Discourse and Downtown Development* (University of Pennsylvania Press, Philadelphia 1991) (In particular Chapter 3 involves a full discussion of Smith) [hereinafter Malloy, *Serfdom*]; Robin Paul Malloy, 'Adam Smith's Conception of Individual Liberty', in *Law and Enlightenment in Britain* (T. Campbell & N. McCormick eds., Aberdeen University Press,1990) [hereinafter Malloy, 'Individual Liberty'] Robin Paul Malloy, 'Invisible Hand or Sleight of Hand? Adam Smith, Richard Posner, and the Philosophy of Law and Economics', 36 *Kan. L. Rev.* 209 (1988) [hereinafter Malloy, 'Invisible Hand'].
4. See Adam Smith, *Lectures on Jurisprudence* 207, 311-30, 401-07 (R. Meek, D. Raphael & L. Stein eds., Glasgow Edition, Liberty Press, Indianapolis, 1978) [hereinafter Smith, *LOJ*].
5. Id.
6. Id.
7. Id.
8. See Malloy, *Serfdom* supra note 3, at 16-29. (This chapter is titled 'The Classical Liberal Perspective' and involves a detailed analysis of Adam Smith's work in the context of the classical liberal tradition).
9. Id.
10. Id.
11. See Adam Smith, *The Theory of Moral Sentiments* 264 (E. West ed., Liberty Press, Indianapolis, 1976) [hereinafter Smith, *TMS*] (first published in 1759).
12. See Smith, *TMS*, supra note 11, at 535-37. Systems of positive law were viewed as the imperfect attempt to articulate natural justice in the sense of capturing a particular historical and contextual notion of social norms. These social norms were evolving and working towards a more perfect system of natural justice.
13. Id. Also consider Smith's conception of progressive stages of development, infra part III of this chapter, and its implications for requiring a dynamic approach to understanding and interpreting law and legal institutions. See Smith, *LOJ*, supra note 4, at 207, 311-30, 401-07 (These are places where he discusses the dynamics of the various stages of economic development and the implications for law).
14. See e.g. Smith, *LOJ*, supra note 4, at 14-37, 200-90, 401-38; Smith, *TWN*, supra note 1, at Vol. I, 420-45, and Vol. II, 231-44.
15. Id.
16. Id.
17. Id.
18. See Adam Smith, *Lectures on Rhetoric and Belles Lettres* (J. Byrce ed., Glasgow Edition, Liberty Press, Indianapolis, 1983) [hereinafter Smith, *LOR*].
19. See supra note 14; Smith, *TWN*, supra note 1, at Vol. 1, 7-26 (discussing the division of labor); Smith, *LOJ*, supra note 4, at 340-55 (discussing how even the poorest members of society benefit from the division of labor).
20. A modern day economist makes an argument similar to that employed by Adam Smith. See J. Galbraith, *The Anatomy of Power*, Houghton Mifflin Co., Boston, (1983).
21. Smith, *LOJ*, supra note 4, at 16.

22. Smith even asserted that this was the key power source of the Catholic Church and that when combined with their religious authority the Church was possibly one of the greatest threats to individual liberty. See Smith, *TWN*, supra note 1, at Vol. II, 325-38. Moving into the age of commerce and the increasing relevance of capital rather than land served to undercut the power of the Church as well as that of all land based overlord systems.
23. See Smith, *TWN*, supra note 1, at Vol. I, 111-44, 157-58, 276-78; Vol. II, 161-65.
24. Smith, *TWN*, supra note 1, at Vol. I, 144.
25. Id. at 278.
26. Smith, *LOJ*, supra note 4, at 208.
27. Smith, *TWN*, supra note 1, at Vol. II, 236.
28. See e.g. Smith, *TWN*, supra note 1, at Vol. II, 302-03.
29. Id. at 302-09.
30. Id.
31. Id.
32. Id. See also, Rosenberg, 'Adam Smith on the Division of Labour: Two Views or One?', 1965 *Economica* 127; West, 'Adam Smith's Two Views on the Division of Labour', 1964 *Economica* 23-32; West, 'The Political Economy of Alienation: Karl Marx and Adam Smith', 21 *Oxford Papers I* (1969). Each of the above articles addresses various aspects of Adam Smith's work relating to his theory of alienation.
33. Smith, *TWN*, supra note 1, at Vol. II, 302-03.
34. See Malloy, 'Icons', supra note 2: Malloy, 'Individual Liberty', supra note 3.
35. See Smith, *TWN*, supra note 1, at Vol. II, 302-09.
36. See Malloy, *Serfdom*, supra note 2, at 16-29.
37. See Smith, *TMS*, supra note 11, at 166-69.
38. See Smith, *LOJ*, supra note 4, at 7.
39. See e.g. Smith, *TWN*, supra note 1, at Vol. II 231-44; Smith, *TMS*, supra note 11, at 126-32; Smith, *LOJ*, supra note 4, at 208.
40. See generally, Malloy, *Serfdom*, supra note 3; Friedrich A. Hayek, *The Road to Serfdom* (University of Chicago Press, Chicago, 1944, 1972 edition); Friedrich A. Hayek, *The Constitution of Liberty* (University of Chicago Press, Chicago, 1960); [hereinafter Hayek, *Constitution of Liberty*] Friedrich A. Hayek, *Law, Legislation and Liberty: Vol. I Rules and Order* (University of Chicago Press, Chicago, 1973), Vol. 2 *The Mirage of Social Justice* (University of Chicago Press, Chicago, 1976), Vol. 3 *The Political Order of a Free People* (University of Chicago Press, Chicago, 1979); Milton Friedman, *Capitalism and Freedom* (University of Chicago Press, Chicago 1962); Milton Friedman and Rose Friedman, *Free to Choose*, (Harcourt, Brace, Jovanovich, New York, 1980).
41. Smith, *TMS*, supra note 11, at 166.
42. Id. at 169.
43. Id. at 236.
44. See Robin Paul Malloy, *Law and Economics: A Comparative Approach to Theory and Practice* 14-47, 60-68, 126-147 (West Publishing Co., St. Paul, Minn. 1990) [hereinafter Malloy, *Law and Economics*] (discussing basic economics, Kaldor-Hicks and Posnerian analysis).
45. Smith, *TMS*, supra note 11, at 300-01.
46. Id. at 305.
47. Id. at 162.
48. Id. at 204.
49. Id. at 205.
50. Id. at 264.
51. See Malloy, 'Invisible Hand', supra note 3, at 217-220.
52. See Smith, *TWN*, supra note 1, at Vol. II, 399-400.

53. Id.
54. See Malloy, 'Invisible Hand', supra note 3, at 217-20.
55. See Smith, *LOJ*, supra note 4, at 271. (For related discussion see id. at 270-79, 314-15). Smith also said that the judicial power must be separated from the executive power to preserve liberty and to create a system that could be viewed as delivering impartial justice that was free of personal and political influences. See generally, Smith, *TMS*, supra note 11, at 264-271, 274-82; Smith *TWN*, supra note 1, at Vol. II, 237-44.
56. See Smith, *LOJ*, supra note 4, at 314-15 (law and an independent judiciary help insure individual freedom); Smith, *TMS*, supra note 11, at 264-71, 274-82 (general rules and norms); Smith, *TWN*, supra note 1, at Vol. II, 49-50, 125 (securing liberty under law allows for a more just society as well as a more industrious and prosperous society).
57. See Hayek, *Constitution of Liberty*, supra note 40, at 220-28. Hayek endorses this view of Smith and finds that Smith was a supporter of general rules. See also Malloy, *Serfdom*, supra note 3, at 53-60. (discussing the idea of general and specific rules).
58. See Smith, *TMS*, supra note 11, at 264-271, 274-82; Smith, *TWN*, supra note 1, Vol. II 237-44.
59. Id.
60. Important Austrian school economists include Friedrich Hayek, Carl Menger, Israel M. Kirzner, Ludwig von Mises, and Murray N. Rothbard, among others. For an introductory reader on the Austrian School see Alexander H. Shand, *The Capitalist Alternative: An Introduction to Neo-Austrian Economics*, (New York University Press, New York 1984).
61. Smith, *TWN*, supra note 1, at Vol. I, 477-78.
62. Smith, *TMS*, supra note 11, at 304 (Discussion of this point covers some ten pages. Id. at 297-307).
63. Id. at 161-62. Smith felt that selfishness was not a proper motive. Id. at 499-508. He even criticized Hobbes because he felt Hobbes' theory was based on self-love. Id. at 161-65 (self interest was different from selfishness).
64. See Malloy, 'Icons', supra note 2.
65. Donald McCloskey has made important contributions to economics by pointing this out in his work on rhetoric. See Donald N. McCloskey, *The Rhetoric of Economics*, (University of Wisconsin Press, Madison 1985); Donald N. McCloskey, *If You're So Smart: The Narrative of Economic Expertise* (University of Chicago Press, Chicago 1990). See also, Malloy, 'Legal Economic Discourse: A Review of *If You're So Smart - The Narrative of Economic Expertise by Donald N. McCloskey*', 42 *J. Legal Ed.* 324 (1992) (forthcoming).
66. Malloy, *Serfdom*, supra note 3; Malloy, *Law and Economics*, supra note 44, (a basic text for those people seeking to learn more about this subject); Robin P. Malloy, 'Expanding Boundaries: Law and Economics as Creative Discourse', in *III Semiotice and the Human Sciences* (R. Kevelson ed., Peter Lang, New York, 1992); Robin P. Malloy, 'Freedom From Authority - Discovering 'The Discovery of Freedom' by Rose Wilder Lane', in *II Semiotics and the Human Sciences: Action and Agency* (R. Kevelson ed., Plenum Publishers, New York, 1991); Malloy, 'Individual Liberty', supra note 3; Malloy, 'Icons', supra note 2; Robin P. Malloy, 'Market Philosophy in the Legal Tension Between Childrens' Autonomy and Parental Authority', in *Perspective of the Family* (R. Moffat et al. eds., Edward Mellen Press, Lewiston, N. Y., 1990) (originally published at 21 *Ind. L. Rev.* 889 (1988); Robin P. Malloy, 'Planning for Serfdom - An Introduction to a New Theory of Law and Economics', 25 *Ind. L. Rev.* 621 (1992); Robin P. Malloy, 'Planning for Serfdom - An Epilogue on Law, Economics, and Values', 25 *Ind. L. Rev.* 825 (1992); Robin P. Malloy, 'If Pigs Could Fly Where Would They Go? A Reply to Professor Posin', 38 *Wayne L. Rev.* 83 (1991) (addressing the Coase Theorem); Robin P. Malloy, 'Letters From the Longhouse: Law, Economics and Native American Values', 1992 *Wisc. L. Rev.* 1569 [hereinafter Malloy, 'Letters From the Longhouse'; Robin P. Malloy, 'Toward a New Discourse of Law and Economics', 42 *Syracuse L. Rev.* 27 (1991) [hereinafter

Malloy, 'New Discourse'] (a special symposium issue on Law and Economics, and Semiotic Process); Robin P. Malloy, 'Is Law and Economics Moral? - Humanistic Economics and a Classical Liberal Critique of Posner's Economic Analysis', 24 *Val. U. L. Rev.* 147 (1990) (this issue the Law Review published a full debate between myself and Judge Posner concerning the humanistic elements of legal economic reasoning); Robin P. Malloy, 'The Limits of "Science" in Legal Discourse - A Reply to Posner', 24 *Val. U. L. Rev.* 175 (1990) (part of the debate between myself and Judge Posner); Robin P. Malloy, 'Equity Participations and Lender Liability Under *CERCLA*', 25 *Colum. J. Envtl. L.* 301 (1989); Malloy, 'Invisible Hand', supra note 3; Robin P. Malloy, 'The Merits of the Smithian Critique: A Final Word on Smith and Posner', 36 *Kan. L. Rev.* 266 (1988); Robin P. Malloy, 'The Political Economy of Co-Financing America's Urban Renaissance', 40 *Vand. L. Rev.* 67 (1987); Robin P. Malloy, 'Equating Human Rights and Property Rights - The Need for Moral Judgment in an Economic Analysis of Law and Social Policy', 47 *Ohio St. L. J.* 163 (1986); Robin P. Malloy, 'The Secondary Mortgage Market: A Catalyst for Change in Real Estate Transactions', 39 *SW. L. J.* 991 (1986); Robin P. Malloy, 'The Economics of Rent Control - A Texas Perspective', 17 *Tex. Tech L. Rev.* 797 (1986); Robin P. Malloy & Michael H. Hoeflich, 'The Shattered Dream of American Housing Policy - The Need for Reform', 26 *B.C.L. Rev.* 655 (1985); Robin P. Malloy, 'Lender Liability for Negligent Real Estate Appraisals', 1984 *U. Ill. L. Rev.* 53 (1984); Robin P. Malloy, 'The Interstate Land Sales Full Disclosure Act: Its Requirements, Consequences, and Implications for Persons Participating in Real Estate Development', 24 *B.C.L. Rev.* 1187 (1983); Robin P. Malloy, 'Mortgage Insurers Should be the Risk Takers', 17 *Real Est. Rev.* 94 (1987); Robin P. Malloy, 'Creative Financing Exposes Lenders to Developers' Liabilities', 15 *Real Est. Rev.* 60 (1985).

67. See e.g. Malloy, *Serfdom*, supra note 3; Malloy, 'Humanistic Economics', supra note 66.

68. See Malloy, 'Invisible Hand', supra note 3; Malloy, 'Humanistic Economics', supra note 66. These ideas will be explored more fully in the section of this chapter addressing Judge Posner's work and in the last chapter of this book which includes a reprint of my debate with the Judge.

69. See e.g . Malloy, *Serfdom*, supra note 3; Malloy, *Law and Economics*, supra note 44; Malloy, 'New Discourse', supra note 66.

70. See supra note 69.

71. See Friedrich A. Hayek, *The Counter-Revolution of Science: Studies on the Abuse of Reason* (Liberty Press, Indianapolis, 1952).

72. See Kuttner, 'The Poverty of Economics', *Atl. Monthly*, Feb. 1985, at 74.

The study of who gets what and why, unlike the study of plants or planets, cannot help being an ideologically charged undertaking. Despite the laborious techniques and scientific pretensions, most brands of economics are covertly ideological. Marxian economics, with its labor theory of value, assumes the inevitability of class conflict, and hence the necessity of class struggle. Keynesianism, with its conviction that industrial capitalism is systematically unstable, offers an equally "scientific" rationale for government intervention. Neoclassical economics, with its reliance on the efficiency of markets, is a lavishly embroidered brief for laissez-faire.

Id. at 83.

73. See text supra page 116-122.

74. See text supra page 116-122.

75. See text supra page 122-127.

76. See text supra page 114-116.

77. See Malloy, *Serfdom*, supra note 3.

78. Id. at 30-37.

79. Id.

80. The classical argument for freedom in economic affairs rests on the tacit postulate that the rule of law should govern policy in this as in all other spheres. We cannot understand the nature of opposition of men like Adam Smith or John Stuart Mill to government "intervention" unless we see it against this background. Their position was therefore often misunderstood .... [t]hey did not mean that government should never concern itself with any economic matters ....

To Adam Smith and his immediate successors, the enforcement of the ordinary rules of common law would certainly not have appeared as government interference; nor would they ordinarily have applied this term to an alteration of these rules or the passing of a new rule by the legislature so long as it was intended to apply equally to all people for an indefinite period of time... There is perhaps no aim which they would not have regarded as legitimate if it was clear that the people wanted it; but they excluded as generally inadmissible in a free society the method of specific orders and prohibitions.

Hayek, *Constitution of Liberty*, supra note 40, at 220-21.
81. See Malloy, 'New Discourse', supra note 66.
82. Id.
83. See Malloy, *Serfdom*, supra note 3; Malloy, 'Political Economy', supra note 66.
84. See supra note 83.
85. Id.
86. See supra note 80.
87. See Malloy, *Serfdom*, supra note 3, at 53-60 (a detailed discussion of general vs. specific rules).
88. See text supra page 118-122 (reference to Smith's similar observation).
89. See Malloy, 'Letters From the Longhouse', supra note 66 (application of my approach to law and economics to issues of concern to Native Americans).
90. Judge Posner's writings are extensive. Listed here are a few of his important books - many of which are based on numerous articles authored by the Judge. See e.g Richard A. Posner, *Sex and Reason* (Harvard University Press, Cambridge, Mass. 1992); Richard A. Posner, *Economic Analysis of Law* 4th Ed. (Little, Brown and Co., Boston, 1992); Richard A. Posner, *The Problems of Jurisprudence* (Harvard University Press, Cambridge, Mass. 1990); Richard A. Posner, *The Economics of Justice* (Harvard University Press, Cambridge, Mass. 1983) [hereinafter Posner, *Economics of Justice*].
91. See Malloy, *Law and Economics*, supra note 44, at 38-42, 60-68, 126-147; Posner, *Economics of Justice*, supra note 90, at 48-118.
92. See 'Debate: Is Law and Economics Moral?', infra Part II of this book.
93. See Posner, 'Utilitarianism, Economics and Legal Theory', 8 *J. Legal Stud.* 103, 135-36 (1979).
94. See Malloy, 'New Discourse', supra note 66.
95. Id.
96. Id. See also Malloy, *Law and Economics*, supra note 44, at 48-59.
97. See e.g. Posner, *Economics of Justice*, supra note 90, at 86 (slavery), 84-85 (racial, ethnic and religious minorities), 76 (feeble minded and infirm). See also Posner, 'Wealth Maximization Revisited', 2 *Notre Dame J. L. Ethics*; 7 *Pub. Pol'y* 85 (1985) (as to slavery being inefficient but not immoral or wrong).
98. See text supra pages 116-127 (regarding Smith and self interest).
99. See text supra pages 120-121 (text and footnotes address Smith's concern for education and his analysis is not based on any conception of wealth maximization).
100. See Richard A. Epstein, *Takings: Private Property and the Power of Eminent Domain*, (Harvard University Press, Cambridge, Mass. 1985) [hereinafter Epstein, *Takings*].

101. See Richard A. Epstein, *Forbidden Grounds: The Case Against Employment Discrimination Laws* (Harvard University Press, Cambridge, Mass. 1992).
102. See Malloy, *Law and Economics*, supra note 44, at 86-92; Malloy, *Serfdom*, supra note 3, at 61-83.
103. See Epstein, *Takings*, supra note 100, at 1-31.
104. Id.
105. Id.
106. Id.
107. Id.
108. Id.
109. See text supra page 114-116.
110. See Epstein, *Takings* supra note 100.
111. See text supra pages 116-121 (Smith's theory of the stages of development).
112. See text and footnotes supra pages 122-127, 128-132.
113. See Malloy, *Law and Economics*, supra note 44, at 69-75 (discussing Ackerman's liberal approach).
114. Bruce A. Ackerman, *Reconstructing American Law* (Harvard University Press, Cambridge, Mass. 1984) [hereinafter Ackerman, *Reconstructing*]. For other books of interest by Ackerman see Bruce A. Ackerman, *We the People: Foundations*, (Belknap Press, Cambridge, Mass. 1991); Bruce A. Ackerman, *Social Justice in the Liberal State* (Yale University Press, New Haven, 1980) [hereinafter Ackerman, *Social Justice*].
115. See Ackerman, *Reconstructing, supra note 114, at 1-22.*
116. Id. at 23-45.
117. Id. at 21-22.
118. Id. at 23-45.
119. Id. at 24.
120. Id. at 78.
121. Id. at 97-98.
122. See text supra pages 116-122.
123. See text supra pages 116-127.
124. See Ackerman, *Reconstructing, supra note 114.*
125. Id.
126. See Ackerman, *Social Justice*, supra note 114, at 66-68 (rejecting social contract theory).
127. See Ackerman, *Reconstructing*, supra note 114, at 24.
128. Id. at 46-110.
129. For an introduction to CLS see Malloy, *Law and Economics*, supra note 44, at 76-85; Malloy, *Serfdom*, supra note 3, at 70-76; *Critical Legal Studies* (Allan C. Hutchinson, ed., Rowman & Littlefield Publishers, Totowa, N.J. 1989); *The Politics of Law: A Progressive Critique* (revised edition, David Kairys, ed. Pantheon Books, New York, 1990); Mark Kellman, *A Guide to Critical Legal Studies* (Harvard University Press, Cambridge, Mass. 1987).
130. See Malloy, *Law and Economics*, supra note 44, at 76-85; Malloy, *Serfdom*, supra note 3, at 61-83.
131. See Kennedy, 'Form and Substance in Private Law Adjudication' 89 *Harv. L. Rev.* 1685 (1976) [hereinafter Kennedy, 'Form and Substance'].
132. Id. at 1713.
133. See Smith, *TMS*, supra note 11, at 71-72.
134. Kennedy, 'Form and Substance', supra note 131, at 1714.
135. Id. at 1716.
136. Id. at 1717.
137. See text supra pages 122-127.
138. See Kennedy, 'Form and Substance', supra note 131, at 1728-59.

139. Id. at 1751.
140. Smith, *TWN*, supra note 1, at Vol. I, 278.
141. Many of my ideas have been formulated and assisted by earlier works on Smith. While this chapter represents a new work it has been aided by earlier projects including; Malloy, 'Icons', supra note 2; Malloy, *Serfdom*, supra note 3; Malloy, 'Individual Liberty', supra note 3; Malloy, 'Invisible Hand', supra note 3.

Syracuse University, College of Law

ROBIN PAUL MALLOY

INTRODUCTION TO PART TWO

As we have seen in the first part of this volume, Adam Smith's views on law and economics are complex. This complexity has made his writings a continual source of interpretive investigation and dispute. The historical significance of Smith, however, remains unquestioned as his ideas are foundational to much of the structure of western capitalistic society. Turning our attention away from the historical Smith we now seek to further understand the 'living Smith', the Adam Smith that continues to play an active role in modern day policy debates. Thus, in Part Two, we will focus on Smith as he actually enters the discourse.

We have reproduced a published debate between Robin Paul Malloy and Richard A. Posner in order to give context and meaning to the way in which Adam Smith's work continues to be an active part of public policy making. Our task here is somewhat different from a purely academic inquiry into the historic understanding of Smith. Here we approach Smith's work not as the direct subject of analytical inquiry but as the often times implicit and sometimes explicit foundations for competing approaches to law and economics. In the context of the Malloy/Posner debate, we examine another dimension to the problem of interpreting Adam Smith. Instead of reporting on Smith or analyzing what others are saying about Smith, we get to see Adam Smith as part of the rhetoric itself. We believe that this is valuable because the debate presented here is representative of the larger intellectual debate within law and economics. Furthermore, we believe that this is important because the law and economics movement continues to grow in size and in its influence on law and legal institutions.

After presenting both sides of the debate and the response and rebuttal of each respective party, Jerry Evensky will offer some thoughts regarding the exchange between Malloy and Posner. He will also conclude the book with a chapter that brings together issues and themes from Part One and Part Two.

R.P. Malloy and J. Evensky: Adam Smith and the Philosophy of Law and Economics, 151.

ROBIN PAUL MALLOY

IS LAW AND ECONOMICS MORAL?--HUMANISTIC ECONOMICS AND A CLASSICAL LIBERAL CRITIQUE OF POSNER'S ECONOMIC ANALYSIS

If in the long run we are the makers of our own fate, in the short run we are the captives of the ideas we have created. Only if we recognize the danger in time can we hope to avoid it.[1] ***F.A. Hayek***

The question posed for tonight's discussion is whether law and economics is moral. The problem with this question, and I suppose with this topic, is that it presumes that there is a given agreed upon set of rules, norms, principles, standards, etc., that is *law and economics*. Herein lies one of the central problems with the phrase--law and economics--and herein resides one of the themes of my recent articles and books in this area.[2] Law and economics is not a given nor even an agreed upon undertaking. Rather, it is an inquiry or study concerning the relationship between law and economics; between our understanding of legal relationships and economic relationships; between our understanding of legal institutions and economic institutions; between our use of legal metaphors and economic metaphors.[3]

The work of Judge Posner reflects one view of the relationship between law and economics. Judge Posner's work reflects a conservative ideological approach to law and economics and has a focus centered on wealth maximization and the promotion of market efficiency.[4] Judge Posner's view of law and economics is, however, only one view. Other notable writers that come clearly within the field of law and economics offer viewpoints which are in contrast to the philosophy offered by Judge Posner. Bruce Ackerman of Yale,[5] for instance, offers a liberal perspective on the relationship between law and economics while Richard Epstein of Chicago presents a libertarian model of legal economics.[6] Both Ackerman and Epstein, like myself, are offering alternative approaches to understanding the relationship between law and economics. While all of us are offering alternative approaches to law and economics, each of us is *doing* law and economics. Law and economics is not, after all, the domain of any one person. Nor is law and economics properly identifiable with any political, philosophical, or ideological viewpoint. Law and economics is a diverse and colorful marketplace of competing ideas.

R.P. Malloy and J. Evensky: Adam Smith and the Philosophy of Law and Economics, 153–166.

To make an analogy, law and economics is like learning to put puzzles together. Law and economics does not consist of everyone sitting down to deal with the same puzzle; with some people being better or worse, faster or slower in figuring out how to put all the pieces together. Rather, law and economics consists of each of us sitting down to a different, perhaps a unique, puzzle. Some of us may discover that we are completing a picture puzzle of an ocean scene; others, of a country landscape; and still others, of an urban skyline. In this sense, of everyone working separate (different) puzzles, we are all learning something about the method of doing puzzles, about the process of relating individual pieces to a spatial, color, and shape oriented whole--that is law and economics.[7] We are all engaged in a similar process or method even though we are all working on different puzzles, on different viewpoints.

From this simple starting point I argue that there are many philosophical and ideological approaches to law and economics.[8] Law, as a derivative field of study, presupposes that a person with a Marxist view of economic relationships, for instance, will have a decidedly different view of law and legal institutions than will a person with a capitalist free market oriented world view. In other words, there is a direct relationship between one's ideological and subjective world view and one's view of law and legal institutions within that world.

Consequently, in the discourse of !aw and economics one can hear many voices--conservatives,[9] liberals,[10] libertarians,[11] neo-Marxist,[12] left communitarians,[13] and classical liberals.[14] Even scholars of the Critical Legal Studies (CLS) movement can be said to be engaging in law and economics because their neo-Marxist views on law, power and resource allocation are essentially discussions on alternative economics. Such an inclusive view of law and economics is possible once one realizes that law is a derivative field of study. That is, a person's view of law and legal institutions is derived from their view of economic and political relationships. Within each of the many ideological categories of law and economics there is diversity--not all conservatives think alike just as not all CLS writers think alike. The key is that within any given ideological framework one can study law and economics--that is, study the relationship between law and economics in conservative theory, liberal theory, libertarian theory, Marxist theory, classical liberal theory, and etc. Once, and only once this is understood can we hope to answer the question--'Is Law and Economics Moral?'

In this context, in this chorus of voices rising and swelling to the diverse measures, chords, and syncopations of economics, the question, 'Is Law and Economics Moral?' becomes a loaded and almost meaningless question. For it seems that morality must be measured from both inside and outside of a particular ideological framework. Few, if any, philosophers hold the view that their own philosophy is immoral. Consequently, understood within its own structural context, any well thought out system of beliefs will include a *moral validator* which, when understood within its own ideological context, allows its proponents to assume the 'morally' correct position on pressing social issues.

Corresponding to the existence of an internal moral validator there is an entire set of *external evaluators* of any given theoretical viewpoint.[15] For example, conservative theories of law and economics may contain their own internal moral validators--such as the creation of wealth, the maximization of that wealth, and the promotion of market efficiency. However, these moral validators, and conservative theory in general, can be subjected to the systematic critique of an alternative belief system. In contrast to conservative theory, for example, a liberal theory of law and economics seeks to promote equality and fairness of outcome rather than wealth maximization. As such, a liberal might well question the conservative system of wealth maximization and efficiency on grounds that it leads to perpetually 'unfair' and 'unequal' allocations of scarce social resources for certain poor and disenfranchised groups such as Blacks and Hispanics.

Thus, from the liberal's vantage point the conservative theory of wealth maximization is immoral--immoral on liberal terms. Likewise, a Marxist, a libertarian, or classical liberal will have their own internal definition of morality--morality as understood and measured within their own consistent theory of law and economics. When the Marxist, the libertarian, or the classical liberal looks at conservative approaches to law and economics or when they look at one another's competing approaches to this subject matter, they may very well discover that their own internalized moral validator is different than the 'morality' at work in the alternative viewpoints. In this regard, the charge of immorality of a particular view of law and economics must be understood within a particular context. This means that while Judge Posner's theory of wealth maximization may be viewed as internally moral from the point of view of its proponents, it can nonetheless be viewed as immoral from the contextual vantage point of an alternative philosophical vision of the relationship between law and economics.[16]

If any belief system can be viewed as both internally moral and yet potentially immoral when viewed from a position outside of the theory, what then is the point of tonight's debate? As I see it--the question--'Is Law and Economics Moral?'--really asks us to consider what ideas we seek to promote as individual human beings. It asks us to compare and contrast competing philosophical world views, each with its own internal moral validator. We are not here, therefore, to *resolve* nor really to debate the morality of law and economics. We are here to engage in a dialogue about values--the alternative values and understandings of morality that exist and are fostered by the acceptance or rejection of competing theories of the 'good' and 'just' society.

Thus, my contention is that while Judge Posner may understand his theory of wealth maximization to be moral on his own terms, his is an ideological approach to law and economics which fails to promote the understanding of morality that I offer in my writings on a classical liberal approach to law and economics.[17] Measured from my perspective as a classical liberal in the *humanistic* tradition of Adam Smith, the Posnerian vision of law and economics is, shall we say, uninviting; uninviting because of the *values and potential consequences* of the values at work in Judge Posner's theory of wealth maximization. My disagreement with Judge Posner's view of law and economics is a disagreement on values. I believe in the humanistic and moral philosophy of Adam Smith; a philosophy that demonstrates that social welfare concerns need *not* be inconsistent with the desire for, and the promotion of, properly conducted free market capitalism.[18] Unfettered laissez-faire was never a viewpoint offered by Smith. Smith's writings, in fact, support many types of government regulation and intervention into the marketplace.[19] For Smith, and for classical liberals, the market, efficiency, and wealth maximization were never ends to be achieved for their own sake, but rather, means to a higher and more noble end--the ends of liberty and freedom. While these terms, individual liberty and freedom, are open textured, it is clear that Adam Smith *was not*, and the modern day Smithian *is not*, a wealth maximizer in the Posnerian sense. To the contrary, Adam Smith's emphasis throughout his life and in his many books was an emphasis on moral philosophy and not economic rhetoric. It is only when one ignores the life long work of Smith as a moral philosopher that one can be misled into believing Adam Smith's philosophy could support the anti-humanistic and anti-libertarian aspects of a theory such as wealth maximization. I will not go into detail on these points tonight for I addressed these ideas in detail in an article I wrote two years ago.[20] In that earlier work I carefully outlined the humanistic and moral underpinnings to Adam Smith's understanding of the relationship between law and economics, and I demonstrated the disconnectedness between Smithian/classical liberal values and the values fostered by Judge Posner's theory of wealth maximization.

In tonight's exchange with Judge Posner, I want to speak in more general terms about the competing values, at work in each of our views of law and economics. In discussing these competing values, we must acknowledge that there is no scientifically agreed upon way to reduce all of our values to quantitative form. Thus, there can be no *scientific* answer to the question confronting us tonight. But, does this lack of scientific certainty mean that my theory, my approach, is more subjective, more political, more personal, than the theory of wealth maximization offered by Judge Posner? *I think not*. Judge Posner has expressly indicated that his theory is both political and subjective. He has stated for instance, that with respect to *his* theory of wealth maximization: 'It must also be emphasized that it is a *political* (emphasis added) philosophy that I am (he was) expounding.'[21] Furthermore, in his reply to an article of mine, Judge Posner repeatedly asserted that economic efficiency, wealth maximization, and cost-benefit analysis were not the only factors to consider in trying to use law to resolve pressing social and legal problems.[22] In other words, there are many personal, subjective and political factors to consider that are outside of the theoretical approach he is most noted for. Judge Posner indicated that some of these other factors are drawn from intuition and some apparently from elsewhere.[23] We are never quite sure what all the factors are, where they come from, nor how Judge Posner might go about applying such additional factors. We are, in other words, given no specific guidance as to what rights or values will trump the theory of wealth maximization. By replying to my *Kansas Law Review* article in this way, Judge Posner acknowledged that he has *no* special claim to a *correct or scientific approach*--he offers only his own political and subjective view of what law *ought* to be.

Thus, we are left with an ongoing dialogue--a dialogue about morality, about law and economics, and about the good and just society. How, in such a setting, are we to know what 'rules' of law and social conduct are good and morally worthy of support? The answer, as provided by Adam Smith, *is experience*. Smith in his classic work *The Theory of Moral Sentiments* tells us the general rules of morality:

> are ultimately founded upon experience of what, in particular instances, our moral faculties, our natural sense of merit and propriety, approve or disapprove of. We do not originally approve or condemn particular actions, because, upon examination, they appear to be agreeable or inconsistent with a certain general rule. The general rule, on the contrary, is formed by finding from experience that all actions of a certain kind, or circumstanced in a certain manner, are approved or disapproved of.[24]

Thus, Smith tells us, and I repeat, we must learn from experience--we must learn good values from bad values, good philosophies from bad philosophies, morality from immorality based on experience. From my own life experience I have drawn my values. Each of us has done the same, some more consciously than others.[25]

From my own experiences, some of them painful, some of them happy, I have tried to articulate and promote a theory that identifies certain values within its morality. These values are consistent with the philosophy of Adam Smith and I would suggest are the types of values supported by many people in our society. These values include:

> The recognition that all people are special; that we are all created equal, and we should all enjoy the natural and inalienable rights to life, liberty and the pursuit of happiness. This means there are certain basic rights that all people have which are *not* dependent upon their current wealth or lack thereof.

The recognition that individual liberty and freedom are meaningless without a conception of *human dignity*, and that we cannot avoid our responsibility in this area by invoking 'scientific' forms of conversation that remove human dignity from the social discourse.

The recognition that free market capitalism is merely a *means* to an end (it promotes liberty and freedom through diversity and counter-balancing power sources), but it is not an end in itself.

The recognition that *no* person, under any circumstance, ought to be the slave of another. Slavery, in other words, is simply wrong.

The recognition that *no* person, no matter how feeble minded, no matter how unfortunate, no matter how poor or lacking in education or resources, should be told that they are without any moral and legal claim to help from a civilized and prosperous community.

The recognition that our government, our economic institutions, and our laws are worthy of praise only to the extent that they recognize the intrinsic rights of all people to participate in a free society; that participation is *not* dependent upon the current possession of wealth nor is one without wealth to be relegated to simple charity and made to feel subservient and beholding to those with wealth.

These are some of my general values; values I try to write about, and *values that I believe can only be supported and promoted in a capitalist free market society*. I argue that if one believes in these values--if experience has told you that these are at least arguably worthy values, then one must experience difficulty with the core, internal morality of the theory of wealth maximization as articulated by Judge Posner.[26] While I, and many others, have elsewhere criticized many of Judge Posner's ideas, let me mention only a few specific items for consideration tonight.[27]

In contrast to the values that I am trying to promote, Judge Posner has expressed some seemingly very different values in his book *Economics of Justice*.[28] In that book, Judge Posner tells us the following about his theory of wealth maximization:

Another implication of the wealth maximization approach, however, is that people who lack sufficient earning power to support even a minimum decent standard of living are entitled to no say in the allocation of resources unless they are part of the utility function of someone who has wealth. This conclusion may seem to weigh too heavily the individual's particular endowment of capacities. If he happens to be born feeble-minded and his net social product is negative, he would have no right to the means of support even though there was nothing blameworthy in his inability to support himself.[29]

(In short, if you have no wealth, if you have no resources, you have no right to claim anything. You must rely on charity and be thankful for whatever others voluntarily give you.)

If Nazi Germany wanted to get rid of its Jews, in a system of wealth maximization, it would have had to buy them out. There would be no more economic basis for coercion here than there is in the usual (that is, low-transaction cost) eminent-domain context.

But one must not overlook the possibility of extending the logic of certain nuisance cases to Jews, Blacks, and other racial, religious, or ethnic minorities. If a funeral parlor can depress land values, because people living near it are upset to be reminded of death, and on this ground can be condemned as a nuisance, likewise the presence of Jews or Blacks in a neighborhood might so upset their neighbors as to depress land values by an amount greater than the members of the minority would be willing to pay to remain in the neighborhood. In these circumstances some form of segregation would be wealth maximizing.[30]

(Thus Posner turns the conversation about rights, and about human dignity, into the process of dickering about price.)

In another passage concerning the economic approach to upholding voluntary contracts, Judge Posner tells us that slavery can, in a limited situation, be consistent with wealth maximization.[31] And, from a different source Judge Posner tells us that, under a system of wealth maximization, the primary objection to slavery is that it is inefficient--*not* that it is morally wrong in all circumstances.[32] Again, the Posnerian conversation turns away from natural and inalienable rights and reduces human dignity and individual liberty to a question of price--the costs and benefits of slavery are treated in as dehumanized a manner as the cost and benefits of toothpaste manufacturing.

While Judge Posner may tell us that he personally does not like these results, his theory, the theory of wealth maximization which he has promoted, is a theory that, by his own words, expressly legitimates the terrible consequences just outlined. Instead of saying that these are reasons to reject his theory, Judge Posner says such things as, 'It is unlikely that ostracism, expulsion, or segregation of a *productive* (emphasis added) group would actually increase a society's wealth.'[33] The consequences, in other words, are not inherently wrong or immoral, rather, they are *unlikely*--unlikely because to treat Jews or Blacks in extremely harsh ways is *unlikely* to increase society's wealth. Of course, the poor, the unemployed, the unemployable, and the feeble-minded *just might* fall prey to this *unlikely* calculation because they are in fact *unproductive*, and Posner's caveat is that certain outrageous consequences are unlikely to occur with respect to *productive* groups.

Importantly, we should ask, why should any of us promote a theory that cannot simply say slavery, maltreatment of the poor, of Jews, of Blacks, of any human being is wrong. Has not our own personal life experience and our national-cultural experience indicated that these actions are wrong? Is it not a failure of principle to avoid the condemnation of these results by inserting a cursory statement that such results are *unlikely*? I think history proves Judge Posner to be wrong. Where a theory or an ideology promotes 'rational and scientific' outcomes which are inhumane, it is not unlikely that the inevitable gruesome consequences may in fact materialize. Slavery and civil rights violations in the United States, and statist anti-libertarian ideologies during and since World War II, are just a couple of easy illustrations of this point.

The theory of wealth maximization offered by Judge Posner is in many ways analogous to the Frankenstein Monster.[34] In the book *Frankenstein*, a noble-minded Dr. Frankenstein creates something and then independent of any good or bad intentions on the doctor's part, the Monster takes on a life of its own; a life that even with its tender moments is ultimately uncontrollably destructive. Likewise, the theory of wealth maximization is a moral monster that can lead even the most noble and good spirited people to conclusions that affront our basic social values. Unfortunately, the theory of wealth maximization is a theory that its chief proponent says can lead to many atrocities; a theory for which its chief proponent fails to articulate clear and specific criteria for its application and its limitations; a theory, in short, which fails to remember that we are all human beings and that we all have a continuing role to play in the humanistic evolution of our community and society.[35]

My own views, derivable from the humanistic and moral philosophy of Adam Smith, stand in sharp contrast to the views of Judge Posner. I believe that freedom, liberty, and human dignity are something more than the cold hard variables of economic calculus, and that these values require us to continually engage in an ongoing discourse of initial first principles. We cannot avoid this responsibility by appealing to concepts of efficiency and wealth maximization because they can play no constructive part in the determination of the basic essence of human dignity.[36] While economics, capitalism, and democracy are all important factors in helping us understand and promote human dignity, we cannot escape our own personal moral obligation to make each of these factors subservient to the higher values they can promote--freedom, liberty, and human dignity. With respect to this point, I think Milton Friedman summed up the classical liberal position best when he said:

> A free society, I believe, is a more productive society than any other; it releases the energies of people, enables resources to be used more effectively, and enables people to have a better life. But that is not why I am in favor of a free society. I believe and hope that I would favor a free society even if it were less productive than some alternative-say, a slave society.... I favor a free society because my basic value is freedom itself.[37]

Yes, our basic value should be freedom itself, and in particular, freedom as understood in the classical liberal tradition of Adam Smith; freedom *of* participation, freedom *from* alienation, freedom *as* human dignity, and freedom *as* a natural right--freedom as *master of*, rather than *servant to*, the alleged scientific principles of economic analysis.

NOTES

1. F. Hayek, *The Road to Serfdom* 2 (1944) [hereinafter Hayek, *Serfdom*]. This particular passage in Hayek's book has always made me stop and pause. Hauntingly, it seems directed at Judge Posner's theory of wealth maximization in as much as Judge Posner has often seemed imprisoned by the desire to pursue the consistency of wealth maximization. His failure to reject slavery as immoral in all circumstances, and his willingness to treat the presence of Blacks and Jews in a neighborhood as analogous to a nuisance problem are simple examples of his captivity within the ideological prison of wealth maximization.

2. In the midst of my varied writings I have addressed this issue in several recent works. See, e.g. R. Malloy, *Law and Economics--A Comparative Approach to Theory and Practice* (1990, forthcoming by West Publishing) [hereinafter Malloy, *Law and Economics*]; R. Malloy, 'Of Icons, Metaphors, and Private Property--The Recognition of "Welfare" Claims in the Philosophy of Adam Smith', in *III Law and Semiotics* (R. Kevelson ed. 1990, by Plenum Publishers) [hereinafter Malloy, 'Icons']; Malloy, 'Invisible Hand or Sleight of Hand? Adam Smith, Richard Posner, and the Philosophy of Law and Economics', 36 *U. Kan. L. Rev.* 209 (1988) [hereinafter Malloy, 'Adam Smith']; Malloy, 'The Merits of the Smithian Critique: A Final Word on Smith and Posner', 36 *U. Kan. L. Rev.* 266 (1988) [hereinafter Malloy, 'Smith and Posner']; Malloy, 'Market Philosophy in the Legal Tension Between Children's Autonomy and Parental Authority', 21 *Ind. L. Rev.* 889 (1988) [hereinafter Malloy, 'Children's Autonomy'] (to be reprinted in *Perspectives on the Family* (R. Moffat, J. Grcic, & Bayles, ed. 1990); Malloy, 'The Political Economy of Co-Financing America's Urban Renaissance', 40 *Vand. L. Rev.* 67 (1987) [hereinafter Malloy, 'Political Economy']; Malloy, 'Equating Human Rights and Property Rights--The Need for Moral Judgment in an Economic Analysis of Law and Social Policy', 47 *Ohio St. L.J.* 163 (1986) [hereinafter Malloy, 'Moral Judgment']; R. Malloy, *Planning for Serfdom--A Contextual Theory of Law, Economics, and the State* (forthcoming by the University of Pennsylvania Press in 1990 [hereinafter Malloy, *Planning*]; R. Malloy, 'Adam Smith's Conception of Individual Liberty', in *IVR '89 Congressional Proceedings on Enlightenment, Rights and Revolution* (T. Campbell & N. MacCormick, ed. 1990, by Aberdeen University Press) [hereinafter Malloy, 'Individual Liberty'].

3. See Malloy, 'Icons', supra note 2. This work explores the use of the market metaphor in the defense of private property rights. It outlines the metaphor of the market and the 'invisible hand' as used by Adam Smith and then demonstrates the misuse of that metaphor by such people as Richard Posner, Richard Epstein, and Duncan Kennedy. It is clear from Smith's work that he recognized the right of welfare claims by individuals and that wealth transfers were a part of government's function. This side of Smith is generally omitted by those who seek to invoke him and his market metaphors as a defense against welfare claims, or, as in the case of Duncan Kennedy, those who seek to critique classical individualist market philosophy by invoking an inaccurate and one dimensional representation of the views of people like Smith. See also Malloy 'Children's Autonomy', supra note 2 (This essay is an application of market theory as a metaphor for discussing power relationships within the family setting.).

4. See, e.g., R. Posner, *The Economics of Justice* (1983) [hereinafter Posner, *Economic Analysis*]; Posner, 'Utilitarianism, Economics, and Legal Theory', 8 *J. Legal Stud.* 103 (1979) [hereinafter Posner, 'Legal Theory']; Posner, 'The Law and Economics Movement' 77 *Am. Econ. Rev.* 1 (1987); Posner, 'Some Uses and Abuses of Economics in Law', 46 *U. Chi. L. Rev.* 281 (1979); Posner, 'Wealth Maximization Revisited', 2 *Notre Dame J. L. Ethics & Pub. Pol'y* 85 (1985) [hereinafter Posner, 'Revisited']; Posner, 'An Economic Theory of the Criminal Law', 85 *Colum. L. Rev.* 1193 (1985).

5. See, e.g., B. Ackerman, *Social Justice in the Liberal State* (1980); B. Ackerman, *Reconstructing American Law* (1984); Ackerman, 'Law, Economics and the Problem of Legal Culture', 1986 *Duke L.J.* 929; Ackerman, 'Law in an Activist State', 92 *Yale L.J.* 1083 (1983);

Ackerman, 'The Marketplace of Ideas', 90 *Yale L.J.* 1131 (1981).
6. See, e.g., R. Epstein, *Takings–Private Property and the Power of Eminent Domain* (1985); Epstein, 'Past and Future: The Temporial Dimension in the Law of Property', 64 *Wash. U.L.Q.* 667 (1986); Epstein, 'The Fundamentals of Freedom of Speech', 10 *Harv. J.L. & Pub. Pol'y* 53 (1987); Epstein, 'Why Restrain Alienation?', 85 *Colum. L.Rev.* 970 (1985).
7. For a discussion of the theory of the method of methods see R. Kevelson, *Foundations of Semiotics–Charles S. Pierce's Methods of Methods* (1987).
8. See Malloy, *Law and Economics*, supra note 2.
9. See. e.g., supra note 4; S. Macedo, *The New Right V. The Constitution* (1986); W. Williams, *The State Against Blacks* (1982); T. Sowell, *Civil Rights: Rhetoric or Reality?* (1984).
10. See. e.g., supra note 5; R. Dworkin, *Taking Rights Seriously* (1978); R. Dworkin, *Law's Empire* (1986); J. Rawls, *A Theory of Justice* (1971).
11. See, e.g., supra note 6; *Freedom, Feminism, and the State* (W. McElroy ed. 1982); R. Lane, *The Discovery of Freedom–Man's Struggle Against Authority* (1984); A. Nock, *Our Enemy, the State* (1983); R. Nozick, *Anarchy, State, and Utopia* (1974); M. Rothbard, *For a New Liberty–The Libertarian Manifesto* (1978).
12. See. e.g., M. Kelman, *A Guide to Critical Legal Studies* (1987); Bender, 'A Lawyer's Primer on Feminist Theory and Tort', 38 *J. Legal Educ.* 3 (1988); Binder, 'On Critical Legal Studies as Guerilla Warfare', 76 *Geo. L.J.* 1 (1987); Kennedy, 'Cost–Benefit Analysis of Entitlement Problems: A Critique', 33 *Stan. L. Rev.* 387 (1981); Kennedy, 'Form and Substance in Private Law Adjudication', 89 *Harv. L. Rev.* 1685 (1976); Kennedy & Klare, 'A Bibliography of Critical Legal Studies', 94 *Yale L.J.* 461 (1984); Tushet, 'Critical Legal Studies: An Introduction to its Origins and Underpinnings', 36 *J. Legal Educ.* 505 (1986).
13. See generally supra note 12.
14. See, e.g., supra note 2; M. Friedman, *Capitalism and Freedom* (1962) (reissued 1982) [hereinafter Friedman, *Freedom*]; M. Friedman & R. Friedman, *Free to Choose* (1980); F. Hayek, *The Constitution of Liberty* (1960) [hereinafter Hayek, *Liberty*]; Hayek, *Serfdom*, supra note 1; Friedman, 'Free Markets and Free Speech', 10 *Harv. J.L. & Pub. Pol'y* 1 (1987) [hereinafter Friedman, 'Free Speech']; Gray, 'F.A. Hayek and the Rebirth of Classical Liberalism', 5 *Literature of Liberty* 19 (1982).
15. For a related concept regarding the internal and external points of view in dealing with the Rule of Recognition and Legal Validity see H. Hart, *The Concept of Law* (1961).
16. See Malloy, 'Adam Smith', supra note 2, at 242-54; Malloy, 'Smith and Posner', supra note 2, at 267-74.
17. See supra note 2.
18. See Malloy, 'Adam Smith', supra note 2; Malloy, 'Smith and Posner', supra note 2; Malloy, 'Icons', supra note 2. See also Malloy, 'Individual Liberty', supra note 2 (based on a paper delivered to the 14th World Congress of the International Association for Philosophy of Law and Social Philosophy at Edinburgh University). Adam Smith identified both a relative and non-relative component to individual liberty. As a non-relative right, individual liberty meant a natural right to fair and just treatment as well as the right to respect and participation. As a relative right, individual liberty focused on the historical, economical, and political context to assess the basic minimum amenities to which every individual in a particular society was entitled. In addition, Smith sets out a role for government to play in providing certain services to individuals because the services are fundamental to individual liberty. Smith uses the example of a free education and says that the state must provide it even if it provides no benefit to the state; the benefit is to the individual and the benefit is one that is owed. See also A. Smith, *An Inquiry into the Nature and Causes of the Wealth of Nations* Vol. 2 at 302-09 (E. Cannon ed. 1976) [hereinafter Smith, *Wealth of Nations*] (first published in 1776; now in two volumes).
19. For a concurrence to this conclusion see Hayek, *Liberty*, supra note 14, at 220-28. Hayek writes:

The classical argument for freedom in economic affairs rests on the tacit postulate that the rule of law should govern policy in this as in all other spheres. We cannot understand the nature of the opposition of men like Adam Smith or John Stuart Mill to government "intervention" unless we see it against this background. There position was therefore often misunderstood by those who were not familiar with that basic conception; and confusion arose in England and America as soon as the conception of the rule of law ceased to be assumed by every reader. Freedom of economic activity had meant freedom under the law, not the absence of all government action. The "interference" or "intervention" of government which those writers opposed as a matter of principle therefore meant only the infringement of that private sphere which the general rules of law were intended to protect. They did not mean that government should never concern itself with any economic matters. ...

To Adam Smith and his immediate successors, the enforcement of the ordinary rules of common law would certainly not have appeared as government interference; nor would they ordinarily have applied this term to an alteration of these rules or the passing of a new rule by the legislature so long as it was intended to apply equally to all people for an indefinite period of time....There is perhaps no aim which they would not have regarded as legitimate if it was clear that the people wanted it; but they excluded as generally inadmissible in a free society the method of specific orders and prohibitions.

Id. at 220-21.

20. See Malloy, 'Adam Smith', supra note 2. (In this article I provide detailed references to the many works of Adam Smith and to other secondary sources. The books written by Smith include: A. Smith, *Wealth of Nations*, supra note 18; A. Smith, *Essays on Philosophical Subjects* (J. Bryce & W.P.D. Wightmen eds. 1980); A. Smith, *The Theory of Moral Sentiments* (E. West ed. 1976) (first published in 1759) [hereinafter A. Smith, *Moral Sentiments*]; A. Smith, *Lectures on Jurisprudence* (R. Meek, D. Raphael & L. Stein eds. 1978); A. Smith, *Lectures on Rhetoric and Belles Lettres* (J. Bryce ed. 1983). See also Malloy, 'Icons', supra note 2; Malloy, 'Smith and Posner', supra note 2; Malloy, 'Individual Liberty', supra note 2; Malloy, *Planning*, supra note 2.

21. See Posner, 'Revisited', supra, note 4, at 103.

22. See Posner, 'The Ethics of Wealth Maximization: Reply to Malloy', 36 *U. Kan. L.Rev.* 261 (1988) [hereinafter Posner, 'Reply']. See also Malloy, 'Smith and Posner', supra note 2.

23. See Posner, 'Reply', supra note 22.

24. See A. Smith, *Moral Sentiments*, supra note 20, at 264.

25. See generally, Malloy, 'Children's Autonomy', supra note 2. In that article, I explore the idea of thinking of the family as a metaphorical marketplace where scarce resources are controlled by one or both parents and the children are subject to the monopolistic power of the parents. Within the family, for instance, if only the male spouse works he controls the economic resources of the family. He has the power to act like a monopolist or like a dictator because there are few if any effective competing sources of power that the other family members can draw on.

I grew up, for instance, in a large lower class family with a father that was an abusive alcoholic. He exercised complete control over our lives and engaged in constant abuse. He regularly stole our milk money and our school lunches which my mother eventually took to hiding in different parts of our house. Most nights he would return home late in the evening and proceed to abuse and harass us until the early morning hours leaving us tired for school but grateful that we survived another night. His idea of "baby sitting" was taking us along to his favorite bars, and there were many nights, as a youngster and grade schooler, that I fell asleep on a bar stool between my father, slumped over in a drunken stupor, and some two-bit whore or drinking companion that was putting the moves on his wallet. My childhood experience, in short, left me with many vivid memories of the fear of uncontrolled power.

As just one specific example, I remember a time when my mother was confined to a wheel chair with a full leg cast that went from her toes to around her waist. It was a cold winter night in upstate New York and eight of us lived in a small house with less than 800 square feet of regular living space. Our home was on an isolated and rural road where my father was able to exercise more abusive control than would be possible if we had lived in the more populated neighborhoods nearby. To make a long story short, that night my father came home early, unusual in itself, and started his usual abusive antics of violence. The evening culminated in frostbitten darkness with my father beating my mother and throwing her out of her wheel chair and into a snowbank with only a nightgown and her leg cast to cover her. He locked the house door and beat the daylights out of all of us because we wanted to help my mother. Through the foot high snow, my mother crawled and dragged herself the quarter mile or so to the neighbor's house and found shelter. These events were frequent occurrences and for the longest time I thought they were normal. When I finally figured out that they were not quite normal I figured that I was somehow to blame. Eventually I came to see that my family experiences represented all of the evils of a mini-dictatorship--of a "marketplace" subject to an intolerable monopoly of power.

I don't reveal this story because I think it is unusual, rather I think it is all too typical of the negative experience of monopoly power that many of us have. The point is that we are all shaped by our personal experiences and our understanding of law and of economics will be affected by such experiences. For me, my many experiences as a child revealed the need for competing sources of power, of a metaphorical market structure that hindered if not defeated the power of market monopoly; political dictatorship; parental abuse. I came to believe that the marketplace, the metaphor of competition and of individual liberty, was vitally important to the exercise of freedom and free will. At the same time, I realized that all people, my mother, my brothers and sisters, all people are special. Being a human being means you should not be subjected to unwarranted abuse or coercion, that your failure to be educated, your lack of resources, your inability to control wealth, should not deny you the legal and humane claim to scarce social resources. It taught me that you cannot reduce human dignity to simple cost calculating numbers. It also revealed to me that human dignity cannot be treated by emotionless and inhumane analogies to nuisance law, to condemnation proceedings, or to simple minded cost and benefit analysis.

For me, government programs have always been essential. The government has represented an alternative source of power for protecting people from the coercive abuse of private individuals, groups, or businesses; just as private sources of wealth and power protect individuals from the potential abuse of an all too powerful state. The government has an active role to play in protecting freedom, individual liberty, and human dignity. We cannot simply endorse theories that dehumanize the individual, that deny the legitimate claims of the poor and disenfranchised. As much as I admire the spontaneous social order and liberating features of the marketplace, I cannot endorse a theory such as that offered by Judge Posner; and, I cannot endorse a person that finds himself unable to clearly and unequivocally renounce the most outrageous consequences of the theory he offers. I believe that the writings of Adam Smith and the traditions of free market theory support my humanistic approach to law and economics--I do not believe Judge Posner can accurately make the same claim.

26. For a detailed discussion of the assumptions and values of neoclassical economics see Malloy, 'Adam Smith', supra note 2, at 242-44; Malloy, *Law and Economics*, supra note 2, at ch. 2 & 3.

27. See, e.g., Minda, 'Toward a More 'Just' Economics of Justice--A Review Essay', 10 *Cardozo. L. Rev.* 1855 (1989); Baker, 'Posner's Privacy Mystery and the Failure of Economic Analysis of Law', 12 *Ga. L. Rev.* 475 (1978); Baker, 'The Ideology of the Economic Analysis of Law', 5 *J. Phil. & Pub. Aff.* 3 (1975); Buchanan, 'Good Economics--Bad Law', 60 *Va. L.*

Rev. 483 (1974); Dworkin, 'Is Wealth A Value?', 9 *J. Legal Stud.* 191 (1980); Kronman, 'Wealth Maximization as a Normative Principle', 9 *J. Legal Stud.* 227 (1980); Leff, 'Economic Analysis of Law: Some Realism About Nominalism', 60 *Va. L. Rev.* 451 (1974); Michalman, 'A Comment on Some Uses and Abuses of Economics in Law', 46 *U. Chi. L. Rev.* 307 (1979); West 'Authority, Autonomy, and Choice: The Role of Consent in the Moral and Political Visions of Franz Kafka and Richard Posner', 99 *Harv. L. Rev.* 384 (1985).

28. R. Posner, *Justice*, supra note 4.

29. Id. at 76.

30. Id. at 84-85.

31. Id. at 86. What is most interesting and disturbing about Posner's position on slavery is that he still justifies it. In a day and age when almost all civilized societies have rejected slavery, Judge Posner presents a theory that provides a justification for it. In so doing he confirms the importance of continuing a debate on this issue.

32. Posner, 'Revisited', supra note 21.

33. R. Posner, *Justice* supra note 4, at 85.

34. See M. Shelley, *Frankenstein, or the Modern Prometheus* (1818).

35. Wealth maximization of a *conversation of exclusion*. It offers scientific pretensions and economic jargon as a means of excluding other forms of social discourse. It reduces people to, and human existence to, imaginary variables for calculation. In this mythical world 'mystics' rule as only they are able to derive the proper quantifiers, select the appropriate input variables, and decipher the mysterious outcomes. I think E. F. Schumacher makes insightful of the extensive efforts to reduce all human behavior and rights to market formulations. Schumacher says that in 'the market':

Everything is equated with everything else. To equate things means to give them a price and thus make them exchangeable. To the extent that economic thinking is based on the market, it takes the sacredness out of life, because there can be nothing sacred in something that has a price. Not surprisingly, therefore, if economic thinking pervades the whole of society, even simple non-economic values like beauty, health, or cleanliness can survive only if they prove to be 'economic.'

To press non-economic values into the framework of the economic calculus, economists use the method of cost/benefit analysis...[I]t is a procedure by which the higher is reduced to the level of the lower and the priceless is given a price. It can therefore never serve to clarify the situation and lead to an enlightened decision. All it can do is lead to self-deception or the deception of others; for to undertake to measure the immeasurable is absurd and constitutes but an elaborate method of moving from preconceived notions to foregone conclusions; all one has to do to obtain the desired result is to impute suitable values to the immeasurable costs and benefits. The logical absurdity, however, is not the greatest fault of the undertaking; what is worse, and destructive of civilization, is the pretense that everything has a price or, in other words, that money is the highest of all values.

E.F. Schumacher, *Small is Beautiful--Economics as if People Mattered* 45-46 (1973).

36. See generally Malloy, 'Moral Judgment', supra note 2.

37. Friedman, 'Free Speech', supra note 14, at 7. See also M. Friedman, *Freedom*, supra note 14. In this book Friedman gives us more insight into his views. Friedman comments:

Viewed as a means to the end of political freedom, economic arrangements are important because of their effect on the concentration or dispersion of power. The kind of economic organization that provides economic freedom directly, namely, competitive capitalism, also promotes political freedom because it separates economic power from political power and in this way enables the one to offset the other....

History suggests only that capitalism is a necessary condition of political freedom. Clearly it is not a sufficient condition. Fascist Italy and fascist Spain, Germany at various times in the last seventy years, Japan before World Wars I and II, czarist Russia in the decades before World War I--are all societies that cannot conceivably be described as politically free. Yet, in each, private enterprise was the dominant form of economic organization.

Id. at 9-10.

Syracuse University, College of Law

RICHARD A. POSNER

LAW AND ECONOMICS *IS* MORAL

Thank you Dean Bodensteiner, Mr. Henke, Professor Malloy, ladies and gentlemen. It is a great pleasure to be here. My real name is Doctor Frankenstein. I am very proud of my monster and I hope to say some words in defense of him. Actually, the differences between Professor Malloy and me are, I think, largely semantic. And the semantic differences are rooted in an aesthetic one. Some people like to talk in moral terms--like to use a moral vocabulary. They like to denounce slavery, and the Nazis, and the Ku Klux Klan; it makes them feel good to denounce the causes, the organizations, the activities, and the ideologies of which there are, after all, no present-day defenders in respectable society. That to me is not a very interesting activity. I find it more interesting to explore the ambiguities in these terms. What exactly do you *mean* by slavery? Is it really the case that slavery is always and everywhere immoral?

I am going to say four things, and I hope they will serve adequately as my side of this debate. First, I am going to offer you my view of what Adam Smith stands for. Second, I will explain what I stand for or think I stand for. I will then show how wealth maximization--the Frankenstein Monster--fits in to what I will be saying about Smith and about myself. I will close, if time permits, by taking some whacks at natural rights.

There are two intellectual dimensions to Adam Smith that have ensured his historical significance. The first is his opposition to mercantilism, and the second is his discovery and articulation of the invisible-hand mechanism. Mercantilism, which was the dominant economic ideology of the eighteenth century, is the view that a nation's proper objective is to maximize its gold reserves. This is done by trying to maximize exports, by conquests, and by other ways of getting foreigners to buy your goods, while minimizing your own imports so that you have a positive balance of trade and foreigners have to give you gold because you are selling them more goods than you are taking back. Mercantilism struck the leaders of eighteenth century European nations as the self-evident way of maximizing a nation's welfare. Adam Smith showed that, in fact, it had the opposite effect. It tended to impoverish a nation; a nation with a positive balance of trade was manufacturing goods for consumers in other countries and getting in return a largely worthless hunk of metal. There is still great mercantilist sentiment in the countries of

R.P. Malloy and J. Evensky: Adam Smith and the Philosophy of Law and Economics, 167–177.

the world. It is an important factor in American public policy. It is behind a lot of the hysteria about our negative balance of trade, and behind pressures for restricting imports. It is fueled, this mercantilist policy, by the self-interest of particular economic groups--for example, workers and employers in declining American industries. Adam Smith was intensely conscious of the element of self-interest in the mercantilist philosophy--not the self-interest of the citizenry as a whole, but the self-interest of particular manufacturers and workers. Mercantilism implies a *dirigiste* state--a powerful central government that regulates trade, has a large army and navy, and generally throws its weight around internationally. Adam Smith was hostile to all of these things and in consequence was hostile to large government. He was a small government man. So number one is Adam Smith's anti-mercantilism and corresponding hostility to governments, which he recognized as frequently the captives of special-interest groups. Second, and from a scientific standpoint more interesting, is Adam Smith's demonstration that economic activity can be coordinated without central government planning and regulation. This is the invisible hand--the equilibrium of independent producers and consumers that ensures, for example, for a vast city like New York, a daily supply of all the products that people purchase there without any government going around and placing orders and directing producers and transportation companies, grocers, etc., to make sure there is enough milk, enough coffee, enough scallions, and so forth, every day for New York consumers. In showing this Adam Smith was providing a complementary demonstration to his opposition to mercantilism, because he was showing not only that big government was a bad thing but that small government was entirely feasible and was consistent with a smooth-running economic system coordinated through the free market. There is a Newtonian cast to Adam Smith's invisible hand portrait of the economy, a balance that resembles the balance among all those heavenly bodies which somehow are kept the right distance from each other by the equilibrium of opposing centripetal and centrifugal forces. Adam Smith, like most eighteenth century intellectuals, was suffused with the type of thinking that had been responsible for Newtonian physics.

The demonstration that mercantilism is wealth minimizing, and the demonstration that an economic system can operate without central direction, are, I think, the basic contributions of Adam Smith to economic thought and public policy. He made a number of other economic points that remain of enduring importance; there is also, as Professor Malloy suggested, a great deal more to Smith than economics. He was a distinguished moral philosopher, and he also wrote on jurisprudence. He was a Scotsman, with some typical Scottish qualities such as hostility to ostentation. All these veins of thought are in Smith's writings. In the diversity of his interests, as well as in the specific form of his economic thought, he again resembles Newton, who as many of you know had a profound interest in theology and also in astrology. We do not think that the meaning of Newtonian physics is inextricably entwined with Newton's theological and astrological views. We can similarly distinguish Adam Smith's contribution to economic science from his moral, philosophical, and ethical views. Whether they are right or wrong, they are not organic to the durable part of Adam Smith's thought, the part that has shaped not only modern economics in the scientific, the descriptive sense, but also the modern free-market position that is hostile to mercantile policies--hostile to tariffs and the like.

To ask whether if Adam Smith were alive today would he support this or that view seems to me utterly fatuous. Adam Smith lived 200 years ago, the product of enormously different historical circumstances. If he were alive today he would have 200 more years of experience and he might have forgotten what he knew so clearly in 1776. The game of taking famous dead people and listing them on your side in current debates over public policy is, I have come to think, a chump's game, whether you do it with the founders, or, as some years ago a professor did to Justice, now Chief Justice, Rehnquist, with Herman Melville, author of (among other great works) *Billy Budd*. The implication of the attack was that if Herman Melville were alive today and writing about law, he would cast Chief Justice Rehnquist in a villainous role. We do not know how people who are the product of different cultures would think about our current problems. This by the way is one of the decisive objections to originalism in constitutional interpretation. We just do not know what people like Hamilton and Madison would think if they were alive today. To ask what Hamilton would have thought of "Dial-a-Porn" just is not a very fruitful exercise.

So let us put Adam Smith aside and talk about me. I will give you my credo. I consider myself to be a pragmatic economic libertarian. Let me explain those words, taking them in reverse order. By libertarian, I mean someone who believes in minimum government--as little government as possible. I mean someone who is suspicious of public intervention, who thinks that people should look to themselves rather than to their government for their happiness, their future, their success in life. I mean a practitioner of laissez faire in a general sense, not in a literal sense. I mean a small-government person. That to me is what a libertarian is, although, as Professor Malloy has explained, libertarians come in all stripes and some would not consider me one of them.

The reason I affixed the adjective 'economic' is not that I am protective only of economic liberty--in fact, I do not see any sharp distinction between economic liberty on the one hand and personal or political liberties on the other hand--but that I use economic theory to try to figure out what the appropriate boundaries of the minimum state are. Basically my view is that the role of government is to intervene and correct, the best it can, serious market failures. I will give two examples. First, when people engage in a career as thieves they obviously do not consider the costs they impose on the victims of their crimes, costs to the rest of society, costs to the taxpayer, costs in self-protection--in alarm systems, locks, and all the rest. This kind of inconsiderate conduct that imposes costs on other people provides an apt occasion for governmental intervention. Indeed, the prevention of private aggression within the country, and the protection of the country from foreign aggressors, constitute the core governmental functions and define a truly minimum government, what is sometimes called the 'nighwatchman' state. There are also more subtle forms of market failure that provide occasions for government intervention. One of these is the general area of education. Suppose there is a promising child--intelligent, energetic, and so forth--but the child has very poor parents. It would not be feasible for the parents or the child to finance the child's education by promising to pay the financier out of the child's future earnings. The enforcement of such a promise would lead us into a system of slavery (for what if the child defaulted?). Because of these difficulties, it is very hard for society to realize the economic potential of children without some public intervention for education. This does not necessarily imply public schools; education may be as well or better furnished through a system of subsidized private education. Government intervention appears to be indicated here for the additional reason that education confers benefits on more than the recipient. Educated people make it easier for others to transact with them.

My third term, pragmatic, comes from my opening remark about not being enthusiastic about moral discourse. I do not derive my economic libertarian views from a foundational moral philosophy such as the philosophy of Kant, or Locke's philosophy of natural rights, or utilitarianism, or anything of that sort. I regard moral philosophy as a weak field, a field in disarray, a field in which consensus is impossible to achieve in our society. I do not think it provides a promising foundation for a philosophy of government. You can if you want describe wealth maximization or libertarianism or laissez faire as moral philosophies. My point is only that I do not intend to try to derive my free-market views from something more fundamental, more rigorously philosophical. And the consequence of this lack of foundations is that I am not dogmatically attached to any of my free-market views. I do think the minimum state defined by the economic analysis of market failure is the state that works best to achieve the common goals of most people in the world. I think that in the disintegration of the communist states and the failures of socialism in a variety of noncommunity countries such as Argentina, Israel, France, and Greece, we find strong pragmatic support for the concept of limited government--as we do also in the failures of many of our own social programs, the experiments of a free society. But if you can show me that socialism really works well and achieves more of what most of us want than capitalism, then I shall be happy to give socialism a close look.

How does wealth maximization fit into the picture that I have presented of Smith and of myself? It is merely a way of operationalizing, of making concrete, the idea of economic libertarianism. It is an analytic tool. What it does primarily--and that is one of the things that disturbs Professor Malloy--is strip away distributive considerations. It strips away the complications introduced in public policy analysis when you think of dollars as being worth different amounts, in some ethical sense, depending on who has each dollar.

I will give you an example of how a distributive consideration--the attempt to weigh dollars according to who holds them--complicates public policy analysis, and how wealth maximization provides a cleaner approach. The example I will give is monopoly. If you have studied antitrust or cognate fields you know that the technique of monopoly is to restrict output, for by doing so the monopolist drives up market price. The monopolist thus creates an *artificial* scarcity of goods. The result of raising price over a smaller output is to increase the profits of the monopolist, and of course to reduce the wealth of consumers because they now have to pay high prices. There is thus a transfer of wealth from consumers to the monopolist producer or the cartel of producers. If you ask what is the public policy significance of this transfer of wealth you quickly get into what I regard as essentially insoluble problems in the interpersonal comparison of worth or desert. Should consumers be wealthier than producers? Who are these consumers? Maybe they are the idle rich and the goods they are buying are luxury toys for the rich. The producers perhaps employ worthy poor people to manufacture these baubles. Maybe it is a good thing that wealth is being redistributed from these consumers to producers; or maybe not. Maybe the consumers are poorer, and maybe poorer people deserve some break relative to the rich. That is a complicated subject--how we decide how income should be equalized. It is the socialist prescription, which Professor Malloy is rightly troubled by. But the economist looking at the monopoly problem will tend to say, let us forget about the transfer of wealth from consumers to producers. Let us treat a dollar as worth the same in the hands of the consumer as in the hands of the producer. So the impoverishment of the consumer by the monopolist is offset by the enrichment of the monopolist. Let us forget about that. There is still a very serious objection to monopoly. When the monopolist creates his artificial scarcity of goods, some consumers continue to buy the monopolist's product at a higher price, but others are deflected to substitute products. They reconsider the alternatives to the monopolist's product now that product is more costly. Some of them will substitute one of the alternatives. The alternatives, however, look attractive only because the monopolist is charging a high price. If the alternative products are being sold by competitive producers, the cost to society of producing these goods may be higher than the cost of the monopolist's goods. So one has an inefficient reallocation of resources; consumers' wants are satisfied at higher overall social cost. In addition, if you allow monopolization--if you dangle this pot of gold consisting of monopoly profits in front of sellers--they will invest resources in becoming monopolists. These resources (other than those devoted to obtaining monopoly by innovation or other means that benefit consumers) are like the resources that thieves invest in their burglar tools and way of life; they are sterile investments, made to effect redistributions of wealth. So, as I say, even if you abstract from all distributive considerations and you consider that sellers are as good as consumers and money in their hands is worth the same as money in the consumer's hands, you can still have an economic argument against monopoly, an argument for government intervention, and I think a more powerful argument precisely because it abstracts from highly controversial distributive considerations.

It is the same in the accident field. There are a number of colorful nineteenth century cases involving damage to crops caused by fires set by locomotive sparks. The question for law was, how to adjust this destructive interaction between railroads and farmers? One answer is to look at the cost that these railroad fires are inflicting, the costs in burned-up crops, and then see what it would cost if railroads were induced by the threat of tort liability to purchase spark-arresting equipment. If the spark-arresting equipment would cost less than the expected damage to crops, and also less than the cost to the farmers of growing fire-resistant crops or of not using their land at all, then we would say, well here is a case for government to intervene and maximize social wealth by imposing liability on the railroad. That is our tort system in a nutshell.

Now it is easy, as one casts one's mind across the entire range of public policy from a wealth-maximization standpoint, to find areas of uncertainty. Should a state pass a law requiring motorcyclists to wear helmets? As a first approximation, the wealth maximizer might say that if the motorcyclist falls on his head and breaks it, the harm is to the motorcyclist himself and he can balance that harm against the cost of buying a helmet. But in the second round of analysis one may wish to point out that many of the medical costs of American society are paid for today by government through the medical tax deduction, through Medicaid and Medicare, and hence, are not fully financed by the beneficiaries of medical care. So some of the costs of this injured motorcyclist will in fact be borne elsewhere. These are external costs analytically similar to that imposed by thieves. So maybe there is a case for government intervention. But on the other hand, maybe to intervene continually in order to correct previous interventions is wrong. Maybe what we really need is a system of medical care that makes people pay for their own care. If you pay for your own injuries there is no reason as a matter of wealth maximization to forbid you to behave in a self-destructive fashion.

The point I wish to make is that once you abstract from controversial issues having to do with the distribution of wealth and the appropriate role of paternalism in government decision making--once you focus on the allocative effects of government policies--you have a powerful analytic tool with which to derive a system of optimal government, a system more limited than what we have, though more extensive than the classical laissez faire state urged by the nineteenth century English economists. But is the system that one comes up with immoral? In the passages from *The Economics of Justice* that Professor Malloy quoted and in much else that he could quote from my writings, I have wrestled with this issue and I have pointed out, not by way of reluctant concession but in a curious and concerned spirit, that the unflinching pursuit of wealth maximization will indeed lead to results that would be widely regarded as immoral or, at the least, highly controversial. One of these that is very much in the news is surrogate motherhood. In the first round of analysis, which is not likely to be the last round, the wealth maximizer sees in surrogate motherhood a contract between willing buyers--the father-to-be and his wife, and a willing seller, the woman who agrees to be the surrogate mother, to carry the fetus fathered by the husband to term and then give the child up to the father and his wife. Now clearly in the enforcement of such a contract there are substantial issues that a wealth maximizer would be concerned with. For example, should specific performance be used to enforce these contracts? But with regard to the basic issue, the propriety of the contract, it strikes the wealth maximizer as a perfectly sensible, because wealth-maximizing, arrangement. There are many couples in which the wife is infertile yet the couple want to have a child. And there are many women who, for a price, are willing to bear a child for another couple and give it up to them upon birth. Although there have been of course some famous controversies arising from surrogate motherhood--the most famous being the *Baby M* case in New Jersey--in fact most surrogate mother contracts are carried out uneventfully and everybody seems to be happy. So the wealth maximizer is apt to say--I would say--that surrogate motherhood is fine. But if you go a few steps beyond that--if you ask, for example, whether people should be able to sell babies--the analysis get trickier. Suppose a woman conceives by accident and carries the baby to term and does not want to keep it. Should she be allowed to charge a price if people want to adopt it? I think this is a form of transaction that would be wealth maximizing and would repair a serious imbalance in the supply and demand for babies for adoption. We have in this country an enormous production of illegitimate births and, on the other hand, a terrible shortage of babies for adoption. This is clearly a disequilibrium, and it results in part from refusing to allow an explicit trade in babies. But this proposal is so disturbing to people, so shocking, that I have never advocated baby selling beyond an experiment that would consist of allowing adoption agencies to take a portion of the fee they charge to adoptive parents and pass it on to pregnant women as an inducement to the women to carry their fetus to term rather than have an abortion. With an experiment like that, we might test the depth of the moral concern in baby selling. But I do not deny that there *is* that moral concern, and I do not suggest that wealth maximization *should* override it. And similarly with the quotation Professor Malloy gave about racial exclusionary zoning. It would be possible in a system unflinchingly dedicated to wealth maximization to come up with results that would be deeply, perhaps universally, offensive. That obviously would and should give one pause.

What I have particularly emphasized in my writings and what Professor Malloy has not mentioned at all is that wealth maximization is an especially useful tool for guiding common law adjudication. I gave you the example of locomotive-spark cases. We can think more systematically about contract law, property law, tort law, and the branch of criminal law that comes down to us from the common law, in wealth maximization terms. Judges are reluctant to get enmeshed in distributive controversies, see prosperity and efficiency as relatively neutral social goals and ones within the judicial capacity to implement, and therefore, I think, consciously or unconsciously focus their efforts on trying to achieve efficient adjustments in these areas.

As Professor Malloy emphasized, the wealth maximization perspective is particularly disturbing to people who have strong sense of natural rights. The whole economic vocabulary is so removed from considerations of natural rights that it seems the economist must be missing something fundamental. I do not question the depth of moral sentiment in areas where that sentiment may be opposed to efficient solutions to social problems. But I do deny that natural rights provide a coherent, cogent, sensible, alternative method of framing questions and of public policy. The natural rights view that Professor Malloy alludes to and that I think remains most influential in current natural rights thinking in American law is the view of natural rights that comes from John Locke. It starts from the notion that before there was society, when people were in a state of nature, they had a natural liberty to do what they wanted, and that society should be viewed as a compact in which people surrender just so much of their own liberty as is necessary to protect the equal liberty of the other people in society. For Locke, the social contract imagined in such a way leads to the minimum nighwatchman state, basically a police force. But in modern thinking, theorists often will expand the range of natural rights, as Professor Malloy attempted to do, and come up with a larger conception of the state. On the other hand, Professor Richard Epstein, whom Malloy mentioned, uses the

Lockean view to derive a sense of minimum government smaller than even I think appropriate.

I do not think natural rights talk really gets anywhere at all. It is extremely porous. Almost any public policy, however interventionist, socialistic--what have you--can be justified in natural rights lingo. For example, if we have a substantial program of redistributing wealth to the poor financed by progressive income taxes, we could call this basically a police measure designed to keep the poor quiet. This is like paying for police, and since the rich have most of the property they should pay most of the cost of any general police measure. Almost every socialist nostrum can be defended as the sort of police measure that, within a Lockean system of natural rights, is a proper function of government.

Natural rights theory also, although often embellished in democratic jargon, is fundamentally anti-democratic; it greatly curtails the role of democracy and representative government. The more rights people have, the less the scope for the people's representatives to deliberate on public policy issues. In some versions of natural rights theory, where the scope of government and the activities of government are highly predetermined, there really is no role for democratic debate except to pick the individuals to administer the machinery of the state. The machinery itself is determined by the natural rights theory. You have to have urban renewal or you cannot have urban renewal, or you have to have a large army, or you have to regulate television or cannot regulate television. If you decide exactly what you have to have, and what you cannot have, in government, there is very little left for elected officials to do.

Third, I do not think nature in fact is an important source of human wealth, and therefore it is difficult to criticize government when it takes something away that we had in nature. In nature we were glorified monkeys running around and throwing stones at each other. The wealth of society is a function of social interaction, making it hard to have a 'natural' benchmark for the allocation of rights. Slaves in society are better off than free people in the state of nature.

And, fourth, and most basically, I do not know why natural rights or nature *should* be the benchmark for answering public policy questions. Why nature? Locke had religious reasons for believing in natural rights. He was a devout Christian and much of his work is actually devoted to the exegesis of the Bible, from which he got many of his views. Adam Smith was not a religious person, and although there is natural rights talk in Adam Smith, it does not appear to have any theological source.

So natural rights as a concept seems to me to be porous, groundless, perverse in many ways, and basically useless; natural rights talk in the concrete is sentimental, contradictory, and also pretty useless. Professor Malloy said, for example, that slavery is wrong *in all circumstances*. It is easy to say things like that. We do not have slavery in the United States. We do not have a big slavery lobby. If you denounce slavery in the United States, you are on pretty safe ground. I happened to read recently the graduation address of the president of Yale University. He said you young people going out into the world would have to deal with very difficult problems, show a lot of moral courage, and therefore he wanted to address a significant moral question. This turned out to be American Negro slavery, and he talked about what a terrible system it was. He gave many examples. Everything he said was right, but to use that as the touchstone of a lecture on moral courage seemed very dubious to me, since there was no one in the audience, no one in Yale University, indeed no one in the United States as far as I know, who wishes to restore slavery. But when one speaks of slavery as being wrong in all circumstances one betrays a historical naivete and a semantic simplicity. One can easily point to historical circumstances in which slavery was not wrong, slavery was an improvement. If you go back to the earliest times of human warfare, you will find that the practice of the victors was to kill the captives whom they took in battle, and if they were lucky enough to conquer an enemy village or an enemy state they would kill the entire male population and take the women as concubines. Then someone had the bright idea of putting captives to work rather than killing them. When slavery took the place of genocide in warfare, that was a moral advance.

What is true is that slavery is abhorrent in modern society for a wide variety of reasons, and indeed in the society we have had for the last several hundred years, including the period when we had slavery in this country. But what is slavery? Slavery is the name for forms of involuntary servitude that we disapprove of. There is plenty of involuntary servitude; if we approve of it, we just do not call it slavery. We do not say, for example, that children are the slaves of their parents. We do not say that prisoners who are forced to work in prison are the slaves of the United States. (There are, in fact, almost a million people in American jails and prisons today and many of them are required to work.) We do not say, well in America we do not have as many slaves as we did in 1860, but we have several hundred thousand slaves. When people volunteer for Army duty, even in peacetime, they are not free to leave at will; they are subject to involuntary servitude. So it seems that while you can say, and you can feel good saying, that slavery is always and everywhere bad, and wrong, and evil, the truth is that many forms of involuntary servitude are approved in our society and all societies, and there have been times when far more extensive forms of involuntary servitude were moral advances.

There is a reason why people who like a moral vocabulary are prone to focus on cases, like slavery, as to which there is a moral consensus. The reason is that when one gets to contested moral questions the power of moral discourse runs out. When one talks about abortion, or when one talks about welfare rights, or when one talks about the appropriate provision for the retarded, or when one talks about surrogate motherhood, or affirmative action, or any one of a dozen other highly controversial moral issues, moral discourse turns out not to provide any sort of solution to these problems. It merely provides a vocabulary in which people can express views that have deep emotional roots. While I do not deny the force of those views and I do not deny that government policy makers should take them into account, I do not think they are analytically fruitful. Wealth maximization is analytically fruitful and I think it has a large, although not an unrestricted, domain of application to law and to public policy in general. Thank you.

United States Court of Appeals for the Seventh Circuit

ROBIN PAUL MALLOY

THE LIMITS OF SCIENCE IN LEGAL DISCOURSE-- A REPLY TO POSNER

In the course of its slow development in the eighteenth and early nineteenth centuries the study of economic and social phenomena was guided in the choice of its methods in the main by the nature of the problems it had to face.... Students of political economy could describe it alternatively as a branch of science or of moral or social philosophy without the least qualms whether their subject was scientific or philosophical.

During the first half of the nineteenth century a new attitude made its appearance. The term *science* came more and more to be confined to the physical and biological disciplines which at the same time began to claim for themselves a special rigorousness and certainty which distinguishes them from all others. Their success was such that they soon came to exercise an extraordinary fascination on those working in other fields, who rapidly began to imitate their teaching and vocabulary. Thus, the tyranny commenced which the methods and technique of the sciences in the narrow sense of the term have ever since exercised over the other subjects.[1] *F.A. Hayek*

I wish to make several comments in response to Judge Posner, and I will first address comments made concerning Adam Smith. Adam Smith, as I assert, is relevant to today's discussion because his work is the foundation of many of our society's underlying assumptions about law and social order. Furthermore, as I pointed out in my *University of Kansas Law Review* article, Judge Posner erroneously cites Adam Smith for support of wealth maximization in his own work.[2] But this is not the essence of my response. First, let me respond to Judge Posner's linking of Adam Smith, John Locke, Richard Epstein, and myself in connection with the concept of the social contract. It is true that John Locke developed a theory of social contract that has played a significant role in many discussions of the proper role and function of the state. The social contract theory, however, was expressly rejected by Adam Smith and plays no part in my analysis of law and economics.[3] Thus, Judge Posner's imagined criticism of me on this score is misplaced.

Second, Judge Posner asks us to question the relevance of Adam Smith as an economic scientist some two hundred years after his work on *The Wealth of Nations*.[4] As an economic scientist, it is true that Adam Smith, like the other classical economists and Karl Marx, was wrong in relying on a labor theory of value. Despite the errors of classical economists

R.P. Malloy and J. Evensky: Adam Smith and the Philosophy of Law and Economics, 179–185.

such philosophers as Adam Smith are still relevant. The fact is that Adam Smith and Karl Marx give us useful insight into conceptions of organizing society, of thinking about rights, and of thinking about the allocation of scarce resources. Just as many people still find Marx's philosophy useful, I too find Adam Smith's philosophy useful. The mere fact that a source is from the past does not discredit the source nor its usefulness--the common law, after all, is a system entirely based on reference to prior and sometimes ancient doctrines and opinions.

I am certainly not the only person to find Adam Smith's philosophy of continuing importance. Two recent Nobel Prize winning economists, Friedrich Hayek[5] and Milton Friedman,[6] rely to a great extent on the work of Adam Smith. For them, Smith's original writing two hundred years ago is still important and vital, not to find out what Smith would say if he were here today and confronted with a particular issue or problem, but to say, there is a framework here that is useful for thinking about today's pressing social issues. I think this is an important distinction.

It is a distinction that is also relevant to the original intentions argument alluded to by Judge Posner.[7] We do not (or should not) for instance, study what Thomas Jefferson said about a particular law two hundred years ago in hopes of applying that 'original intention' to the application of a law today. Today's problems may have been totally unpredictable by Jefferson and there would be no telling what he would have said if confronted with today's problems. On the other hand, we can still study Thomas Jefferson's theory of government to find out if he offers us any useful insights that are helpful today in understanding a proper organization of society. So there is a distinction that I think is important concerning what I am doing. I am not just trying to ask 'what would Adam Smith say today?' I am trying to find out if our social discourse can be assisted by going back to Smith's original work. I think it can.

My interest in law and semiotics gives rise to another important distinction between my work in law and economics and that of Judge Posner.[8] This distinction pertains to my focus on the metaphorical aspects of economics as well as the scientific. I think it is accurate to say the Judge Posner's work on the relationship between law and economics is predominantly focused on the scientific application of economic analysis to questions of whether particular legal rules are efficient and wealth maximizing. In contrast to Judge Posner, I think it is vitally important to consider the analytical power of economics as a metaphorical process for engaging in a discourse on the proper relationship between individuals, the state, and the community.

I would like to illustrate this distinction between economics as science and economics as metaphor by considering Judge Posner's example of the problem of monopolies. As Judge Posner presents issues of monopoly, he considers them as economically undesirable for 'scientific' reasons. Monopoly is harmful because monopoly is inefficient and inefficiency results in a less than optimal use of scarce resources and thus the inability of society to make full use of the resources available to it. In addition to this scientific analysis of the inefficiency of monopoly, there is an important metaphorical critique of monopoly. This metaphorical analysis is consistent not only with my earlier work but also with the works of Adam Smith, Friedrich Hayek and Milton Friedman. Using economics in the metaphorical sense, monopoly is detrimental because it represents a unified dominating source of power that is able to inhibit the liberty of individuals precisely because there are no competitive and counterbalancing sources of effective power. (For a personal example *see supra* footnote 25 of Malloy, *Is Law and Economics Moral?--Humanistic Economics and a Classical Liberal Critique of Posner's Economic Analysis*). In contrast to monopoly, market theory tells us that if you have competition, if you have competing forces, if you have many capitalists and a democratic government, you can protect individual freedom because each of those sources of power acts as a check on the abuse of the exercise of power by any one person, group or organization. Such an environment of tension, of interaction and competition, protects individuals and the problem with monopoly is not so much inefficiency as it is the concentration of power which can potentially destroy all freedom; be it destroyed efficiently or inefficiently.

Turning away from the science/metaphor distinctions between my work in law and economics and the work of Judge Posner, let us now consider the matter of moral discourse and first principles. It seems that people have historically engaged in moral discourse and that we might as well try and figure out how to make that discourse more valuable. While economics can be a helpful analytical tool or metaphor there are certain moral questions that cannot be answered by economic science; these questions I consider matters of first principles. We ask first principle questions, for example, when we ask, 'Do people have a right to housing; do people have a right to a minimal level of medical care?'[9] Economics does not tell us the answer to these difficult first questions. If, however, we can come to some agreement as a community concerning a particular first principle then economics is a powerful tool and method that can help us analyze alternative approaches to solving the moral and social problems that confront us. If we choose option 'A' as a means of providing housing, what are the likely consequences? Who will actually end up paying? What will be the distributional effects? Where is the tax ultimately hidden? Is option 'A' better than option 'B'--the discussion and selection between all these choices is helped by the powerful scientific and metaphorical principles of economics but the first principle choice of what we should be doing in the first instance is not helped by the science of economics.[10]

My last point of discussion in this brief reply to Judge Posner, is to point out that there was in his presentation, and I think there is in general, a mistaken portrayal of wealth maximization as not requring moral decisions. Despite the lack of an express moral dialogue in wealth maximization discourse, the movement to a model or a metaphor of economics as a science incorporates within it many assumptions and many moral choices. In the brief time that I have, I will give you two examples of the underlying moral choices reflected in the concept of wealth maximization.[11] First, consider that a neoclassical market model operates on the assumption of rational individuals acting in their own self-interest, that is, making choices that are wealth maximizing as to themselves. Furthermore it is assumed that the sum of all these individual choices, in the aggregate, results in the best use of resources for the community. As such, the market model of neoclassical economics and of wealth maximization defers to and legitimizes the aggregation of numerous individual choices concerning the way in which we divide our scarce social resources. We may agree with this affirmation of resource allocation. We may think that this is the best way to do things but many people today would disagree. Many people believe that experts, that social planners or central committees should decide on the appropriate use and distribution of scarce social resources. For them property should not be controlled nor resources allocated based on the aggregate determination of individuals acting with wealth in the marketplace. While I may think it is important to focus on the individual, the point of this example is to demonstrate that a moral choice has been made. A moral choice has been made concerning the validation of individual choices and power involving the use and distribution of such basic and valuable resources as the air, the water, and mineral rights.

A second example of moral decision in wealth maximization discourse is its validation of past distributions of income and wealth. This is reflected in the neoclassical economists' market model by virtue of efficient outcomes being judged in terms of casting dollars as votes. People with wealth cast their votes in the marketplace and move resources and goods towards their 'highest' or most valued use. In so doing, if I start out with lots and lots of resources, I have more votes, thus my particular definition of highest use is more persuasive. The theory of wealth maximization, thus, validates the outcomes generated and defined as highest in value by those that already have the most votes to cast.

Now, one can take the position that this market model is the best that we can do even if it is imperfect but the mere acceptance of this model is a moral decision to accept the process by which past distributions and wealth accumulations occurred. Even Adam Smith, however, recognized that law emerged in a socio-historical context.[12] According to Smith, property rights under law emerge in order to enhance the power of people that already have property to the detriment of those who do not have property.[13] Thus, even Smith recognized the distributional problems of the market just as do many current members of the conference on Critical Legal Studies. As a consequence, I think it is wrong to view wealth maximization as not making a first set of moral decisions and value judgments. And this erroneous view is compounded when we go around talking about issues in terms of a language of efficiency and cost and benefit analysis. Such a form of discourse makes it too easy to forget the underlying morality invoked by the theory of wealth maximization. And I think, as a rhetorical matter, this is precisely the goal of wealth maximization discourse--to marginalize and extinguish our conscious cognitive participation in moral decision making.

I think that one of the reasons for the success of Judge Posner's model of wealth maximization is that it allows one to ignore the inherent moral choices being made. Once the model is accepted, one can transform the world and all legal conversation into a mere collection of 'facts' and fact determinations.[14] Legal inquiry becomes a factual attempt to find out what is the most efficient outcome. Legal uncertainty is reduced to a fact discovery process and we are 'allowed' to forget about underlying moral questions. With respect to Judge Posner's example of surrogate motherhood, for example, wealth maximization allows us to engage in a fact sifting process without ever asking the difficult questions raised by feminist jurisprudence and Critical Legal Studies--difficult questions about the woman's role in society and the ability of women to 'freely' engage in a voluntary exchange of this type. We never need to ask how the market and law have historically treated women. Likewise, wealth maximization discourse can ignore the issue of whether Blacks or Hispanics have anything to bargain about when the 'relevant facts' require us to switch to a discourse about upholding contractual bargains. Consequently, when wealth maximization validates the 'voluntary' contract or transaction it simultaneously validates a failure to ask whether some people have been systematically deprived of an opportunity to acquire the wealth and resources necessary to engage in a bargain.

Now, I think that on some of the issues discussed tonight Judge Posner and I may not be so far apart but in many respects I think we are. On the one hand, for instance, we are both engaging in moral discourse; that is, we are both presenting theories of law and economics that embody certain values and moral judgments. It is evident, however, that we not only disagree on the nature of many of these values and judgments but that I prefer to keep these issues in the forefront of my discussion of law and economics while Judge Posner seeks to eliminate such discussions from his wealth maximization discourse. The elimination of these issues from the forum of express debate reduces our ability to comprehend the complex and humanistic nature of both law and economics. Likewise, it unduly restricts the practitioners of wealth maximization by limiting their vocabulary to the "scientific" dimensions of economics which is ill-equipped to handle the first principle conflicts that underlie our most pressing social problems.

NOTES

1. F. Hayek, *The Counter-Revolution of Science: Studies on the Abuse of Reason* 20-21 (1952) [hereinafter Hayek, *Abuse of Reason*]. (Hayek's point is not to argue against science but rather to point out the limits of science and to show how the social sciences have in many ways fallen prey to a scientifc abuse of reason).
2. See Posner, 'Utilitarianism, Economics, and Legal Theory', 8 *J. Legal Stud.* 103, 135-36 (1979).
3. See A. Smith, *Lectures on Jurisprudence* 207, 311-30, 401-07, (R. Meek, D. Raphael & L. Stein eds. 1978) [hereinafter Smith, *Jurisprudence*]. See also Malloy, 'Invisible Hand or Sleight of Hand? Adam Smith, Richard Posner and the Philosophy of Law and Economics', 36 *Kan. L. Rev.* 209, 238-40 (1988) [hereinafter Malloy, 'Adam Smith'].
4. See Malloy, 'The Merits of the Smithian Critique: A Final Word on Smith and Posner', 36 *U. Kan. L. Rev.* 267-74 (1988) [hereinafter Malloy, 'The Merits'].
5. See, e.g., F. Hayek, *The Constitution of Liberty* (1960); Hayek, *Abuse of Reason*, supra note 1; F. Hayek, *Law Legislation and Liberty: Rules and Order* (1973); F. Hayek, *Law, Legislation and Liberty: The Mirage of Social Justice* (1976); F. Hayek, *Law, Legislation and Liberty: The Political Order of a Free People* (1979); F. Hayek, *The Road to Serfdom* (1944); F. Hayek, *The Fatal Conceit: The Errors of Socialism* (1989).
6. See, e.g., M. Friedman, *Essays in Positive Economics* (1953); M. Friedman, *Capitalism and Freedom* (1962); M. Friedman, *Bright Promises, Dismal Performance* (W. Allen, ed. 1983); M. Friedman & R. Friedman, *Free to Choose* (1980); M. Friedman & R. Friedman, *Tyranny of the Status Quo* (1984); Friedman, 'Free Markets and Free Speech', 10 *Harv. J. L. & Pub Pol'y* 1 (1987).
7. See Malloy, 'The Merits', supra note 4, at 270-71.
8. Semiotics, the study of signs, is related to law in that it involves the study of legal discourse. It is a study of the process by which certain forms of legal discourse become accepted as valid and persuasive. As a dynamic process, semiotics investigates the discovery and creation of new forms of legal discourse and of the creation of new forms of legal actions. At the same time, law and semiotics is also concerned with the process by which established forms of legal argument lose their validity and power of persuasion over time. Thus, for example, consider the legal concept of 'caveat emptor.' That legal phrase is a 'sign'--a symbolic representation of an idea and a concept. Law and semiotics is concerned with the nature of such a sign as it is used and understood in legal discourse. Law and economics is also concerned with the dynamic and evolutionary process by which such signs or legal terms go from having a tremendous role in old consumer law cases to a position of relative weakness in a modern day transaction involving similar facts. (Legal 'facts'" themselves are signs in semiotics and one can study the process by which facts are established and dealt with in legal discourse.). For a path breaking book in the area of law and semiotics see R. Kevelson, *The Law as a Sysytem of Signs* (1988). See also Malloy, 'A Sign of the Times--Law and Semiotics: A Review of R. Kevelson's *The Law as a System of Signs*', 64 *Tul. L. Rev.* 211 (1990).
9. See Malloy, 'Equating Human Rights and Property Rights--The Need for Moral Judgment in an Economic Analysis of Law and Social Policy', 47 *Ohio St. L.J.* 163-77 (1968) [hereinafter Malloy, 'Human Rights'] (In this article I raised many of these type questions and argued by example that economics, as a science, is unable to resolve these and many other of our most pressing social problems).

10. See id. See also Malloy, 'The Political Economy of Co-Financing America's Urban Renaissance', 40 *Vand. L. Rev.* 67-134 (1987) (This article addressed this issue and applied my theory of law and economics to a particular context--urban development. The article demonstrated the way in which the theory can be used in analyzing specific social and legal issues.); R. Malloy, *Planning for Serfdom: Legal Economic Discourse and Downtown Development* (1991 University of Pennsylvania Press) (elaborating on similar themes and containing a full discussion of Adam Smith and Classical Liberal Theory).

11. See Malloy, 'Adam Smith', supra note 3, at 242-44. (This part of the article spells out six different major underlying assumptions of neoclassical economics and then details the value judgments at work in each of these assumptions. Furthermore, the article shows how Posner's theory of wealth maximization is essentially and critically linked to the neoclassical economic model, its assumptions, and values.). See also R. Malloy, *Law and Economics: A Comparative Approach to Theory and Practice* Chapters 1-3 (1990).

12. See Malloy, 'Adam Smith', supra note 3, at 216-38. (This part of the article gives detailed references to Smith's work. It details Smith's analysis of the evolution of society and of legal, economic, and political arrangements within society as they develop relative to a specific historical context. This article also sets out the dualistic nature of the relative and non-relative aspects of individual liberty in the work of Smith and establishes the recognition by Smith of certain welfare obligations that are to be carried out by the government). See also R. Malloy, 'Of Icons, Metaphors, and Private Property--The Recognition of 'Welfare' Claims in the Philosophy of Adam Smith', *III Law and Semiotics* (R. Kevelson ed. 1990).

13. See A. Smith, *An Inquiry into the Nature and Causes of the Wealth of Nations* Vol. II 231-44 (E. Cannon ed. 1976) (first published in 1776 and now in two volumes); A. Smith, *The Theory of Moral Sentiments* 126-32 (E. West ed. 1976) (first published in 1759); A. Smith, *Lectures on Jurisprudence* 208 (R. Meek, D. Raphael & L. Stein eds. 1978).

14. By transferring our inquiry into a factual search for efficiency we make the process of law look scientific. In this manner Posner makes law look more natural, more objective, and more determinate. But as we know, there is much less here than meets the eye. The "facts" themselves are subjective interpretations and they are submitted to an indeterminate mode of economic analysis which is itsels resting upon very certain assumptions and value judgments. While such an approach may provide additional comfort for doctrinal practitioners, seeking to formalistically apply law without thinking about the people involved, it can hardly be viewed as scientific in any form other than rhetorical.

Syracuse University, College of Law

RICHARD A. POSNER

REBUTTAL TO MALLOY

The question I would like to leave with you is, if we took the word "moral" out of Professor Malloy's vocabulary, would he be rendered speechless? I do not think moral discourse is productive, and I do not think the fame and Nobel Prizes of Friedrich Hayek and Milton Friedman are due to their side-careers as moralists. Milton Friedman received the Nobel Prize for his work on the consumption function, in which he showed that the propensity to save does not increase as one's income rises, which was a key tenet of Keynesianism; and also for his work on monetarism, that is, on the effect of the money supply on the price level and on output. Now in addition to being a first class economic scientist, Milton Friedman is a person of strong political convictions and a great articulator of those convictions. As an advisor to Presidents, as a spokesman for the free-market philosophy, as a popularizer and advocate of a variety of political and economic principles and policies, he has relied heavily on a moral vocabulary. Friedrich Hayek also had a dual career. His Nobel Prize is for the work that he did in the 1930s on the role of the market as a means of generating information. His somewhat counterintuitive proposition, which history has proved correct, is that a decentralized market is more efficient at generating information about the economic system than a centrally planned economy is. Now Hayek, in addition, is a polemicist, a political advocate, the author among other things of a famous historically flawed book, *The Road to Serfdom*, written right after World War II, where he predicted that England would become a totalitarian state as a consequence of its socialist policies. He predicted communist totalitarianism and history delivered Margaret Thatcher.

I do not agree that the way to start in thinking about surrogate motherhood or the Department of Housing and Urban Development is by first taking a moral stand. I think the way to look at these issues is factually; and because there is, in fact, a high degree of moral consensus among Americans on a lot of issues, often the appearance of moral controversy will dissipate if only one can find the facts.

For example, to deal with the question raised by Professor Malloy of whether women are incapable of giving informed consent to participation in surrogate motherhood arrangements because of the history of discrimination against women, why do we not look factually at what the surrogate mothers do with the money they get for surrogate motherhood? Do they use it to buy food or medicine? Are they desperate people? Or in fact do they use it to build a wing on their house, or a garage, or send their children to private school? In fact, of course, it is the latter sort of thing, because the people on the buying side of the surrogate-motherhood market, the prospective father and his wife, do not want to deal with a poor woman. They do not trust her to deliver herself of a healthy child. The surrogate mothers like Mrs. Whitehead of the *Baby M* case are middle-class women. I think that middle-class women are capable--with some exceptions, as is true for everyone--of making rational choices with regard to procreation. But I do not want to defend surrogate motherhood here. I want simply to assert that the productive way to look at these problems is factually. Let us look at what we gain and what we lose by forbidding surrogate motherhood contracts. Perhaps we gain very little because, in fact, the law has no effect on these deals. These are victimless crimes so to speak. If there is money to be had for surrogate motherhood there will be surrogate mothers. It might be that efforts to outlaw surrogate motherhood will prove as quixotic as efforts to prohibit the drinking of alcoholic beverages. With any question you care to address--rights to medical care, rights to housing, whatever--if we are very careful to consider the cost and likely benefits of the proposed government policy, I believe that nine times out of ten most people will come to the same conclusion. The great power of wealth maximization, and of economics generally, is in clarifying the costs and the benefits of a proposed course of action, eliminating or at least reducing the element of factual uncertainty, and in that way minimizing, the area of genuine irreducible moral debate. Once we get down to that genuine irreducible element of moral debate, I do not think economics will help; nor I think, will moral philosophy. But I do not think we will have that large a residuum of the irresolvable if we attend carefully to the economics of these proposals.

United States Court of Appeals for the Seventh Circuit

JERRY EVENSKY

PROFESSOR MALLOY, JUDGE POSNER, AND ADAM SMITH'S MORAL PHILOSOPHY

1. INTRODUCTION

As with any debate between two thoughtful and articulate scholars, there is much in the arguments of Professor Malloy and of Judge Posner that has merit and draws us toward their respective positions. The question I address here is: How close is the work of each of these men to the intellectual tradition of Adam Smith.

Both claim to be working in the Smithian tradition. Can either legitimately make such a claim? What can we learn about the respective positions of Malloy and Posner by comparing each with the ideas of Adam Smith?

Malloy claims the Smithian mantle quite explicitly, stating that:

> My disagreement with Judge Posner's view of law and economics is a disagreement on values. I believe in the humanistic and moral philosophy of Adam Smith; a philosophy that demonstrates that social welfare concerns need *not* be inconsistent with the desire for, and the promotion of, properly conducted free market capitalism. Unfettered laissez faire was never a viewpoint offered by Smith.[1]

Posner places himself in the Smithian tradition by setting the scene for his presentation as follows:

> There are two intellectual dimensions to Adam Smith that have ensured his historical significance.... [N]umber one is Adam Smith's anti-mercantilism and corresponding hostility to governments, which he recognized as frequently the captives of special-interest groups. Second, and from a scientific standpoint more interesting, is Adam Smith's demonstration that economic activity can be coordinated without central governmental planning and regulation. This is the invisible hand...
>
> The demonstration that mercantilism is wealth minimizing, and the demonstration that an economic system can operate without central direction, are, I think, the basic contributions of Adam Smith to economic thought and public policy.[2]

Then in the course of his presentation Posner writes:

R.P. Malloy and J. Evensky: Adam Smith and the Philosophy of Law and Economics, 189–197.

How does wealth maximization fit into the picture that I have presented of Smith and of myself. It is merely a way of operationalizing, of making concrete, the idea of economic libertarianism.[3]

Clearly, both Posner and Malloy see themselves as working well within the intellectual tradition of Adam Smith. In fact however, while the ideas of both Malloy and Posner embody elements of the work of Adam Smith, neither man fully appreciates Smith's legacy. Choosing to work within different dimensions of the full space of Smith's ideas; each man arrives at a position that is not only at variance with that of the other, but that is also at variance with and less enlightening than Smith's. In what follows I make this case.

Section 2, 'Malloy's Moral Beings', compares Malloy's view on the moral foundation of society with Smith's. Section 3, 'Posner's Wealth of Nations', compares Posner's wealth maximization standard for public policy with Smith's conception of the standard for public policy. The Conclusion, 'The Nexus of Wealth and Values', sets the ideas of Malloy and of Posner into the larger Smithian perspective.

2. MALLOY'S MORAL BEINGS

Malloy's position correctly identifies and shares several features with Smith's work that are fundamental to Smith's moral philosophy: 1) An appropriate moral system is crucial to the functioning of a constructive classical liberal society; 2) there are many moral systems within and across societies, and 3) societies evolve. Where Malloy and Smith part company is on the issues of causation in social evolution and of the structure of the moral system that is so essential for a constructive classical liberal society to sustain itself.

It is clear that Malloy believes that if society is to evolve in a constructive way, it must develop the proper moral foundation. It is this notion that motivates his advocacy for a 'moral discourse', for he believes that such a foundation can only emerge from such a general, self-conscious dialogue about the ethics society will enshrine as its system of values. Malloy's logic implies a causation in the evolution of society that begins with the determination of this system of values.

This notion is different from Smith in that Smith saw moral systems as evolving simultaneously with the economic and political conditions. There is no causation from morals to political or economic outcomes. In Smith's analysis the human condition is a simultaneous system within which the social (moral), political, and economic dimensions coevolve.

Or so it was until the 1780s. As Smith gets older he begins to loose faith in the power of the invisible hand to guide humankind through stages toward the constructive classical liberal society that he envisioned.[4] As this faith wanes, Smith turns to the more visible hand of the statesman as the source of constructive development of society.

At this time and place, Smith's Britain in the 1780s, society had reached the classical liberal stage. But Smith worried that the moral system was not strong enough to sustain it in a constructive fashion. Mercantilism seemed to be a dynamic cancer in the system.

Seeing the success of this cancer as the product of a weak moral system (something akin to a weak immune system), Smith turns to a solution not unlike Malloy's moral discourse. He looks to an elite of moral leaders to set an example of virtue that the great mass of society would emulate to the benefit of all. The similarity to Malloy is that the active policy Smith advocates for social improvement is focused on developing a moral order. The difference is that Smith's solution is less democratic than the moral discourse Malloy advocates. Smith does not envision a social discussion of values with the objective of creating consensus. He envisions a moral elite leading the way.

The difference here is not trivial, but difference notwithstanding, Malloy is certainly in the Smithian tradition. This is less true with the structure of the moral system embodied in Malloy's presentation:

Adam Smith's moral system differentiates justice from benevolence.

> The most sacred laws of justice,...those whose violation seems to call loudest for vengeance and punishment, are the laws which guard the life and person of our neighbour; the next are those which guard his property and possessions; and last of all come those which guard what are called his personal rights, or what is due to him from the promises of others. (Smith, *TMS*, 84)

> Justice...is the main pillar that upholds the whole edifice [of society].... [S]ociety cannot subsist unless the laws of justice are tolerably observed.... (Smith, *TMS*, 86-87)

> the violation of justice is injury..../...[thus] the observance [of justice]...may be extorted by force,...[for its] violation exposes to resentment, and consequently to punishment. (Smith, *TMS*, 79, 78)

Benevolence (or beneficence) is a kindness that adds warmth to the cool efficiency of a just society; but, unlike justice, it is not an action to which one can lay claim.

> Beneficence is always free, it cannot be extorted by force, the mere want of it exposes to no punishment; because the mere want of beneficence tends to do no real positive evil...(*TMS*, 78)

Malloy makes no such distinction. In terms of the Smithian taxonomy, Malloy argues that the state must enforce not only justice, but also benevolence. It is not sufficient that the state should protect a person from exploitation in the market place, it must assure a sufficient degree of distributive success.

Smith shares Malloy's valuation of benevolence; but he does not believe that state power should be used to enforce benevolence. Smith's hope for the realization of such an outcome lay more in the development of the values of the citizens of the state. If this were accomplished, the citizenry would insure that all persons were properly cared for by family, by fellow citizens, *or* by the state.

Note that it is not inconsistent with Smith's vision for the state to be an instrument for the benevolence of its citizenry. The key difference between Smith and Malloy is that in Smith's view it is not incumbent on the state to enforce some definition of benevolence, as it must do with justice. The role of government is not, according to Smith, to insure the outcome of the race, but rather to assure that in all aspects the race is fair.

3. POSNER'S WEALTH OF NATIONS

Adam Smith reaches across the centuries to touch Posner with his invisible hand. According to Posner, 'from a scientific standpoint' Smith's invisible hand analysis is the most compelling element of Smith's work.[5] Not a surprising position, since Posner's 'wealth maximization' criteria for public policy is simply another way of asserting that Adam Smith's invisible hand is a better guide to optimal social outcomes than the visible hand of some bureaucrat in Washington.

This places Posner securely in the Smithian tradition; for, *ceteris paribus*, this is certainly the heart of the story of Smith's *Wealth of Nations*. But Smith relaxes the *ceteris paribus* assumption and analyzes the human condition in all of its dimensions (social (moral), political, and economic) simultaneously. This is what it meant to Smith to be a moral philosopher.[6]

The problem with Posner's analysis is that it is, in Smithian terms, a partial analysis. Posner, the 'pragmatic economic libertarian'[7], focuses entirely on economics. As a result, Posner's analysis not only doesn't do Adam Smith justice, which is not Posner's objective; it doesn't do the invisible hand or wealth maximization justice, which *is* Posner's objective.

As a comparison with Posner will demonstrate, Smith's conception of the role of government in society is fundamentally different from and more realistic than Posner's. Smith's analysis of the necessary conditions for maximizing the wealth of the nation include government, but go beyond that dimension of the human condition to encompass the social and economic conditions as well. Lacking this full dimensionality in his analysis, Posner's wealth maximization criteria for public policy is not the 'powerful analytic tool with which to derive a system of optimal government'[8]; it is an invitation to the very kind of mercantilist rent-seeking[9] he rails against.

According to Posner 'the role of government is to intervene and correct, as best it can, serious market failures.'[10] As he labels himself, so one could label his ideal government: it would be 'pragmatic economic libertarian' - providing a minimalist effective reaction to market failures. Posner's government is a problem solver. When market failure (e.g., an externality) or market power (e.g., monopoly) imposes a cost on society, government steps in. It collects the facts, calculates the costs, identifies and quantifies the benefits of alternative feasible solutions, and implements the most efficient solution. Government is reactive in that it only functions once a problem has been anticipated by rational expectations or has actually manifested itself.

Unfortunately, this approach to governing is analogous to treating the symptoms of a disease that has the genius of creative mutation on its side. When the treatment works, the disease adjusts. So, the creative genius of the entrepreneur who is willing to expend resources in pursuit of a distributive advantage (rent-seeking behavior) is constantly engaged in the pursuit of new ways to beat the system by identifying opportunities for exploiting the system that have not occurred to others. And while the government is identifying the cure for this new plague, the creative exploitive entrepreneur is enjoying a rent and planning for the next assault on the system. Thus, Posner's government is always fighting the last war when it comes to controlling problems of market failure or market power.

This approach to government invites inefficiency in two ways that complement one another. Creative exploitation can pay handsomely and thus will attract participants who use potentially productive resources for redistribution rather than production. This in turn requires the government to maintain a constant flow of potentially productive resources into controlling this rent-seeking disease. And, as noted, the government is perpetually one step behind the disease.

But there is a more fundamental problem with Posner's logic that belies the efficiency of a government that is guided by a policy of wealth maximization. As Posner describes it, the adoption of wealth maximization as a policy objective allows policy makers to 'strip away...[the] distributive consideration...[which] complicates public policy analysis...[thereby providing] a cleaner approach.'[11] It is an approach that embodies 'relatively neutral social goals'[12] and is guided by the facts. 'The great power of wealth maximization, and of economics generally, is in clarifying the costs and the benefits of a proposed course of action, eliminating or at least reducing the element of factual uncertainty, and in that way minimizing, the area of genuine irreducible moral debate.'[13]

The role of government in this wealth maximizing model is consistent with small government. It's job is technocratic: it must collect, analyze, and assess the facts; make a cost/benefit calculation; and implement the most efficient policy.

But herein lies the rub: big government, little government; smart government, dumb government; whatever government you can imagine - all governments are is people, people who are doing the work of the state. This fact creates a gap in Posner's logic, and traversing that gap requires a leap of faith. Posner's small, sharp, technocratic government must be different from big governments. Those who work in his government must carry out their mission without becoming 'the captives of special-interest groups'[14] Posner's model of wealth maximization policy depends on this leap of faith, but it seems like a very long jump.

Indeed, if anything, Posner's model of government is particularly vulnerable to capture by private interests. It would be more cost effective for a creative exploitive (rent-seeking) entrepreneur to work with a small, technocratic government than with a big bureaucratic government. In the smaller context a few well placed dollars could alter the 'facts', or the assessment of the facts, or the cost/benefit calculations based on the facts. Rate of returns on such 'participation in government' could be very attractive. Competition for power could be quite fierce. Allocation of potentially productive resources to this fierce battle over distribution could reduce the wealth of the wealth maximizing state dramatically.

Adam Smith recognized this. He despised Mercantilism precisely because it was a rent-seeking disease that caused just such an allocative distortion. But his solution to mercantilism lay not in changing the size or shape of government. Rather he turned his attention to refining the moral system of the citizenry. The central theme of Adam Smith's moral philosophy is that it is not the size or the shape of the government or the society that determines the efficiency of society. There is no government big enough or small enough to constrain or avoid the inefficiencies that come with unbridled self-interest. It is the ethics of the people who make up the government and the society that determines the degree to which a society will realize its constructive potential.[15]

If the ethics of a society evolve towards a proper balance of justice, prudence, and benevolence; the government will mature with its people, and the society will be more fruitful. As a society is more fruitful it will have more time to indulge in the further refinement of its ethical standards, its children, and its government. The evolution of society is a simultaneous system. By Smithian standards, Posner's partial analysis, abstracting from the ethical dimension of societal analysis, is fundamentally flawed. This is of special significance given Posner's position as a federal judge, because judges are central to Smith's conception of constructive government.

Recall Smith's words on justice: 'Justice...is the main pillar that upholds the whole edifice' of society. (Smith, *TMS*, 86) In his model of a government for a constructive classical liberal society, Smith envisions a properly constituted judiciary as the ultimate arbiters and defenders of justice:

When the judicial is united to the executive power, it is scarce possible that justice should not frequently be sacrificed to, what is vulgarly called, politics. The persons entrusted with the great interests of the state may, even without any corrupt views, sometimes imagine it necessary to sacrifice to those interests the rights of a private man. But upon the impartial administration of justice depends the liberty of every individual, the sense which he has of his own security. In order to make every individual feel himself perfectly secure in the possession of every right which belongs to him, it is not only necessary that the judicial should be separated from the executive power, but that it should be rendered as much as possible independent of that power. The judge should not be liable to be removed from his office according to the caprice of that power. The regular payment of his salary should not depend upon the good-will, or even upon the good economy of that power. (*WN*, 722-3)

Thus we see that long before Judge Posner was appointed to the United States Court of Appeals for the Seventh Circuit, Adam Smith was advocating that judges be assured the autonomy Judge Posner enjoys in his position. Smith's concern was not that Judge Posner be free to play wealth maximizer, but rather that he be free to insure that justice prevails. Judges should concern themselves with justice, and let the invisible hand take care of the economy.

4. THE NEXUS OF WEALTH AND VALUES

Smith's view on the moral foundation of the wealth of nations is reflected in the following passage from *The Theory of Moral Sentiments*.

It is thus that man, who can subsist only in society, was fitted by nature to that situation for which he was made. All members of human society stand in need of each others assistance, and are likewise exposed to mutual injuries. Where the necessary assistance is reciprocally afforded from love, from gratitude, from friendship, and esteem, the society flourishes and is happy. All the different members of it are bound together by the agreeable bands of love and affection, and are, as it were, drawn to one common centre of mutual good offices.

But though the necessary assistance should not be afforded from such generous and disinterested motives, though among the different members of the society there should be no mutual love and affection, the society though less happy and agreeable, will not necessarily be dissolved. Society may subsist among different men, as among different merchants, from a sense of its utility, without any mutual love or affection; and though no man in it should owe any obligation, or be bound in gratitude to any other, it may still be upheld by a mercenary exchange of good offices according to an agreed valuation.

Society, however, cannot subsist among those who are at all times ready to hurt and injure one another. The moment that injury begins, the moment that mutual resentment and animosity take place, all the bands of it are broke asunder, and the different members of which it consisted are, as it were, dissipated and scattered abroad by the violence and opposition of their discordant affections. If there is any society among robbers and murders, they must at least, according to the trite observation, abstain from robbing and murdering one another.... Society may subsist, though not in the most comfortable state, without beneficence; but the prevalence of injustice must utterly destroy it....

Justice, on the contrary, is the main pillar that upholds the whole edifice [of society].... [S]ociety cannot subsist unless the laws of justice are tolerably observed.... (Smith, *TMS*, 85-86)

In sum: Justice is the *sine qua non* of social cohesion. A cool efficient society can exist without benevolence, but a 'society [that] flourishes and is happy' must be imbued with benevolence. Benevolence, justice - these are terms that must be defined through a moral discourse. Thus, such a discourse is a prerequisite for the realization of a constructive classical liberal society.

To his credit, Malloy desires such a discourse. Unfortunately, Posner rejects the invitation: 'I do not think moral discourse is productive ....'[16] The frustrated Malloy makes the case that, like it or not - admit it or not, Posner is engaged in a moral discourse because his language is laden with an implicit value system.

And so it goes, they talk at each other, not with each other - they exchange words, but not ideas. But all their talk is not for nought, for those of us who hear them are not trapped in their fight. We can assess their ideas and learn from both. In an effort to do just that, I have examined their respective positions from a Smithian perspective. Smith's moral philosophy embodies and integrates the strengths of both men's perspectives in a way that can inform our current conversations about law, economics, and ethics.

NOTES

1. Malloy, p.156
2. Posner, p. 167-68
3. Posner, p. 171 Posner dissociates himself from any debate over the Smithian mantle , suggesting that '[t]he game of taking famous dead people and listing them on your side in current debates over public policy is...a chump's game.... We do not know how people who are the product of different cultures would think about our current problems.'p. 169 In effect, he claims the tradition and then belittles Malloy for claiming the mantle.
4. See Evensky p. 7-29 for an extended discussion of this evolution in Smith's thought.
5. Posner, 168
6. Posner dismisses moral philosophy as 'a weak field, a field in disarray, a field in which consensus is impossible.' (Posner, 170) But what he rejects is a philosophy of morals. This is not the conception of moral philosophy Smith held.
7. Posner, 169
8. Posner, 173
9. See Rowley, et. al.
10. Posner, 169-70
11. Posner, 171
12. Posner, 174
13. Posner, 188
14. Posner, 168
15. See Evensky, p. 7-29 for an extended description of Adam Smith's moral philosophy.
16. Posner, 187

REFERENCES

Evensky, Jerry
Malloy, Robin Paul
Posner, Richard
Rowley, Charles. Tollison, Robert. and Tullock, Gordon. (eds.) (1988). *The Political Economy of Rent-Seeking*. Boston: Kluwer Academic Press.
Smith, Adam. (1980). *Essays on Philosophical Subjects*, Edited by W.P.D. Wightman and J.C. Bryce; Vol. 3 of *The Glasgow Edition of the Works and Correspondence of Adam Smith*, General editing by D.D. Raphael and Andrew Skinner, Oxford: Clarendon Press.
----. (1978). *Lectures on Jurisprudence*, Edited by R.L. Meek, D.D. Raphael, and P.G. Stein; Vol. 5 of *The Glasgow Edition of the Works and Correspondence of Adam Smith*, General editing by D.D. Raphael and Andrew Skinner, Oxford: Clarendon Press.
----. (1977). *The Correspondence of Adam Smith*, Edited by E.C. Mossner and T.S. Ross; Vol. 6 of *The Glasgow Edition of the Works and Correspondence of Adam Smith*, General editing by D.D. Raphael and Andrew Skinner, Oxford: Clarendon Press.
----. (1976). *An Inquiry into the Nature and Causes of the Wealth of Nations*, Edited in two vol.by W.B. Todd; Vol. 2 of *The Glasgow Edition of the Works and Correspondence of Adam Smith*, General editing by D.D. Raphael and Andrew Skinner, Oxford: Clarendon Press.
----. (1976). *The Theory of Moral Sentiments*, Edited by D.D. Raphael and A.L. Macfie; Vol. 1 of *The Glasgow Edition of the Works and Correspondence of Adam Smith*, General editing by D.D. Raphael and Andrew Skinner, Oxford: Clarendon Press.

Syracuse University, Maxwell School, Department of Economics

JERRY EVENSKY

THE ROLE OF LAW IN ADAM SMITH'S MORAL PHILOSOPHY:NATURAL JURISPRUDENCE AND UTILITY

INTRODUCTION: ADAM SMITH AS EVOLUTIONARY PHILOSOPHER - THE ROLE OF THE REAL AND THE IDEAL:

Adam Smith writes of human action that:

> [W]hen we are determining the degree of blame or applause which seems due to any action, we very frequently make use of two different standards. The first is the idea of complete propriety and perfection, which, in those difficult situations, no human conduct ever did, or ever can come up to; and in comparison with which the actions of all men must for ever appear blameable and imperfect. The second is the idea of that degree of proximity or distance from this complete perfection, which the actions of the greater part of men commonly arrive at. Whatever goes beyond this degree, how far soever it may be removed from absolute perfection, seems to deserve applause and whatever falls short of it, to deserve blame. (*TMS*, 26)

This quotation reflects a fundamental element of Adam Smith's moral philosophy that must be understood if we are to appreciate the role of law in that philosophy. Smith has two images of the world: the real and the ideal. He writes about the real with the ideal in mind, for the ideal is the hope he has for society. Indeed, in all except his last writings, the ideal is more than a hope, it is the limit toward which he believed society is evolving. But while Smith writes with these two images in mind, there is a crucial distinction between them that shapes the way he tells his story of the evolution of society. Smith can know the real[1] in all its detail. He can only know the ideal as generalities, the detail (the invisible 'connecting principles') is left to the imagination.[2]

In broad outline, the ideal is a world in which all people live in harmony with the Deity's design for '[t]he happiness of mankind, as well as of all other rational creatures, seems to have been the original purpose intended by the Author of nature, when he brought them into existence.' (*TMS*, 166) In such a world moral sentiments (that balance of self-love, justice, and benevolence behind every action that would enjoy the perfect sympathy of an impartial spectator) would lead to the greatest possible wealth for the nation. Self-love would spur on the 'race for wealth'[3], justice would

R.P. Malloy and J. Evensky: Adam Smith and the Philosophy of Law and Economics, 199–219.

insure that the race was most fruitful - for the common reward of constructive efforts would be success[4], and benevolence would provide the warmth of kindness for those who do not do well in the competition by no fault of their own.

In this best of worlds the role of Government with respect to laws of justice would be definitional. It would establish clear and concise definitions of property rights and terms of contracts so that individuals are using the same standards and speaking the same language as they interact.

This vision I describe is, as I referred to it above, the broad outline of the ideal. Smith was never so presumptions as to believe that he could know and detail the exact nature of the terms and standards that would prevail in the ideal world[5]. He understood that societal standards, be they legal definitions or ethical principles, are contextual; and that one can only know and appreciate the standards if one knows and appreciates the context. As he put it with respect to ethics:

Every age and country look upon that degree of each quality, which is commonly to be met with in those who are esteemed among themselves, as the golden mean [emphasis added] of that particular talent or virtue. (*TMS*, 204)

Thus, for example, while Smith looks back from his time and condemns Cato's treatment of his slaves, nevertheless Smith appreciates that by the standards of the time Cato was 'a man of the most severe virtue and the strictest observer of the morall rules then in fashion .... ' (*LJA*, 181)[6] From Smith's vantage point, he could know the golden mean of Cato's age and of his own, but he could only imagine what that standard might be like in an age that was only to be imagined. He could no more know the standards of that future world than he could expect Cato to know the standards of his.

If in Smith's moral philosophy the ideal was an unknowable norm; one could, nevertheless, make relative historical comparisons as to which societies in history were closer or further from the norm based on the success of the society in achieving and sustaining high per capita wealth[7]. This proxy works because the approximation of the ideal meant closer and closer approach to the best of all possible worlds. It is this conceptual framework, observation of the real in the context of a proxy for the ideal, that allows Smith to intuit the kinds of standards of justice and benevolence that might prevail in the ideal, and to address the issue Knud Haakonssen cites as central to Smith's moral philosophy:

[T]he problem situation which gave Smith's jurisprudence it's very special character ... derived from Hume's question about the possibility of legal criticism - or of how to avoid a complete relativism - if neither naturally nor divinely given standards were available. (Haakonssen, 2)

In Smith's work these standards exist behind the face of nature - thus they are there but they are not directly observable or knowable. They only reveal themselves in the evolution of society.

This brings us to that other side of Smith's moral philosophical vision - the real side. It is in the pages he devotes to history and evolution of society that we see the real complexity of his vision unfold. This story, drawn from Smith's reading of history, is about the weave of circumstance, chance, and autonomous actions of kings and footmen leading to unintended consequences: the rise and fall of societies and nations, and the evolution of humankind toward the ideal. And as he writes his evolutionary story of the real, he takes pride and care in distinguishing it from the abstraction of the ideal. For example, early in the pages of the *Theory of Moral Sentiments* as he is discussing the way people actually measure the merit or demerit of the action of another he inserts a very long note which includes the following instructive caveat:

> ... [T]he present inquiry is not concerning a matter of right, if I may say so, but concerning a matter of fact. We are not at present examining upon what principles a perfect being would approve of the punishment of bad actions; but upon what principles so weak and imperfect a creature as man actually and in fact approves of it. (*TMS*, 77)

And then he continues in the same note with thoughts that provide a nice introduction to his analysis of the role of justice in 'real' society.

> The very existence of society requires that unmerited and unprovoked malice should be restrained by proper punishments; and consequently, that to inflict those punishments should be regarded as a proper and laudable action. Though man, therefore, be naturally endowed with a desire of the welfare and preservation of society, yet the Author of nature has not entrusted it to his reason to find out that a certain application of punishments is the proper means of attaining this end; but has endowed him with an immediate and instinctive approbation of that very application which is most proper to attain it. The oeconomy of nature is in this respect exactly of a piece with what it is upon many other occasions. With regard to all those ends which, upon account of their peculiar importance, may be regarded, if such an expression is allowable, as the favourite ends of nature, she has constantly in this manner not only endowed mankind with an appetite for the end which she proposes, but likewise with an appetite for the means by which alone this end can be brought about, for their own sakes, and independent of their tendency to produce it. (*TMS*, 77)

Nature 'has endowed him with an immediate and instinctive approbation of that very application which is most proper to attain ... the end which she proposes'; and she does so with that elegant 'oeconomy ... [she uses] upon many other occasions', the guidance of the invisible hand. Smith sees society as evolving, and that evolution is guided by the invisible hand. In what follows I present a series of three propositions that I believe help us to understand Smith's evolutionary story and the role of law in that story. The first proposition sets the foundation of my analysis, and the second builds on that foundation, and the third completes the logic of the argument.

My three propositions are that in Smith's story:
1) Societal Evolution Implies Social Maturation
2) Utility is an Instrumental Variable in the Evolution of the Legal System
3)The Evolution of the Legal System is Instrumental in the Formation of Social Ethics

1. SOCIETAL EVOLUTION IMPLIES MATURATION:

Elsewhere I have demonstrated that the first proposition, societal evolution implies maturation, holds for the social dimension of societal development[8]. Given the topic of this piece, I will focus here on the evolution of law and legal institutions to establish Smith's conception of evolution as consistent with the notion of maturation.

Adam Smith opens his Wednesday, February 23, 1763 lecture on jurisprudence with the following words:

> In the last lecture I endeavoured to explain to you more fully that form of government which naturally arises amongst mankind as they advance in society, and in what manner it gradually proceeded. (*LJA*, 214)

This, as Smith says, is a story of the 'advance in society'. What his students had learned is, in broad outline, as follows: The evolution of government and ultimately of law revolves around the emergence of and growing complexity of property, followed by the necessity of contractual language that individuals can depend on and have enforced if commerce is to proceed. In the most unrefined or rude state of society 'there can be very little government of any sort ....' (*LJA*, 201) What judicial or executive power there was resided in the community as a whole. Internal disputes and decisions regarding intertribal disputes were resolved by consensus. 'The legislative power can hardly subsist in such a state; there could be occasion but for very few regulations, and no individual would think himself bound to submit to such regulations as were made by others, even where the whole community was concerned.' (*LJA*, 202) The reason for this simple form of governance is the simple state of the society. The size and nature of the tribal life made communal meetings possible whenever necessary, and the number of potential disputes was small because the conception of property was very limited: 'Among savages property begins and ends with possession, and they seem scarce to have any idea of anything as their own which is not about their own bodies.' (*LJB*, 460)

This all changes in the next, shepherd's, stage of society. 'Among shepherds the idea of property is further extended.' (*LJB*, 460) 'Those animalls which are most adapted for the use of man ... are no longer common but are the property of certain individualls. The distinctions of rich and poor then arise' (*LJA*, 202) as the rich accumulate property and the poor become dependents of the former. This expanding domain of '[p]roperty makes it [(Government)] absolutely necessary. ... [for property is] the grand fund of all dispute ....' (*LJA*, 208) Government must exist to maintain the property rights of the rich against the poor, and to insure that the poor 'must either continue poor or acquire wealth in the same manner as they [(the rich)] have done.' (*LJA*, 208-9) Thus, '[t]he age of shepherds is that where government properly first commences.' (*LJA*, 202) But even here the legislative function of government is largely missing:

> With regard to laws and the legislative power, there is properly nothing of that sort in this period. There must indeed be some sort of law as soon as property in flocks commences, but this would be but very short and have few distinctions in it, so that every man would understand it without any written or regular law. It would be no other than what the necessity of the state required. Written and formall laws are a very great refinement of government, and such as we never meet with but in the latest periods of it. (emphasis added) (*LJA*, 213)

Here, in the underlined sentence, we see an explicit expression of Smith's notion that evolution is refinement, and in Smith's mind refinement is synonymous with improvement.

If it is in the age of shepherds that 'government properly first commences.' (*LJA*, 202), it is in the age of agriculture that it gets its first major expansion, for it is in this age that 'property receives its greatest extension ....' (*LJB*, 460) With this begins the complex task of settling issues related to means, besides possession, of acquiring property: accession[9], prescription[10], or succession[11]. Smith writes with regard to the first of these: 'Tho the opportunities of accession are but very few in the age of shepherds, yet they multiply to a number almost infinite when agriculture and private property in land is introduced.' (*LJA*, 28) It is only as the law regarding these cases evolves and becomes defined that property rights become more secure and only in that case can the society's economic progress go forward. For in Smith's evolving and maturing world, security of property is essential for progress:

> In the infancy of society, as has been often observed, government must be weak and feeble, and it is long before it's authority can protect the industry of individuals from the rapacity of their neighbours. When people find themselves every moment in danger of being robbed of all they possess, they have no motive to be industrious. There would be little accumulation of stock, because the indolent ... would live upon the industrious, and spend whatever they produced. [And he goes on to note that w]hen the power of government becomes so great as to defend the produce of industry, another obstacle arises from a different quarter. Among neighboring nations in a barbarous state there are perpetual wars ... [so] tho' private property be secured from the violence of neighbours, it is in danger from hostile invasions. In this manner it is next to

impossible that any accumulation of stock can be made. It is observable that among savage nations there are always more violent convulsions than among those farther advanced in refinement. ... Nothing can be more an obstacle to the progress of opulence. (emphasis added) (*LJB*, 522)

Again we see that the progress of society and the progress of opulence go hand in hand. Society's government and law, and its economy must mature together if society is to realize the fruitfulness that progress can bring.

An example of this nexus between legal and economic progress of a maturing society can be found in Smith's description of the role of exclusive privileges of corporation as the protected trades of feudal society mature into the competitive trades of a commercial society. He writes that

[i]t is found that society must be pretty far advanced before the different trades can all find subsistence .... To bring about therefore the separation of trades sooner than the progress of society would naturally effect ... it was found necessary to give them a certainty of a comfortable subsistence. And for this purpose the legislature determined that they should have the privilege of exercising their separate trades without fear of being cut out of their livelihood by the increase of their rivalls. That this was necessary therefore in the 1st stages of the arts to bring them to their proper perfection, appears very reasonable and is confirmed by this, that it has been the generall practise of all the nations in Europe. But as this end is now fully answered, it were much to be wished that these as well as many other remains of the old jurisprudence[12] should be removed. (*LJA*, 86)

Indeed the advancement into and within the commercial stage required a significant maturation of law and legal institutions. For Smith the case in point was England.

In his March 1763 lectures on jurisprudence, Smith reviews the course the evolution of governments in western Europe from the feudal to commercial societies. He notes that '[i]n England alone a different government has been established from the nautrall course of things.--The situation and circumstances of England have been altogether different.' (*LJA*, 265) The English story is indicative of his view, or rather is the empirical foundation of his belief, that societal evolution is a rather quirky process of chance concurrence of circumstance[13] and people[14], the process of evolution selects for success those societies that have the good fortune to develop a more mature social structure.

The story Smith tells about the maturation of English government is one of maturation through evolution. A centerpiece of this story is the Common Law, for it is precisely this character in the Common Law that made it so admirable to Smith. The slow and iterative process of the its development gives it its probity. He seems to see it as the best method humans could create to realize the distillation of the perspective of an impartial spectator. The standards are those of an accumulated wisdom of many who sought to sit and judge from that perspective. As such it is 'more deserving of the attention of a speculative man than any other [system of law], as being more formed on the natural sentiments of mankind.' (*LJA*, 98) This is complemented by the evolution of the court system in England. It has produced an independent judiciary bound by precedent, and employing an exemplary jury process[1516].

Smith also admired other English institutions that have emerged to secure the liberty of English subjects. Included among these is the power to impeach[17], the *Habeas Corpus* Act[18], the 'frequency of elections'[19], and expanded suffrage[20]. All of these realities of English political life are, as Smith tells the story, the result of an evolution that was guided by good fortune of circumstance and the unintended consequences of individual choices. And the consequence of this good fortune in terms of political maturation is a society that enjoys, mercantile impediments notwithstanding, the greatest commercial success in the world:

That security which the laws in Great Britain give to every man that he shall enjoy the fruits of his own labour, is alone sufficient to make any country flourish, notwithstanding these [mercantile impediments] and twenty other absurd regulations of commerce .... The natural effort of every individual to better his own condition, when suffered to exert itself with freedom and security, is so powerful a principle, that it is alone, and without any assistance, not only capable of carrying on the society to wealth and prosperity, but of surmounting a hundred impertinent obstructions with which the folly of human laws too often incumbers its operations .... In Great Britain industry is perfectly secure; and though it is far from being perfectly free, it is as free or freer than in any other part of Europe. (*WN*, 540)

Thus we see Smith's assessment of the state of humankind's evolution: We have made much progress since the rude state of savages. That progress has been possible due to the maturation of our system of government and law. Great Britain is the current standard of maturity in the real world, but we are by no means at the ideal. There are all still the 'hundred impertinent obstructions with which the folly of human laws too often incumber' (*WN*, 540) and there is the constant reality of human frailty which undermines the efficiency of the economic competition.

The next two questions we address are: How does the progress of law occur?, and How does that progress contribute to achieving the more fundamental necessity of societal maturation, the development of an ethical maturity[21] in the people of society? My second and third propositions address these questions:

2) Utility is an Instrumental Variable in the Evolution of the Legal System

3)The Evolution of the Legal System is Instrumental in the Formation of Social Ethics

2. UTILITY IS AN INSTRUMENTAL VARIABLE IN THE EVOLUTION OF THE LEGAL SYSTEM

This proposition is in effect another citing of the invisible hand at work. As the invisible hand does in the world of commerce, so it does in the world of law and legal institutions. The evolution of the legal system is driven by individuals in pursuit of utilitarian (personal or social) objectives, but these autonomous actions lead to unintended consequences. Under the right circumstances, the entire legal system begins to approximate the ideal structure that holds as its standard not utility, but the judgement of an impartial spectator.

I make my case for this proposition by reviewing a case in Smith's analysis. His presentation of the evolution of the English court system is a classic case of utilitarian evolution into impartial spectator justice. Smith reviews this process in lectures in March of 1763 and covers the same subject in his 1766 lectures.

The judiciall power in the kingdom was first given ... [to a] Chief Justiciary, and in France the Mayer de Palais. ... All these three different parts of the judiciall power were united in the Great Justiciary (*LJA*, 275-6) : the power of judging in all civill causes, ... [of trying] all criminall causes; ... [and of trying] fiscall [disputes] ... betwixt the sovereign and the subjects. (*LJA*, 276)

[T]he first defalcation made on the power of the Justiciary [occurred] in the time of King John. ... [A]s the Justiciary attended the king in his progresses thro the kingdom to execute justice, and his court followed that of the kings, it was found necessary to separate one of these powers from him, which was given to the Court of Common Pleas. (*LJA*, 276)

The reason for this change was entirely utilitarian. Since the resolution of civil suits was much slower than criminal suits[22] following the Justiciary as he followed the king was a burden on the people. 'This inconvenience was very soon perceived to require a remedy; it was therefore provided by the Magna Charta in King Johns time that': 'Common pleas shall not follow the King's Court but be held in one fixed place.' (*LJA*, 277-8, 278fn)

But the power of the Justiciary was not much abated by this change. Indeed, that power was such that it was a threat to the kings own power. Indeed,

[w]e see ... that the Mayers de Palais [(the French equivalent to the English Great Justiciary)] during the two first races of the kings of France usurped the kingdom. ... [But in England] Edward the I[st], one of the most prudent of our kings, who seems to have known what he did as well as any one, dreading least the Great Justiciary should serve him in the same way as the Mayer de Palais had done the French kings, abolished his authority all together. (*LJA*, 276)[23]

This is, according to Smith, the point at which the evolution of the English judicial system departed from that found on the continent. This parting of the ways was not based on Edward's philosophical attachment to the notion of courts as impartial or independent, or any of the other characteristic that become admirable in the mature English judicial system. It is simply reflection of Edward's prudence in the face of a potential threat to his power.

> Edward Ist divided the business of the Justiciary into three different courts *vizt*
> The Court of King's Bench
> The Court of Exchequer
> The Court of Common Pleas
> In the last all civil suits were tried. In the first all criminal ones, and to it lay the appeal from the Court of Common Pleas; ... [and t]he Court of the Exchequer judged in all affairs between the king and his subjects .... The Court of Chancery was originally no court at all. The Chancellor was no more than a keeper of breives or writs according to which justice was done. What gave occasion to the keeping of these breives shall now be considered. (*LJB*, 422-3)

Smith has explained the transformation in the structure of the judiciary. Now, with language of evolution and transition he prepares his students to move on to the story of how this new structure matured. And as with the first, the next chapter in this story is one of utility guiding choices that create unintended, and in this case praiseworthy, consequences.

> When Edward had thus broke the judicial power, the persons whom he appointed as judges were generally of the meanest sort of no fortune or rank, who had been bread to the knowledge of the law, and very frequently these were clergy men. ... When therefore this power was in the hands of mean persons ... being all low men who depended on the will of the king, they would be very unwilling and afraid in any shape to go beyond the meaning of the law or any ways to alter it; and therefore in all cases breives and writts were drawn out according to which they decided justice, and exact records of all proceedings were kept in the officina brevium. (*LJA*, 278-9)

This standard of exactness was pushed further by the fact that men of low station were vulnerable to 'bribery and corruption'. In fact, 'Edward himself levi'd at one time by fines for bribery about £100,000 ... so that the bribery must have been very excessive. .... [and t]hey were therefore ordered to judge by the strict law, and were to be tried in their proceedings by their own records ....' (*LJA*, 279)

Here we see utility and irony in Smith's story. The utility is that of judges from 'the meanest sort' turning to precedent as protection from the possible wrath from the king, and the king requiring scrupulous record keeping (essential for a system based on precedent) as protection from the corruption of the judges. The irony is that this makes two characteristics of the court which Smith would abhor, low sorts as judges and lack of independent judges, the very condition which gave rise to another more permanent characteristic of the court that Smith found most essential to the sure administration of justice.

[One] thing which greatly confirms the liberty of the subjects in England ... [is] the little power of the judges in explaining, altering, or extending or correcting the meaning of the laws, and the great exactness with which they must be observed according to the literall meaning of the words .... (*LJA*, 275)

Having examined the causes which 'gave occasion to the keeping of these breives' and the salutary effects of this evolution, Smith then turns to the utility that gave rise to the professionalisation of the courts.

Another thing which tended to support the liberty of the people and render the proceedings in the courts very exact, was the rivalship which arose betwixt them. (*LJA*, 280)

Smith describes how through various methods the several courts were able to encroach on each others jurisdiction (e.g., 'a fiction of a trespass' (*LJA*, 280)). This process was encouraged by the fact that

the whole profits of the courts ... depended on the numbers of civill causes which came before them, [thus] they would all naturally endeavour to invite every one to lay his cause before their court, by the precision, accuracy, and expedition (where agreable) of their proceedings, which emulation made a still greater care and exactness of the judges. (*LJA*, 281)

Again we see the utility of the institution and its members leading to an unintended consequence, the professionalisation of its work: a consequence much to be admired for the maturation it brings to the institution who's raison d'etre is justice - that 'main pillar that upholds the whole edifice' of human society. (*TMS*, 86)

Next Smith addresses the process through which gaps in the existing precedents, the set of briefs, were addressed. And again the process is directed by utility toward the unintended ends of the Deity, the creation of the conditions necessary for a constructive commercial society.

[When] the wrong complained of agreed not with any single brief but was comprehended under any two or more, he [(the Chancellor)] should cause the clerk to make out a new brief in that form. ... In this manner he was as it were the judge of the *point of law*, and the courts had only the matter of fact to examine. Many causes would however occurr in which there was no fact disputed, in which case there could be no use or necessity to carry it before the courts; ... In these cases the Chancellor could give a sufficient remedy. And in this manner it was that the equitable Court of Chancery began. ...

The Chancellor ... soon began to consider those cases which the common law did not comprehend. The first thing he did in this way was to order specifick performance of contracts. These were not sustaind by the common law; all they did was to give the pursuar damages but did not think of forcing specifick performance. (*LJA*, 281-2)

Thus it was that an essential piece of the legal foundation of a commercial society came into being. The evolution of Chancellor's duties were driven by utility; but clearly, in Smith's story, they were guided to fill an important role (the enforcement of contracts) in the maturing of society by the invisible hand. The beauty of this new court is that unlike those unfettered new courts Smith deplores -

All new courts are a great evil, because their power at first is not precisely determined and therefore their decisions must be loose and inaccurate. (*LJB*, 426) -

the Court of Chancery joins an existing system of justice that can act, to a significant degree, as a constraint on any arbitrary judgement it might make.[24]

And finally, Smith's addresses the evolution of what he clearly believes is the most significant and mature element of the English judicial system: the jury. The jury 'curbs the power of the judge ... [because] in all causes ... [t]he matter of fact is left intirely to their determination.' (*LJA*, 283)

The law of England, always the friend of liberty, deserves praise in no instance more than in the carfull provision of impartial juries. ... Nothing can be a greater security for life, liberty, and property than this institution. The judges are men of integrity, quite independent, holding their offices for life, but they are tied down by the law. The jurymen are your neighbours who are to judge of a fact upon which your life depends. (*LJB*, 425)

Smith describes the evolution of juries as follows:

'In the beginnings of the allodial and feudall governments ... the person prosecuted came into court with twelve others; and if he swore he was innocent and these 12 swore also that they believed him to be so, he was acquitted.' (*LJA*, 283)

This method was ultimately undermined by the resentment among the nobles at the fact that they could get no satisfaction of an abridgement of their rights from such a partial process. As a result they turned back to a more traditional method of settlement: 'judiciall combat'. (*LJA*, 283)

The first person to remedy these inconveniencies was Henry 2d, who of all our kings excepting Edwd. Ist. had the greatest legislative capacity. He ordered that instead of [the current system] ... the sheriff should appoint 12 juratores who should be made acquainted with the cause, and having considered it should give in their opinion or verdict, to which the judge should adhere, and pronounce the sentence accordingly from the law. ... Nothing can be more carefull and exact than the English law in ascertaining the impartiality of the jurers. (*LJA*, 283-4)

Here again we see leadership in pursuit of order that results in decisions which transcend their own utility. Henry put in place the mechanism for English justice to approximate the perspective of an impartial spectator, and it is this perspective that lies at the heart of Adam Smith's conception of justice in particular and moral sentiments in general. Smith does not see the English judicial system as perfect[25], but he does believe it is the most mature example of jurisprudence human society had produced as of his lifetime. And he clearly believes that it is the good fortune of secure circumstance (being an island), wise leadership (e.g., Edward Ist and Henry 2nd), and the time to mature that made the system approximate his image of the ideal:

It takes time and repeated practice to ascertain the precise meaning of the law or to have precedents enough to determine the practise of a court. (*LJA*, 287)

I have focused on the evolution of the English judicial system to make the case for my second proposition: that utility is an instrumental variable in the evolution of the legal system. There are many more examples to be found that reflect the same process. I cite a few here, without exploring them, to show the general nature of the proposition.

In his discussion of the House of Commons, Smith says: 'We have now shewn how the government of England turned absolute [('Under the House of Tudor' (*LJB*, 420))]; we shall next consider how liberty was restored, and what security the British have for the possession of it.'(*LJB*, 420) The story that unfolds[26] is one of utility leading to unintended consequences that transcend utility - a government consistent with the security of liberty.

Similarly, in his analysis of the evolution of contracts, he writes that '[i]f we consider now the reasons why contracts were not binding , we will discover also the causes which gradually introduced their validity.' (*LJA*, 89) Again, it is a story of evolution driven by utility that had the unintended consequence of securing a crucial tool of commerce.

Another example can be found in the domain of international law. Smith presents its evolution as a maturation of laws that allow the development and extension of commerce. For example, with respect to the treatment of aliens utility gives rise to civility and legal status:

[W]hen men have a little farther progress in society and the arts and improvements of it, and begin to find the benefit of having foreigners coming amongst them, who carry out what is superfluous of the product of the country and importing the superfluities of their country, which tend either to the convenience or the luxury of the country, then they will find the benefits of foreign commerce and it will be induced to encourage the settling of foreign merchants amongst them. For this purpose it will be absolutely necessary to give them the protection of the laws, both to their persons and their goods. (*LJA*, 307)

There is a characteristic of international law, however, that limits its ability to mature.

[T]he rules which nations ought to observe with one another cannot be treated so accurately as private or public law. We find the rules of property pretty exactly established in every nation. The extent of the sovereigns power, as well as the duty of the subject, so far as justice is concerned, are pretty uniform every where. But with respect to the laws of nations, we can scarce mention any one regulation which is established with the common consent of all nations, and observed as such at all times. This must necessarily be the case, for where there is not supreme legislative power nor judge to settle differences, we may always expect uncertainty and irregularity. (*LJB*, 545)

Smith believed that the evolution of law both followed and led an evolving consensus.[27] His is a vision of a rolling evolution. It begins among the leaders of the nation as they redefine the golden mean of social standards. Those standards then begin to permeate the great institutions of society, e.g, the law. And finally the law, to the degree it can establish its authority with the populace, begins to shape the behavior and ultimately the values of the populace.[28] If the leaders[29] are good (e.g., Solon[30]), and the institutional structures are also good (like those English institutions (the Common Law, the judicial system, the Parliament)), then the golden mean of society will evolve toward the ideal. Indeed, in Smith's vocabulary, good leaders and good institutions are defined as those who and which move society in that direction.

This process was and could only be evolutionary, because there is no 'man of system' [31] with the wisdom to know the Deity's intention. It is all about process. Which brings me to my final proposition.

3. THE EVOLUTION OF THE LEGAL SYSTEM IS INSTRUMENTAL IN THE FORMATION OF SOCIAL ETHICS

As society begins to take form there is very little law, for there is very little need for law. But as social interactions become more complex the scope of individuals with whom one is interdependent grows far beyond the boundaries of one's own family or tribe. And thus, they also grow beyond the reach of traditional values and sanctions. It is this process that leads to the expansion of laws and legal institutions. They fill the void left by the limited reach of traditional values and sanctions - they constrain unethical, unjust, behavior.

The more improved any society is and the greater length the severall means of supporting the inhabitants are carried, the greater will be the number of their laws and regulations necessary to maintain justice and prevent infringements of the right of property. (*LJA*, 16)

The enforcement burden of this job falls to the 'civil magistrate [who] is entrusted with the power not only of preserving the public peace by restraining injustice, but of promoting the prosperity of the commonwealth by establishing good discipline.' (*TMS*, 81) Note the two dimensions of the job: restrain injustice and promote good discipline.

To restrain injustice the magistrate can tap into our natural fear of punishment:

Nature has implanted in the human breast that consciousness of ill-desert, those terrors of merited punishment which attend upon its [(justice's)] violation, as the great safe-guards of the association of mankind, to protect the weak, to curb the violent, and to chastise the guilty. (*TMS*, 86)

At this stage in social development, punishment is an instrumental variable measured out not by the standards of an impartial spectator but by the requisites of social utility. Even a man of humanity, who might be closer in his perspective to the insights of an impartial spectator than the common standards of society have yet realized, must accept that these are the standards necessary in a maturing, but not fully mature, society. Thus,

the man of humanity ... looks upon the centinel [who is executed for falling asleep at his station] as an unfortunate victim, who, indeed, must, and ought to be, devoted to the safety of numbers, but whom still, in his heart, he would be glad to save; and he is only sorry, that the interest of the many should oppose it. (*TMS*, 90-1)

But even as the law and its punishments fall short of the ideal, the process of punishment can drive the maturation of the golden mean for it serves that second responsibility of the civil magistrate: establishing good discipline. The strong hand of the law establishes the authority of the standards:

Written and formall laws are a very great refinement of government, and such as we never meet with but in the latest periods of it. It is a sigh of great authority in the government to be able to make regulations which shall bind themselves, their posterity, and even persons who are unwilling. (*LJA*, 213)

If authority gives rise to allegiance[32], then over time the people come to accept the standards as their values.

Every morall duty must arise from some thing which mankind are conscious of. ... [yet] it is very seldom that one has a distinct notion of the foundation of their duties, but have merely a notion that they have such and such obligations. ... [I]ndeed it will but seldom happen that one will be very sensible of the constitution he has been born and bred under; everything by custom appears to be right or at least one is but very little shocked at it. (*LJA*, 321-2)

The mere weight of the laws authority tends to inculcate it as a standard, and furthermore, '[a]uthority [also serves as] ... the foundation of that of utility or common interest' (*LJA*, 322) to which men appeal when persuading others of the 'virtue' of the law. In this manner the law serves as a tool for the inculcation of values.[33]

Summarizing, the process of evolution in which the law plays an instrumental role in shaping values goes as follows: Leaders of the nation redefine the golden mean of social standards. Those standards then begin to permeate the institutions of society, e.g, the law. And finally the law, to the degree it can establish its authority with the populace, begins to shape the custom and ultimately the values of the populace. If the leaders are good, and the institutional structures are also good; then 'redefine' implies refine, and the golden mean of society evolves toward the ideal. As this occurs the burden on the law begins to lighten.

When society made a still greater progress and the peace and good order of the community were provided for, and tranquillity firmly established, these punishments would again be mitigated and by degrees brought to bear a just proportion to the severall crimes. (*LJA*, 130)

Where once the primary responsibility for constraining individual behavior resided in the law, now that responsibility is shared by a refined ethics. At the limit, in the presence of a perfectly ethical society, the system of law can withdraw to its natural scope and standards. That scope is the definitions, judicial interpretations, and regulations of police necessary for a constructive commercial society. The standards are those set by the sympathy of an impartial spectator.

CONCLUSION:

I have offered three closely related propositions on the nature of Adam Smith's conception of the role of law in moral philosophy:

1) Societal Evolution Implies Social Maturation

2) Utility is an Instrumental Variable in the Evolution of the Legal System

3)The Evolution of the Legal System is Instrumental in the Formation of Social Ethics

If these propositions are correct they suggest the following rhythm of governmental development: little government, maturing and increasingly assertive government, and an easing of government as social ethics mature. In the following extended quotation we see something like this pattern reflected in Knud Haakonssen analysis of Smith's work.

In the most primitive society crime and punishment is purely a matter between the injured and his family and the offender and his family. For good reasons, only serious infringements of the most basic natural rights are acted upon - at any rate they are the only ones which make the surrounding society venture to intervene. ... As government gains strength in shepherd society, the chieftain can enforce such reconciliation and in return for his trouble he will begin to ask for a part of the compensation, in proportion to the severity of the crime. At the same time people will begin to consider crime under two aspects, partly as an injury to the victim and partly as an injury to the peace of society. As governmental authority becomes absolute, the latter aspect is the only one that matters, and via a graduated scale of bodily retaliation all crimes come to be considered treasonable and capital. ... Smith's account of the development of punishment in the major part of our period is, therefore, the story of how the government, far from seeing itself as an impartial spectator, came to consider itself the major party in every dispute .... For the later part of the period he then goes on to show that government eventually becomes so strong that it can allow itself to soften this attitude, considering only actions directly against the state as treasonable and allowing the now independent courts to bring more natural ideas of justice to bear on all other crimes. (Haakonssen, 1981, 174-5)

I believe my analysis extends Haakonssen's by tying the development of social values to this evolution in the role of government.

I also see my thesis as complementing that of John Cairns in his piece on 'Adam Smith and the Role of the Courts in Securing Justice and Liberty'. Cairns offers a wealth of detail on and a rich appreciation for the evolution of that institution. His stress on 'historical continuity' and his careful analysis of that process as represented by Smith is a significant contribution to our understanding of Smith's vision. Clearly my own propositions rest on the notion that Cairns is correct in his analysis.

My propositions regarding the role of utility in Smith's moral philosophy and it's relationship to law and ethics benefitted greatly from reading J. Ralph Lindgren's 'Adam Smith's Treatment of Criminal Law'. I believe Professor Lindgren makes a very strong case that 'the overriding point of criminal law is crime prevention.' (Lindgren, 78) I would simply add to that point another utility of criminal law: It is a tool for shaping social values, and this function is complementary to its function in crime prevention.

This complementarity comes out in a crucial point Professor Lindgren makes:

The criminal law together with the system of courts, prisons, executioners, etc. is one means that governments, as they become more powerful, may use to protect the liberties of citizens from injuries at the hands of one another, but it is not the most promising. Governments are best advised to depend in advancing that objective instead upon the fostering of commerce and manufacturing. (Lindgren, 79)

Citing empirical evidence form London and Paris on crime, Smith asserts that the necessity of police for personal security is not proportional to population but to the 'nature of the manners of the people.' (*LJA*, 332) The more 'retainers and dependents' the more need of police. 'Nothing tends so much to corrupt and enervate and debase the mind as dependency, and nothing gives such noble and generous notions of probity as freedom and independency. Commerce is one great preventative of this custom. ... hence it is that the common people of England who are alltogether free and independent are the honestest of their rank any where to be met with.' (*LJA*, 333) In sum, culture is a better crime prevention device than fear. The 'noble and generous notions of probity ... [that come with] freedom and independency' evolve as commerce does. This is so because these values are necessary for commerce to be constructive and thus flourish. They are the values that secure each and all in their possessions and rights most efficiently. Here we see the importance of values for maintaining the liberal context and the contextual nature of the development of those values.

Kenneth Mackinnon offers new insights into 'Adam Smith on Delictual Liability'. I believe, however, that his excellent analysis on the impartial spectator device can be strengthened by adding another dimension to it. Mackinnon writes that

> there is no reason to be found in his [(Smith's)] basic scheme why the impartial spectator should not take on board policy considerations when determining what is to be approved and what is not. And indeed it does look as if 'under cover' utilitarianism does penetrate into the impartial spectator judgements. ... But once it is acknowledged that spectator (dis)approval can be influenced by policy considerations, the impartial spectator device loses much of its value as a principled criterion of moral or jurisprudential judgement .... (Mackinnon, 100-1)

I think Mackinnon is correct if we understand the 'impartial spectator' to be, as he does, one '[w]earing the guise of the legislator or, more commonly, of the judge ... [who] has to implement the values of the community ....' (Mackinnon, 91) Certainly, Smith thought that people in such positions should act as impartial spectators. But the impartial spectator of Smith's moral system is not an actual person seeking an abstract position. It is a truly abstract position that no one can in fact ever achieve. Understood as the person seeking to be impartial, Mackinnon's assertion regarding the spectator is correct. It is an important insight. But understood as the ideal of impartiality, that spectator is the ever present standard of principled moral judgement. Ironically, we can never observe that standard directly. We can only know that we as a society are moving toward it by the proxy I cited above: the success of the society in achieving and sustaining high per capita wealth.

I would also suggest that Mackinnon may overstate 'Smith's misplaced complacency' in assuming that the 'status quo is ... both fair and desirable ... [a]nd [that] to the extent [he does he] ... perpetuates social injustice.' (Mackinnon, 109) Smith is certainly an elitist and believed in the value of distinction among the ranks of society. Nevertheless, he also firmly believed that the distribution of that wealth should be in a continuous gradient with the possibility of mobility[34] if the greatest per capita wealth was indeed going to be realized.[35] Nevertheless, Mackinnon is correct in the suggestion that Smith does not have a late twentieth century perspective on the gender and racial foundations of social and distributive injustice.

Smith would, I believe, cite this as a classic example of context.[36]

Central to Smith's conception of society is the notion that any given society is a matrix of social, political, and economic customs, laws, institutions, and relationships that are historically determined and are in a constant process of evolution (sometimes very slow, at other times fast). Thus our understanding of the world is inherently contextual. As I noted above regarding Smith's judgement of Cato, even as we judge the past by present standards (our context), we must appreciate that the standards were different in that different context. And as we try to peer into the future we must recognize the limitations of our own context as a perspective from which to see beyond the horizon of our time.

What we can learn from Smith, and the essential fact of his own analysis, is that social change is a story of evolution and in that story we discover the interdependence of context and change. This is a key insight of Robin Paul Malloy's excellent piece on 'Adam Smith and the Modern Discourse of Law and Economics.' Malloy writes that '[i]t will be argued that Smith offered a dynamic and contextual understanding of the relationship between law and economics.' (Malloy, 114) My presentation here is meant to complement and extend Malloy's excellent documentation of this 'dynamic and contextual understanding'.

What are the insights and policy implications to be taken from this analysis of the role of law in Smith's moral philosophy?

Change is necessary, for maturation requires change. Change can be good if it embodies a maturing of the individuals and institutions of society (e.g., the law). Thus, Smith would not be wedded to original intent as a guide for constitutional interpretation. While he certainly rejects arbitrary change, he would reject even more vehemently the notion that a constitution written in one societal context should be perpetually interpreted in the terms of the original context.

Change must come from context. Even change that appears to be revolutionary on the face of it, must have some evolutionary connection to the extant social context if the change is to be maintained. The people of a society cannot be arranged and rearranged as one would pieces on a chess board.

> [I]n the great chess-board of human society, every single piece has a principle of motion of its own, altogether different from that which the legislature might chuse to impress upon it. If those two principles coincide and act in the same direction, the game of human society will go on easily and harmoniously, and it is very likely to be happy and successful. If they are opposite or different ... the society must be at all times in the highest degree of disorder. (*TMS*, 234)

In Smith's moral philosophy it is the role of leaders to build on this coincidence and the rule of law to nurture it. If, as I argue Smith believed, law is shaped by social utility, and then by its authority it in turn serves the utility of shaping the customs/values of the people - it is in this way that harmony of social and legal cited in the quotation above can be realized.

And finally, if change is to be constructive it must me based on a maturation of the golden mean of societal values toward the standards of the impartial spectator. This requires that all participants be educated so that they can appreciate the discourse on values, that all participants feel invested in the course of society's evolution - that they have the opportunity to better themselves, and that good fortune offers a society the circumstance and leadership to shape a system of custom and law which honors liberty and opportunity. Such a fortunate society would then mature toward that best of all possible worlds and the greatest wealth for the nation. In the ideal, the law would provide the language and the institutions through which honorable people could carry on a constructive and fruitful intercourse. This is a lesson not to be lost on all those societies around the world that are seeking the fruitful world of the invisible hand - the image of the ideal Adam Smith offered us over two hundred years ago.

NOTES

1. By 'know the real' here, I mean to accept one's perceptions of the world, including its history as fact.
2. See page 9 of my chapter, 'Setting the Scene' for more on this.
3. *TMS*, 83.
4. See (*TMS*, 166-7) for Smith's assertion that virtue would generally be rewarded.
5. 'Some general, and even systematical, idea of the perfection of policy and law, may no doubt be necessary for directing the views of the statesman. But to insist upon establishing, and upon establishing all at once and in spite of all opposition, every thing which that idea may seem to require, must often be the highest degree of arrogance. It is to erect his own judgement into the supreme standard of right and wrong. It is to fancy himself the only wise and worthy man in the commonwealth, and that his fellow-citizens should accommodate themselves to him and not he to them. (*TMS*, 234).
6. A note on citation form: I cite page numbers from the single volume, *Lectures on Jurisprudence* and note the 'A' and 'B' distinction for the 1762-3 and 1766 terms respectively.
7. Below I will address the issue of distribution and its role in Smith's vision.
8. See for example (Evensky, 1993) on social values.
9. See (*LJA*, 28) or (*LJB*, 460).
10. See (*LJA*, 36) or (*LJB*, 461).
11. See (*LJA*, 37) or (*LJB*, 462).
12. For example law of primogeniture (*LJB*, 465).
13. As an island, '[t]he Union [with Scotland] put them out of the danger of invasions. They were therefore under no necessity of keeping up a standing army; they did not see any use or necessity for it. ... a system of liberty has been established in England before the standing army was introduced ....' (*LJA*, 265, 269).
14. 'Elizabeth, who always affected popularity, was continually unwilling to impose taxes on her subjects. In order to supply her exigencies she sold the royal demesnes .... Her successors therefore standing in need of frequent supplies were obliged to make application to Parliament. The Commons were now to become very considerable, as they represented the whole body of the people, and as they knew the king could not want, they never granted him any thing without in some degree infringing his priviledges. At one time they obtained freedom of speech, at another they got it enacted that their concurrence should be necessary to every law. The king on account of his urgent necessities was forced to grant whatever they asked and thus the authority of the parliament established itself.' (*LJB*, 420-1).
15. Except for the unanimity rule. See (*LJA*, 285) or (*LJB*, 426).
16. This will be explored in more detail below.
17. (*LJA*, 272).
18. (*LJA*, 272), (*LJB*, 480).

19. (*LJA*, 273).
20. (*LJA*, 274).
21. Smith regularly refers to the importance of 'refinement in humanity' (*LJB*, 467) as a crucial element in the evolution of society. See for example (*LJA*, 7, 292) or (*LJB*, 439, 463, 522, 548).
22. A point that Smith finds ironic and consistent with his conception of punishment. See (*LJA*, 276-7).
23. '[I]n every country but England he became as powerfull as the king. But Edward the first saw the danger and got it prevented.' (*LJB*, 422).
24. [T]he Chancellor is certainly as arbitrary a judge as most. But neither is he very dangerous to the liberty of the subject, as he can not try any causes besides those which have no remedy at common law. Nor can he in any case act directly contrary to any method of proceeding laid down by the courts of common law. And from this court as from all others appeals may be carried before the House of Lords. (*LJA*, 283).
25. For example, he criticizes the fact that juries must reach unanimous decisions as a significant defect in the system. See (*LJA*, 285).
26. See footnote 13 above for a bit of that story.
27. Clearly, this is not the only avenue through which this permeation of values travels - religion, for example, is another.
28. There are two constraints on this process of redefinition. First, the 'leaders' lead contextual lives and thus the scope of their own redefinitions is limited by the context from which they come. Second, the people are not pawns. See the 'Conclusion' for more on this second point.
29. '[T]he greatest and noblest of all characters, [is] that of the reformer and legislator of a great state ....' (*TMS*, 232).
30. 'The man whose public spirit is prompted altogether by humanity and benevolence ... [w]hen he cannot establish the right, he will not disdain to ameliorate the wrong; but like Solon, when he cannot establish the best system of laws, he will endeavour to establish the best that people can bear.' (*TMS*, 233).
31. Smith had little trust in the 'man of system'. (*TMS*, 233).
32. See (*LJA*, 318).
33. Similarly, Smith sees the development of social values as process of socialization in which the two essential tools for persuading the immature to accept the virtues of the extant order are appeals to authority and utility. See (Evensky, 1993) for an extended discussion of the socialization of values in Adam Smith's moral philosophy.
34. The classic counterfactual is the slave. With not hope of mobility, of bettering his or her circumstance, the slave was the least productive kind of labor (*LJB*, 523) and the least likely to contribute creative changes to the production process (*LJB*, 526) - the very changes that drive the division of labor (*WN*, 19-20) and the growing opulence of society.
35. Smith writes for example that 'in the present state of things a man of a great fortune is rather of advantage than disadvantage to the state, providing that there is a graduall descent of fortunes betwixt these great ones and others of the least and lowest fortune.' (*LJA*, 196) and 'In order that the innequality of property should have the effect above mentioned [(drive the progress of society)], there must be a graduall declension and subordinate degrees of wealth.' (*LJA*, 262).
36. And, I believe, Smith would assert this as an intellectual insight, not a moral excuse. Smith did not excuse Cato, even as he understood the contextual nature of Cato's values.

REFERENCES

Cairns, John W.. (1994) 'Adam Smith and the Role of the Courts in Securing Justice and Liberty.' in *Adam Smith and the Philosophy of Law and Economics*. Edited by Robin Paul Malloy and Jerry Evensky. The Netherlands: Kluwer Academic Publishers.

Evensky, Jerry. (Forthcoming). 'Adam Smith on the Human Foundation of a Successful Liberal

Society. *History of Political Economy.*

Evensky, Jerry. (1994) 'Setting the Scene: Adam Smith's Moral Philosophy. in *Adam Smith and the Philosophy of Law and Economics.* Edited by Robin Paul Malloy and Jerry Evensky. The Netherlands: Kluwer Academic Publishers.

Haakonssen, Knud. (1981) *The Science of a Legislator.* Cambridge: Cambridge University Press.

Lindgren, J. Ralph. (1994) 'Adam Smith's Treatment of Criminal Law.' in *Adam Smith and the Philosophy of Law and Economics.* Edited by Robin Paul Malloy and Jerry Evensky. The Netherlands: Kluwer Academic Publishers.

Malloy, Robin Paul. (1994) 'Adam Smith and the Modern Discourse of Law and Economics.' in *Adam Smith and the Philosophy of Law and Economics.* Edited by Robin Paul Malloy and Jerry Evensky. The Netherlands: Kluwer Academic Publishers.

MacKinnon, Kenneth A.B.. 1994) 'Adam Smith on Delictual Liability.' in *Adam Smith and the Philosophy of Law and Economics.* Edited by Robin Paul Malloy and Jerry Evensky. The Netherlands: Kluwer Academic Publishers.

Smith, Adam. (1980). *Essays on Philosophical Subjects*, Edited by W.P.D. Wightman and J.C. Bryce; Vol. 3 of *The Glasgow Edition of the Works and Correspondence of Adam Smith*, General editing by D.D. Raphael and Andrew Skinner, Oxford: Clarendon Press.

-----. (1978). *Lectures on Jurisprudence*, Edited by R.L. Meek, D.D. Raphael, and P.G. Stein; Vol. 5 of *The Glasgow Edition of the Works and Correspondence of Adam Smith*, General editing by D.D. Raphael and Andrew Skinner, Oxford: Clarendon Press.

-----. (1976). *An Inquiry into the Nature and Causes of the Wealth of Nations*, Edited in two vol.by W.B. Todd; Vol. 2 of *The Glasgow Edition of the Works and Correspondence of Adam Smith*, General editing by D.D. Raphael and Andrew Skinner, Oxford: Clarendon Press.

-----. (1976). *The Theory of Moral Sentiments*, Edited by D.D. Raphael and A.L. Macfie; Vol. 1 of *The Glasgow Edition of the Works and Correspondence of Adam Smith*, General editing by D.D. Raphael and Andrew Skinner, Oxford: Clarendon Press.

Syracuse University, Maxwell School, Department of Economics

Law and Philosophy Library

1. E. Bulygin, J.-L. Gardies and I. Niiniluoto (eds.): *Man, Law and Modern Forms of Life.* With an Introduction by M.D. Bayles. 1985 ISBN 90-277-1869-5
2. W. Sadurski: *Giving Desert Its Due.* Social Justice and Legal Theory. 1985 ISBN 90-277-1941-1
3. N. MacCormick and O. Weinberger: *An Institutional Theory of Law.* New Approaches to Legal Positivism. 1986 ISBN 90-277-2079-7
4. A. Aarnio: *The Rational as Reasonable.* A Treatise on Legal Justification. 1987 ISBN 90-277-2276-5
5. M.D. Bayles: *Principles of Law.* A Normative Analysis. 1987 ISBN 90-277-2412-1; Pb: 90-277-2413-X
6. A. Soeteman: *Logic in Law.* Remarks on Logic and Rationality in Normative Reasoning, Especially in Law. 1989 ISBN 0-7923-0042-4
7. C.T. Sistare: *Responsibility and Criminal Liability.* 1989 ISBN 0-7923-0396-2
8. A. Peczenik: *On Law and Reason.* 1989 ISBN 0-7923-0444-6
9. W. Sadurski: *Moral Pluralism and Legal Neutrality.* 1990 ISBN 0-7923-0565-5
10. M.D. Bayles: *Procedural Justice.* Allocating to Individuals. 1990 ISBN 0-7923-0567-1
11. P. Nerhot (ed.): *Law, Interpretation and Reality.* Essays in Epistemology, Hermeneutics and Jurisprudence. 1990 ISBN 0-7923-0593-0
12. A.W. Norrie: *Law, Ideology and Punishment.* Retrieval and Critique of the Liberal Ideal of Criminal Justice. 1991 ISBN 0-7923-1013-6
13. P. Nerhot (ed.): *Legal Knowledge and Analogy.* Fragments of Legal Epistemology, Hermeneutics and Linguistics. 1991 ISBN 0-7923-1065-9
14. O. Weinberger: *Law, Institution and Legal Politics.* Fundamental Problems of Legal Theory and Social Philosophy. 1991 ISBN 0-7923-1143-4
15. J. Wróblewski: *The Judicial Application of Law.* Edited by Z. Bańkowski and N. MacCormick. 1992 ISBN 0-7923-1569-3
16. T. Wilhelmsson: *Critical Studies in Private Law.* A Treatise on Need-Rational Principles in Modern Law. 1992 ISBN 0-7923-1659-2
17. M.D. Bayles: *Hart's Legal Philosophy.* An Examination. 1992 ISBN 0-7923-1981-8

KLUWER ACADEMIC PUBLISHERS – DORDRECHT / BOSTON / LONDON

Law and Philosophy Library

18. D.W.P. Ruiter: *Institutional Legal Facts.* Legal Powers and their Effects. 1993
ISBN 0-7923-2441-2
19. J. Schonsheck: *On Criminalization.* An Essay in the Philosophy of the Criminal Law. 1994
ISBN 0-7923-2663-6
20. R.P. Malloy and J. Evensky (eds.): *Adam Smith and the Philosophy of Law and Economics.* 1994
ISBN 0-7923-2796-9

KLUWER ACADEMIC PUBLISHERS – DORDRECHT / BOSTON / LONDON

Printed in the United Kingdom
by Lightning Source UK Ltd.
104328UKS00001B/236